Airport Wayfinding

Heike Nehl Sibylle Schlaich

Airport Wayfinding

niggli

AEP
AGA
ADL
AMM
AMS
ATL
BCN
BER
BKK
BLR
BOM
BSL
BUR
BWI
CAI
CAN
CCU
CDG
CGH

CGN
CGK
CKG
CTU
CPH
DAC
DEL
DME
DEN
DFW
DOH
DUS
DXB
EWR
EZE
FCO
FIH
FRA
GIG

GRU
GUA
GVA
HAN
HAJ
HEL
HFT
HGH
HKG
HND
HRB
IAD
IAH
ICN
IKA
IST
JFK
JNB
KIX
KHI
KMG
KUL
LAP
LAS
LAX
LCY
LED
LGA
LBG
LGB
LGW
LHR
LIM
LIS
LOS
LTN
MAA
MAD
MEM
MEX
MMX
MNL
MUC
MVD
NCL
NKG
NRT
ONT
ORD
ORY
OSL
PEK
PKX
PMI
PTY
PRG
PVG
RAK
RUH
SAW
SEA
SEN
SFO
SGN
SHA
SIN
SNA
STN
STR
SVO
SXF
SZX
THF
TPA
TSN
TXL
VCE
VIE
VKO
WUH
ZRH

Preface

We are very excited that our publisher has made a 2nd edition of our book possible. This gave us the opportunity to update important topics in this rapidly growing and transforming world. It's particularly reflected in the chapter Digital. In 2021 global climate change and the Covid-19 pandemic were two of the most pro-found challenges facing commercial aviation, an industry which has been defined by perpetual fast-paced transformation throughout its eventful first century. Mobility will most certainly remain a hallmark of modern society. Efficient organization in intermodal networks, that encourage connectivity between modes of transport will continuously be developed. There is a great need to continue the integration of new concepts and technologies and significantly reduce the industry's carbon footprint while ensuring the safety of travellers. The transition to a new era of aviation is happening now, and there is no doubt in our minds that design, information design and wayfinding will continue to be essential tools in this fundamental transformation. This was our motivation for publishing a book in 2021.

Throughout our 30-year history as a design agency, our Moniteurs team in Berlin has always considered airport wayfinding to be the ultimate design challenge. After gathering a considerable amount of experience in the field, we are delighted to publish a book dedicated exclusively to this multifarious topic. Moniteurs has worked on large and small projects for seven airports and implemented several additional wayfinding systems that required the design of countless signs. Our fascination and enthusiasm for wayfinding grew with each one. This book is the product of Moniteurs' many years of intensive reflection, analysis and creative work in the wonderfully complex world of airport wayfinding.

In just a few short decades, hundreds of new airports have been built around the world, mostly in Asia. In that same time period, annual passenger numbers have grown exponentially. This growth was propelled by three key trends: first, more globalisation has led to more international connectivity and international travel flows; second, with the permeation of digital tools and automation, passengers are now fully independent agents from booking to boarding; and, third, travelling has become more affordable and accessible, just as airport operators have added alluring commercial and retail attractions transforming airports into lifestyle destinations in their own rite. These three trends have also transformed airport wayfinding into a spatial interface in which travellers use multiple media to navigate a vast, complex and multipurposed structure.

In 2020, we felt the time was right to capture these remarkable developments in a book. The centenary of commercial passenger flight also provided the perfect occasion to trace back the unique evolution of the aviation industry and of wayfinding systems. We were able to speak with some of the most interesting experts from all over the world who share our conviction that effective interdisciplinary collaboration is crucial for good wayfinding. We would like to express our profound respect for our wayfinding collaborators, architects, interior designers, information designers, engineers, sign makers and many others who work closely and tirelessly with airport operators to find workable solutions to complex puzzles. One hundred years have demonstrated that airports are structures in perpetual evolution, as are the instruction manuals that allow us to navigate them, that is, their wayfinding systems.

The demands placed on wayfinding systems by the evolving commercial aviation industry over the past 100 years were always met by high-quality collaborative design solutions. Indeed, design and planning have always focused on solving the challenges of the future. The global climate crisis is no exception as the aviation industry strives to become more energy-efficient and the transport sector seeks to at once decarbonise and provide better connectivity between modes of transport. In 2024 passenger numbers are again at the same level or higher than in 2019.

With this context in mind, the four chapters of this book examine over 100 airports from around the world and explore each of their unique wayfinding solutions.

The first chapter, Evolving, is a journey through 100 years of airport history. We look at how airport typologies have changed during this time and what impact these changes have had on passenger flows and on-site information requirements. We experienced our own iteration of airport evolution during our work on the Berlin Brandenburg Airport BER, which officially opened October 2020 just as we were putting the finishing touches on this book. BER gave us the unique opportunity to develop and adapt a wayfinding system for an airport that evolved and grew even before it was officially opened eight years after the originally scheduled date. In this chapter, we also summarise the ways in which airports, airlines, aircraft, passengers and design can contribute to achieving the goal of zero emissions.

The second chapter, Identity, focuses on how airports have become architectural expressions of a country's character and identity. Indeed, airports have developed into unique brands closely intertwined with the image of the country they serve. The wayfinding system at an airport is a key element in expressing that airport's brand identity, yet it must be equally user-friendly for international as well as local visitors and passengers. An airport's identity is conveyed through its architecture, but also through the wayfinding system—with its colours, fonts and pictograms. These three elements represent the design tradition and history of a specific geographic and cultural region. In this chapter, inspired by our many years of experience as information designers at Moniteurs, we pay special attention to font design and its unique ability to transport both identity and cultural heritage. We also shine a spotlight on pictograms, which perform the challenging task of fulfilling clear functions, while also visualising and reflecting the distinctive characteristics and traditions of a specific location and airport brand.

In our third chapter, Digital, we examine how airports are constantly innovating and integrating the use of digital technology and tools to ensure an excellent passenger experience. As digital technology has permeated all aspects of our daily lives, it has become essential to navigating complex environments such as airports. In this chapter, we explore how airports around the world have become smart and how technology can play a role in achieving cleaner, safer and more efficient transport in the future.

The final chapter, Beyond, explores the interdependent relationship between airports and the cities and regions they serve. We take a look at how airports function as key economic drivers and take stock of how well they connect to other parts of the transport infrastructure. After the boom years of the Jet Age in Europe and the United States and rapid expansion in Asia, we are now entering a new phase where airports will take on additional roles and fulfil new functions.

This book celebrates the centenary of aviation, providing a snapshot of what has been and what is yet to come. Especially in light of the challenges facing the transport sector due to climate change and the Covid-19 pandemic, our aim has been to draw on the lessons learned over the past 100 years to clearly point in an entirely new and innovative direction.

12

Evolving

1

13

The evolution of the aviation industry

This chart depicts worldwide passenger traffic from 1914 to 2024. The numbers show the steady growth of the air travel industry but also reveal some of the setbacks it has suffered.

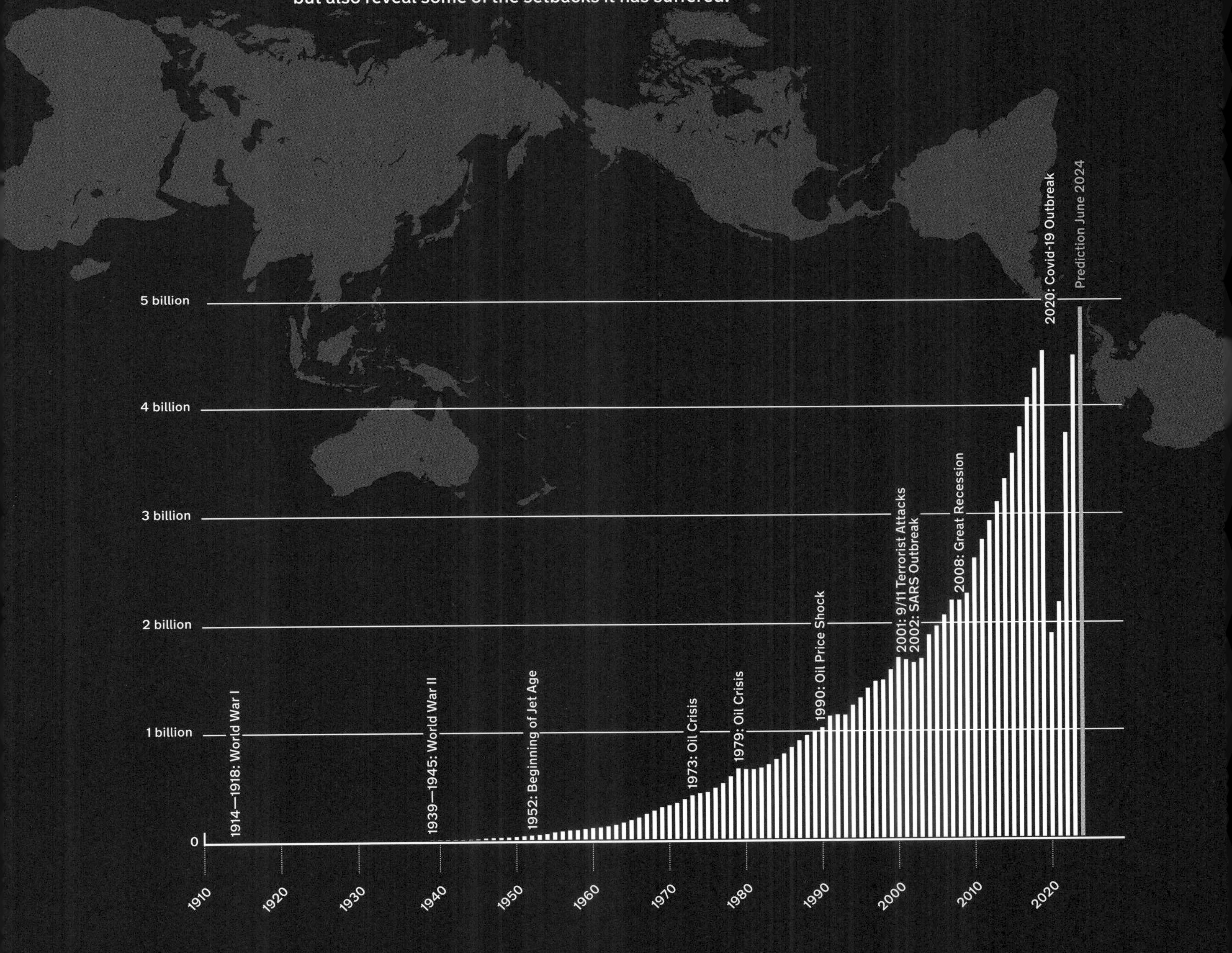

14

A constant state of evolution

15

An airport is a building complex which is never "finished". It is in a constant state of evolution which often takes a completely different direction than originally planned.

To understand this process of perpetual change and how to plan for it, we explore the societal, political and local contexts influencing the evolution of some of the most interesting airports around the world. We also examine historical linkages as well as the developments that influence passenger air travel to this day.

Whereas in the beginning of the 20th century, planners were unable to envisage the exponential growth of air traffic, today it is standard procedure for large airport hubs to be designed with a strategy for doubling or even tripling capacity within the space of a few short years.

At the beginning of civic aviation, a straightforward handling of flights and goods at the airport required no more than a straightforward building structure. With the addition of new processes and services, the structure had to expand or reorganise to accommodate them. This in turn led to the rerouting of passenger flows and an expansion of service information that needed to be integrated into on-site wayfinding.

New demands on airport buildings emerged as the industry evolved and adapted to new circumstances. The separation of land and airside, the separation of passenger flows for departure and arrival, and the need for heightened security procedures all had structural consequences. Services such as shopping, conference facilities and the accommodation of innovative concepts for overnight stays have become mainstays at modern airports. Architects routinely include them in their designs, and the wayfinding system leads the way.

As service requirements have increased in complexity, a simple expansion or doubling of existing building typologies is often not enough. New layouts are required to integrate new processes, new technologies and new information.

As wayfinding designers, we draw from the architectural design principles of the building. They are the basis of our wayfinding solutions. How do passengers move through the complex? What are the goals for passenger flows? What passenger flows can a particular route achieve?

In this chapter, we introduce the main building concepts behind modern and historical airports. We zero in on the three international examples of Berlin Brandenburg Airport BER, Hong Kong International Airport HKG and Los Angeles International Airport LAX to examine the political, historical and geographical contexts leading to the evolution of each airport into a significant international hub. Their examples illustrate that wayfinding systems, too, are never finished, but also in a state of constant evolution and improvement. Finally, we compare future scenarios and perspectives on air travel from the past and the present and consider what visions exist for its future.

A

Design and layout

Despite its short history, the era of passenger aviation has brought forth a variety of different airport building styles, many of which have come to embody local cultures and reflect the political and aesthetic preferences of their times. Architectural styles are defined by specific organisational principles. Our experience shows that there are three distinct designs for airports: linear airports, pier airports and satellite airports.

Each of these three architectural concepts places very different demands on passenger wayfinding systems—in particularly when an existing complex is expanded. In this chapter, we examine and compare these three distinct airport designs as well as their respective layouts and typical characteristics.

1 **JFK** John F. Kennedy International Airport, New York (historical photo). Four of the "Seven Wonders" can be seen on this photo. In front left the TWA building, Terminal 5 with satellite. Behind that the old Terminal 4 by SOM architects and in the back left the legendary Terminal 3, also called Worldport by Ives, Turano & Gardner Associated Architects and Walther Prokosch. Right, a section of Terminal 6, also called The Sundrome by I. M. Pei architects.

2 **TXL** Berlin Tegel Airport. A historical photo of Terminal A, a linear building in the shape of a hexagon by the architects von Gerkan, Marg and Partners.

3 **AMS** Amsterdam Airport Schiphol, with Y-piers in 1967.

4 **BKK** Suvarnabhumi International Airport in Bangkok. An aerial view in 2016 shows that the area for doubling the airport is already strategically planned.

5 **ORD** O'Hare International Airport, Chicago. Visualisation of the winning design by Studio ORD for the new O'Hare Global Terminal in 2019. The extension of the new terminal is planned with satellite buildings.

Design principle

The very first civic aviation structures were essentially single-building ports similar to train station halls. Upon entering the building, passengers found themselves in a familiar environment with each destination within their direct field of vision. There was only one way for travellers to move in these early structures—towards the opposite side of the building and out to the airfield, which was visible from the entrance. This required very few and simple signs indicating the handful of contact points in the building.

Today when entering an airport, each air traveller embarks upon an individual route referred to as the "passenger journey". This is a multi-phase handling process that begins with check-in, then security and perhaps some shopping before arriving at the departure gate correctly designated in both language and numerals by the wayfinding system.

In the early stages of airport planning, owners and architects decided upon one of the three principle designs for the project at hand. Would it have a linear design, pier design or satellite design? The determining factors for the most appropriate design depended on the political vision for the region, the desired passenger capacity, the potential for future expansion and whether or not the airport should function as a transfer hub.

We use the term "layout" here to describe the variants amongst the three design options. A "linear" airport could take the form of a curved layout, as a polygon or even as a closed circle. A "pier" design could be Y-shaped or star-shaped. And a "satellite" design might be built in the shape of a circle or a bar. In this chapter we showcase some of the most eye-catching airport designs and layouts .

In the case of a smaller destination airport that serves a set local region, planners are most likely to opt for a linear design. Larger-scale hub airports with higher passenger numbers more often feature a scalable pier or satellite design which can be expanded to accommodate future growth.

1 **STR** Stuttgart Airport. View of the interior of the departure hall in 1954. Designed by the architect Ernst Sagebiel, completed in 1938 and demolished around 1999. The appearance is reminiscent of a train station hall of that era.

2 **STR** Stuttgart Airport. View of the interior of the check-in hall of Terminal 1. It was opened in 1991 and has a light, airy atmosphere. The terminal roof is supported by columns designed by the architects von Gerkan, Marg and Partners to resemble trees.

1

2

Design

Linear

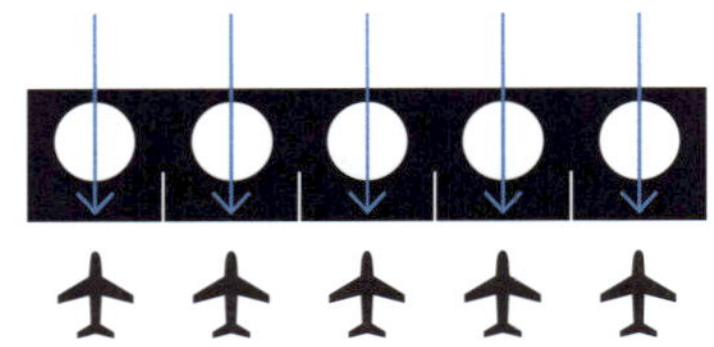

The design principles: linear, pier, satellite

The linear airport design features a decentralised passenger handling process carried out at counters dedicated to a particular destination or aircraft. Here check-in, baggage check, passport and ticket control are all centralised in one location. Passenger distances are minimal and aircraft can approach the terminal directly. Passengers can also board and disembark directly at the building.

Pier designs are different. Here, passenger handling processes are centralised in a dedicated location within the terminal building. The departure gates and their access routes are located in the piers, which spread out like fingers from the central terminal building. Boarding and disembarking take place in the pier sections of the building.

Satellite buildings function much like the piers, with the sole difference that they are not connected to the terminal but built as separate structures. Trains, people movers, tunnels or bridges provide access to the satellites. Passenger check-in and handling is first conducted at a central area of the terminal building.

Understandably, each of the three designs and their respective layouts place different demands on wayfinding systems. Planning begins with identifying and naming the most important goals for the airport. Planners make editorial decisions by filtering the destination points to ensure a smooth passenger journey and selecting them for a specific sign location. The wayfinding system translates user flows, services and destination points into a visual language that enables travellers to gain a clear spatial understanding of their surroundings from any point within the airport complex. The wayfinding system thus contributes not only to the style and visual appearance of the structure, but also to passengers' sense of wellbeing and security.

Layout

Polygonal layout

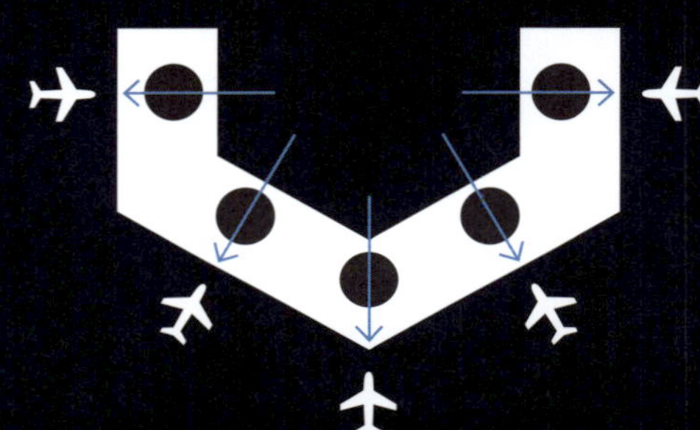

Curved layout

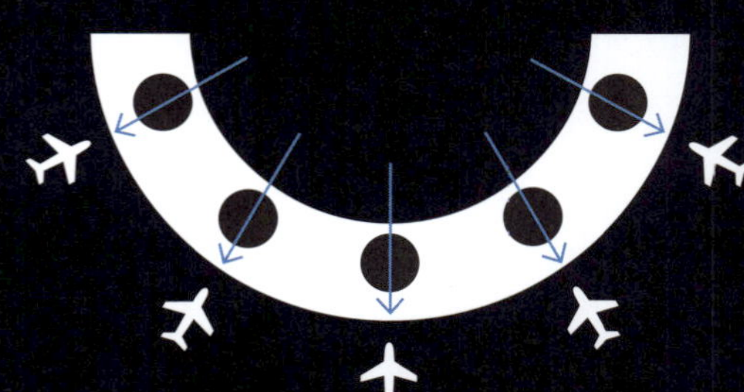

Pier

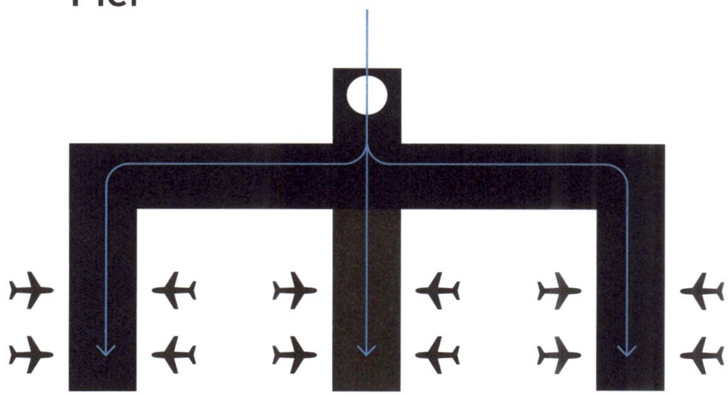

Satellite

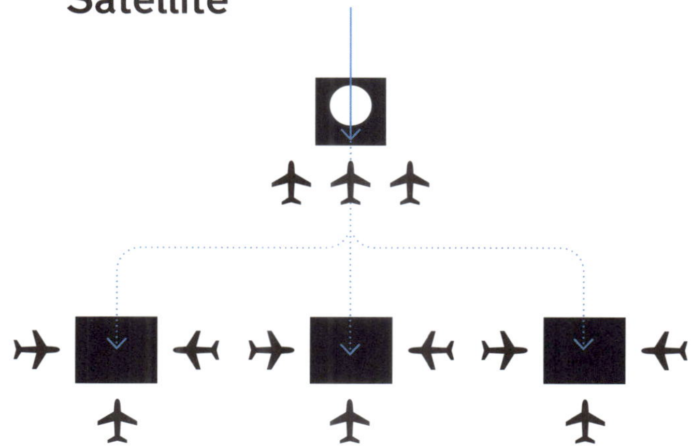

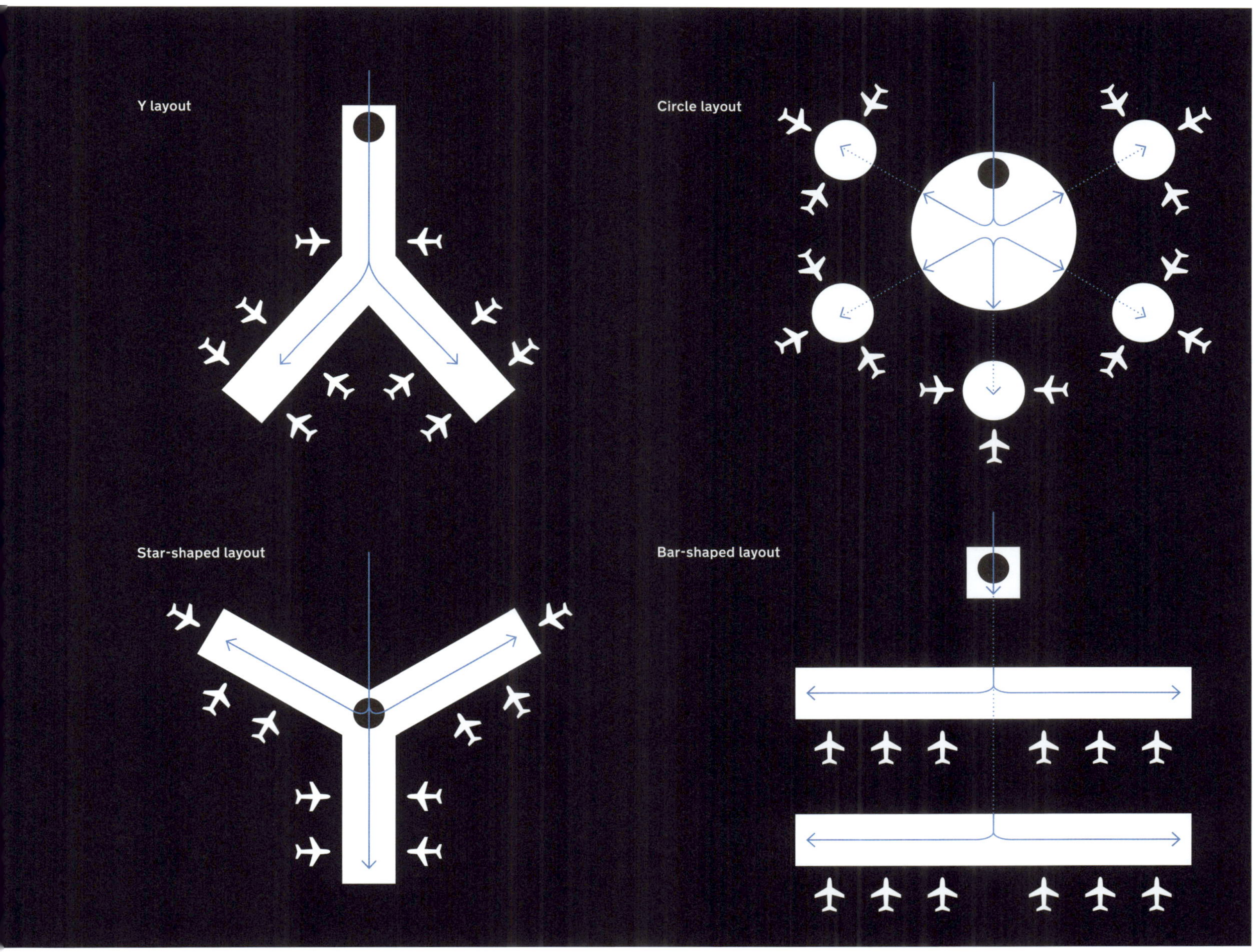

Pax flow

In the best case scenario, the passenger flows are already examined and optimized together with the wayfinding designer during the architectural design phase. How should the passenger flows work through the space and how should the space be allocated? A passenger flow or “pax flow” diagram illustrates the sum of all passenger movements through the airport: for example, international passengers in transit or with connecting flights will take different paths than domestic passengers who have already reached their destination.

One way of accommodating the two key directions in which travellers move, arriving and departing, is to organise pax flow on separate floors of the airport complex. The vertical separation of passengers on different floors can be advantageous for accommodating security procedures and to achieve better destination clarity by avoiding two-way passenger flows. One of the unique challenges wayfinding systems face in such buildings is to clearly and effectively identify the stairs, escalators and elevators so that visitors can choose the right option to correspond with their individual mobility abilities.

In addition to providing clear and effective guidance to destinations, wayfinding systems also organise the pace of the passenger flows and the so-called pax journey. The goal here is to maintain a steady flow and minimise wait times at the boarding gates. One requirement is delivering passengers a short and direct path to their destination, which avoids encounters with passenger flows in the opposite direction. A wayfinding system must also ensure that travellers are able to take full advantage of their time in the complex by making use of the wide range of entertaining activities and shopping

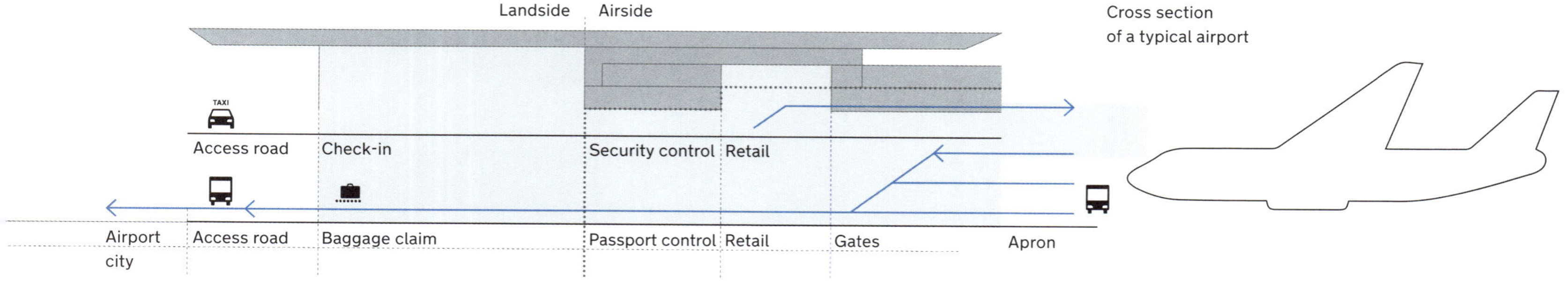

Cross section of a typical airport

options of a modern airport. They should be able to enjoy uninterrupted pax flow throughout their entire journey without encountering any congestion.

The pax flow is also influenced by the airport's check-in and handling concept and by the means and length of the transport routes passengers must use to get to their aircraft, whether this be by foot, by bus, through tunnels, via boarding bridges or with special transfer vehicles. Ideally, wayfinding systems should be developed simultaneously with the pax flow concept as dictated by the chosen building design. When the facility is expanded or updated, wayfinding specialists should be consulted early on in the process. Large airport hubs with capacities of 25 million pax or more are routinely designed so that terminal or pier buildings can either be doubled symmetrically or by adding new rows of piers or satellites alongside the existing structures. Common logic dictates that passenger orientation is easier in symmetrical buildings. However, this is not necessarily the case as destination points to the left and to the right can look very similar. Adding eye-catching objects or landmarks that are visible from a significant distance is a helpful technique to enhance passenger orientation and render the space more easily recognisable. Such tools can be included in passenger flow diagrams.

Destination points and decision points

Forecasted pax flows help planners to determine target and decision points and select the appropriate information for each location. The key questions here are the following: Where are the passengers going? Which direction are they moving in? Which destination points will they seek out when they arrive at a specific location?

In the first step, we identify the key decision points along a specific path by selecting appropriate locations or by designing them to serve this function. In the second step, we select the target information and locate the best visual axes for visibility from a distance. The goal of any airport wayfinding system is to have travellers find their way instinctively, rather than having to search for it!

Naming

All of the destination points in an airport layout should be identified and named according to a logical nomenclature that is unique to each individual layout. If these pre-defined names are applied consistently throughout the complex, this results the best possible orientation. A seamless and consistent chain of information that repeats location names clearly throughout the complex helps passengers to find their destinations instinctively one step at a time. A stringent categorisation of information into a clear and hierarchical structure is a prerequisite for effective information design.

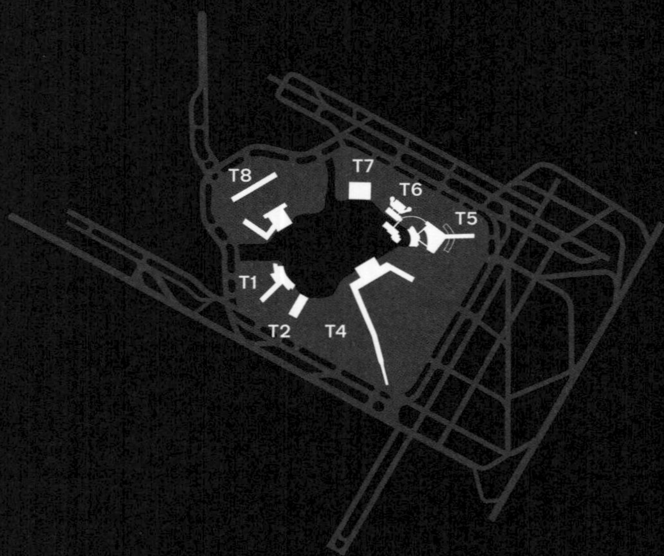

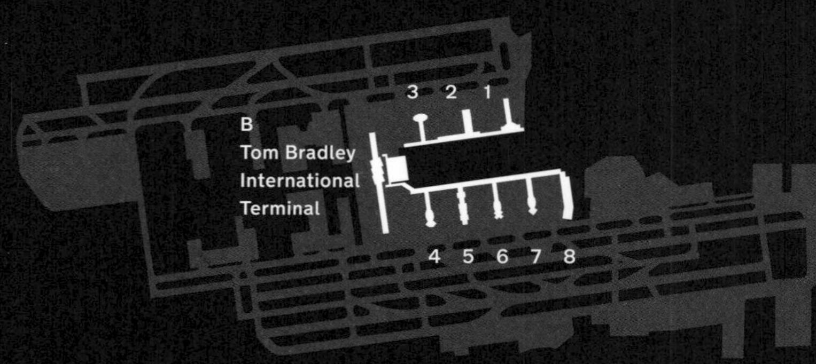

JFK
John F. Kennedy International Airport, New York
Pax 2019: 63 million > 62.5
Pax 2023: 62.4 million

Terminal 1
Terminal 2
Terminal 3
Terminal 4
Terminal 5
Terminal 6
Terminal 7
Terminal 8

fig. 1

LAX
Los Angeles International Airport
Pax 2019: 88.0 million
Pax 2023: 75.0 million

Tom Bradley International Terminal
Terminal 1
Terminal 2
Terminal 3
Terminal 4
Terminal 5
Terminal 6
Terminal 7
Terminal 8

fig. 2

Airport building completed
Airport building in the planning stage
Airstrip

All airports shown here are depicted
in proportion to one another
in a north-facing position

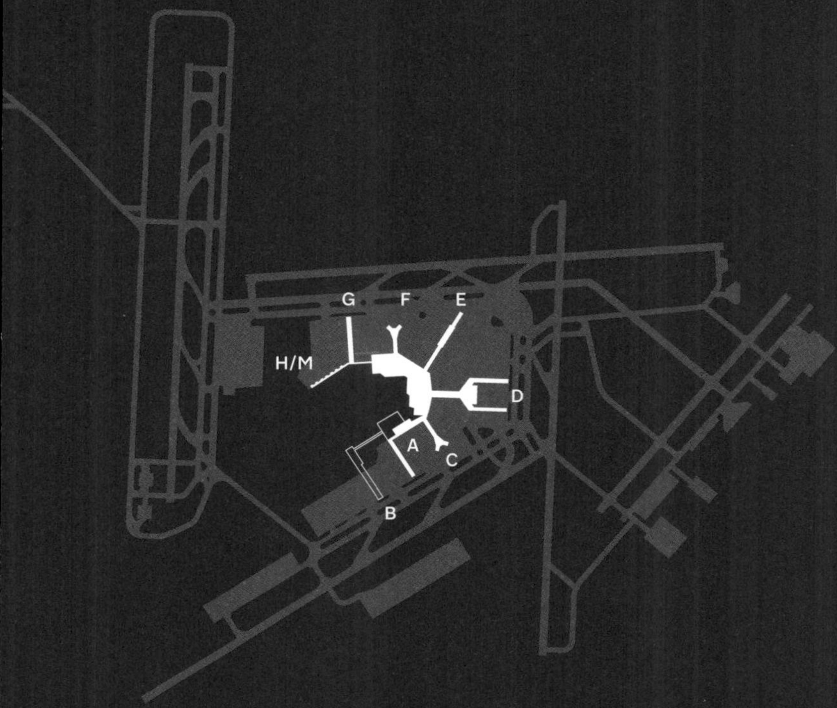

AMS
Amsterdam Airport Schiphol
Pax 2019: 71.7 million
Pax 2023: 61.8 million

Gates A
Gates B
Gates C
Gates D
Gates E
Gates F
Gates G
Gates H/M

fig. 3

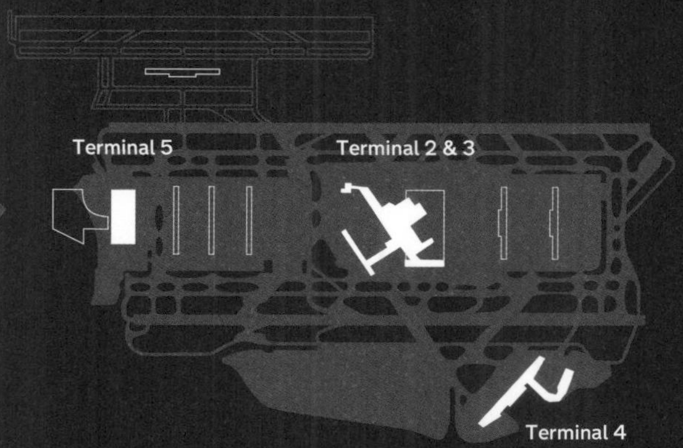

LHR
Heathrow Airport, London
Pax 2019: 80.9 million
Pax 2023: 79.1 million

Terminal 2, originally Europa Building
Terminal 3, originally Oceanic Building
Terminal 4
Terminal 5

fig. 4

Airports

Most airports have interesting histories involving stories of growth and evolution into more complex structures with the integration of new procedures and services. In many cases, airports have undergone changing ownership or operating entities over the decades. Different architectural teams have also done their part to influence airport functionality and left behind a mix of architectural styles that exist side by side.

Taking existing airports to the next level

No matter how heterogeneous the airport, an intelligent wayfinding concept will always be designed to make passenger guidance as clear and unambiguous as possible. On pages 24/25 and 28/29, we feature some airports that are currently preparing for quantitative and qualitative updates in response to new international requirements. In some cases, new buildings will be integrated into existing layouts; in others, existing buildings will undergo renovation or additions. In further cases, the airport layout itself will be transformed in the process and the relationships between the buildings will change. This is particularly true of larger hub airports as they introduce new mobility concepts such as people movers and sky trains.

Many necessary transformations to airport functions, such as the integration of new security procedures both inside and outside the buildings are often possible without changing the buildings' structure.

New trends in passenger mobility are another good example. Not so long ago, travellers would arrive at the airport by taxi. Today, ride sharing and buses are more attractive options and seamless connections to public transport networks are essential. Airports are never truly finished. There is always work to do.

Airline terminals

JFK The master plan developed in the 1950s for what later became the John F. Kennedy International Airport in New York envisaged seven terminals arranged in a ring. It was a concept that gave important airlines their own terminal and their own custom-made signage. At the time, the airlines held such a large degree of economic sway that "their" airport terminal buildings were integral parts of a larger marketing and brand strategy. Each of these buildings is unique in its design, but each has long since ceased functioning as a modern airport terminal. They are simply too small by today's standards and cannot be expanded. Currently the airport is undergoing a comprehensive redesign of the airport as part of the Transforming JFK project.

↗ see fig. 1 p. 24

LAX Unlike JFK, all six satellite buildings at Los Angeles International Airport, which opened in 1961, were almost identical in their pill shape. Over the years, these satellite structures were converted into eight pier buildings capable of processing a far larger volume of aircraft. In 1984, LAX inaugurated the Tom Bradley International Terminal, the largest terminal to date at the top end of the U-shaped building complex. The airport's 1961 master plan envisaged passengers arriving by car using a U-shaped access road to the ticketing buildings. Car parks and the imposing Theme Building were located in the middle of the semicircle to minimise the distance between the parked cars and the terminal building.

↗ see fig. 2 p. 24

Today, the ticketing/terminal buildings are connected to one another at landside and airside. This change to the design was undertaken to facilitate connections between aircraft at different terminals. When the present construction is completed, a people mover will connect the buildings to one another with an access road. To this day, the wayfinding systems in the individual terminals are not uniform. Instead, each design reflects the preferences of the airline located in the respective terminal. As the buildings continue to grow closer together, the wayfinding system, too, should become more consistent throughout the complex.

Flexible-use terminals

↗ see fig. 3 p. 25

AMS From above, Amsterdam's Schiphol Airport appears to comprise several terminal buildings in a row. In fact, the airport layout is a one-terminal system. All of the important check-in and handling facilities are located in a single building, with the gate areas situated in individual piers. In contrast to JFK and LAX, the plan at Schiphol was never to line the buildings up next to one another. The airport actually had to purchase extra land in order to grow and this is reflected in its wayfinding system; the airside paths for travellers are indicated primarily via gate names/letters and only secondarily via the terminals. At the moment, Schiphol's Master Plan 2025 foresees a new terminal building between piers B and C as well as a new pier building in the structure itself.

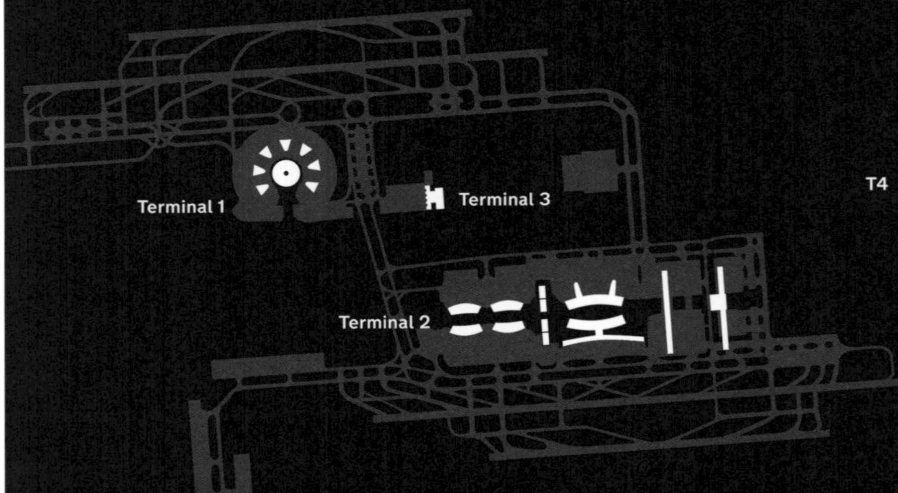

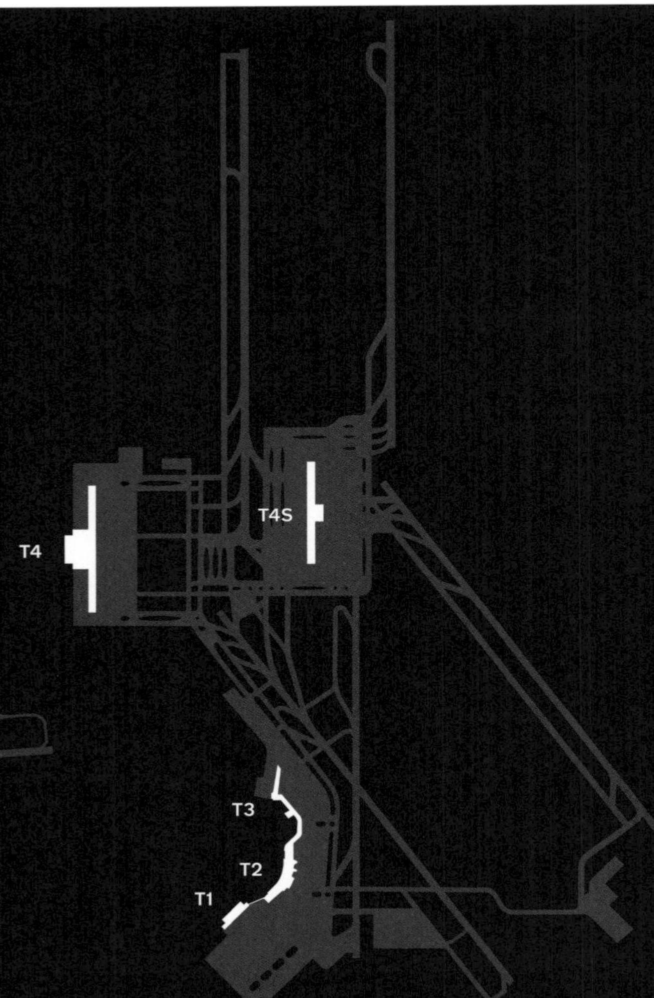

CDG
Charles de Gaulle Airport, Paris
Pax 2019: 76.1 million
Pax 2023: 67.4 million

Terminal 1
Terminal 2 A
Terminal 2 B
Terminal 2 C
Terminal 2 D
Terminal 2 E
Terminal 2 F
Terminal 3

fig. 5

MAD
Adolfo Suárez Madrid-Barajas Airport
Pax 2019: 61.7 million
Pax 2023: 60.2 million

T1
T2
T3
T4
T4S
Terminal T1
Terminal T2
Terminal T3
Terminal T4a
Terminal T4S

fig. 6

Airport building completed
Airport building in the planning stage
Airstrip

All airports shown here are depicted
in proportion to one another
in a north-facing position

ORD
O'Hare International Airport, Chicago
Pax 2019: 84.6 million
Pax 2023: 73.8 million

Terminal 1
Terminal 2
Terminal 3
Terminal 5

fig. 7

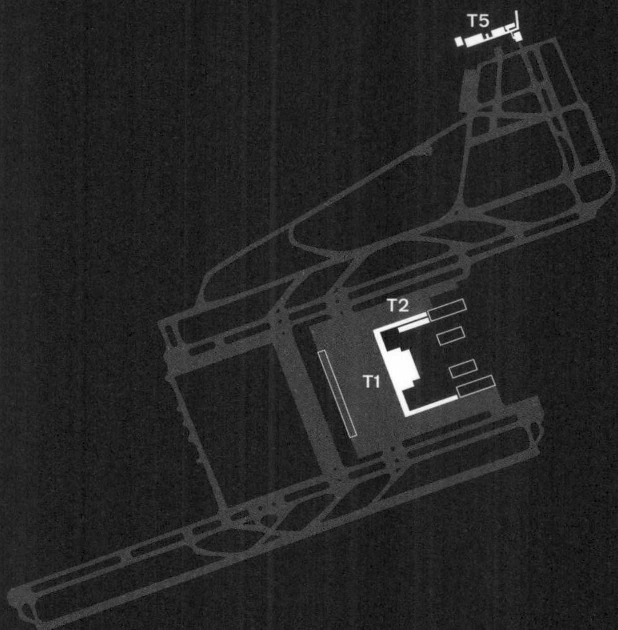

BER
Berlin Brandenburg Airport
Opened October 2020
Pax TXL and SXF 2019: 36 million
Pax BER 2023: 23.0 million

Terminal T1
Terminal T2
Terminal T5

fig. 8

LHR As far back as 1947, London's Heathrow Airport was planned as a group of buildings (Terminals 1, 2 and 3) organised around a diamond-shaped central area between star-shaped double runways. In the early days of the airport, the terminals had names: the Europa Building and Oceanic Building, indicating their function as international or intra-European hubs. After originally being conceived with a system of buses for transporting passengers to their aircraft, the airport soon transformed into a pier system. Lined up at the periphery of the diamond, growth within the airport's central area was limited. For this reason, the newer terminals 4 and 5 were set up outside the diamond-shaped area. In a massive construction process that lasted several years, the ensemble was restructured. Then Terminal 1 was demolished in 2015 to make room for the extension of Terminal 2. Terminal 3 has been renovated again and again since the 1960s and is scheduled to be continuously upgraded over the next years. During the long construction period, the wayfinding system was a crucial tool to navigate passengers to the correct gates amidst all the renovation work around the restricted areas. The master plan, entitled Heathrow Expansion, is currently being executed. In addition to building a third runway, this plan also envisages the gradual demolition of the old terminals to make space for new buildings. However, since passenger numbers have fallen because of Covid-19, the third runway is no longer a priority and it could take 10 to 15 years before it is needed.

↗ see fig. 4 p. 25

CDG The revolutionary satellite layout of Terminal 1 at Charles de Gaulle Airport in Paris opened in 1971. This multi-storied building had one ultimate goal—to enable the most comfortable transition from car to plane. To this day, cars still park centrally in the terminal building, directly above the check-in and handling area. For passengers, the shortest path to the airport is a vertical one using an elevator from the car park to the check-in counters. The planning team sought to achieve the most fluid pax flow possible. Once inside the terminal, passengers should encounter no obstacles, nor should they ever have the need to reverse their direction of movement. Seven satellite gate areas were arranged in a circle around the spherical terminal building. Unfortunately, the round shape of Terminal 1 did not lend itself to expansion. The plan therefore was to replicate the same structure four more times adjacent to one other. But ultimately, exponential growth in passenger numbers resulted in the construction of Terminal 2 with an entirely new layout. This consisted of a row of identical bow-shaped building pairs west of Terminal 1. Recognising that a terminal comprising several building parts requires a very clear naming scheme, the letters A to E were added to the Terminal 2 numbers for better orientation.

↗ see fig. 5 p. 28

The passenger wayfinding system guides travellers between the three terminal areas to the train station and car parks.

MAD At the Barajas Airport site near Madrid, it is easy to trace the growth of the complex over the years and determine the age of the terminal buildings. Since the 1970s, the number of passengers has increased continuously and it became obvious that the linear layout of terminals 1, 2 and 3 would not enable the airport's expansion into an international hub. Linear growth was no longer an option. Instead, the solution was found 2.5 kilometres away in a new, larger-scale terminal with a satellite connected by bus and underground train. Terminal 4, which opened in 2006, was designed to allow for expansion in phases. The wayfinding system features colour designations to mark the gate areas and the terminals as well.

↗ see fig. 6 p. 28

ORD Chicago's O'Hare International Airport was one of the first airports to feature a purely pier-based layout. Three terminal buildings, each with Y-shaped piers for boarding and disembarking, promised a great degree of flexibility, particularly to accommodate the growing size of aircraft that followed the airport's opening in 1963. Terminal 1 was replaced in 1987 by two new buildings situated parallel to one another and connected with tunnels. Terminal 2 will be replaced in the coming years. Due to its size and layout, the new terminal should provide more cohesion to the complex which can often feel somewhat disparate. The new design is a terminal that comprises piers and satellite buildings laid out in a dynamic Y-shape resembling the symbol used in Chicago's city marketing to represent the Y-shaped confluence of the Chicago River. In the new terminal, the point at which the three Y axes converge into a central junction will feature the spectacular Oculus, a massive skylight built into the roof and a lush indoor park below. The Oculus and the park will create a spectacular landmark and provide a simple orientation point for passengers and visitors.

↗ see fig. 7 p. 29

BER The new Berlin Brandenburg Airport was built to replace the city's three smaller airports, Berlin Tempelhof Airport THF, Berlin Tegel Airport TXL and Berlin Schönefeld Airport SXF. It opened in 2020 and has been given the IATA abbreviation BER. In 2015, the operators decided to integrate Schönefeld's existing terminal building into BER in order to meet new capacity requirements. BER opened with the terminals 1, 2 and 5. The BER master plan foresees the addition of two terminal buildings (3 and 4) by 2040. These will be connected to the main terminal via the north and south piers. BER will also be able to undergo further expansion with the addition of adjacent satellite buildings.

↗ see fig. 8 p. 29

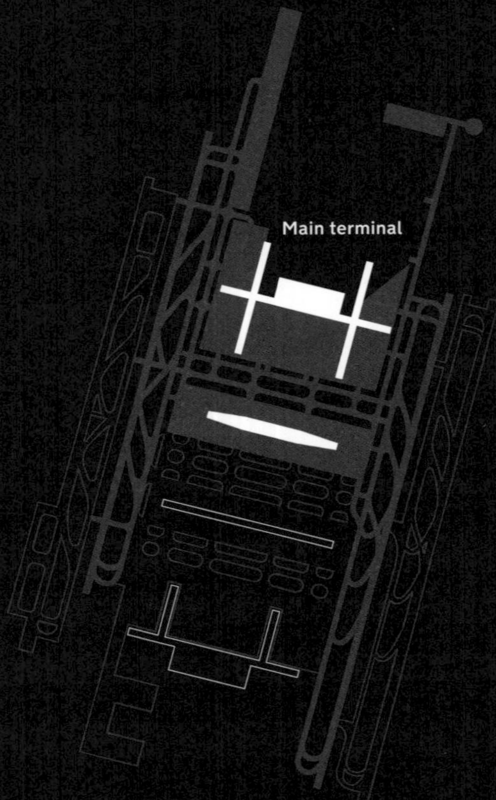

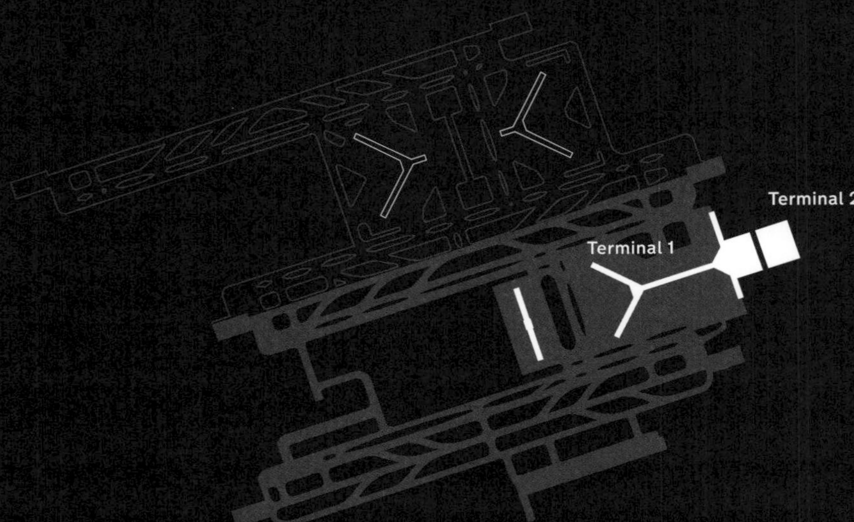

BKK
Suvarnabhumi International Airport, Bangkok
Pax 2019: 65.4 million
Pax 2023: 51.6 million
Planned final expansion stage: 100 million

Main terminal
Concourse A
Concourse B
Concourse C
Concourse D
Concourse E
Concourse F
Concourse G

fig. 9

HKG
Hong Kong International Airport
Pax 2019: 71.4 million
Pax 2023: 39.4 million
Planned final expansion stage: 100 million

Terminal 1
Terminal 2

fig. 10

Airport building completed
Airport building in the planning stage
Airstrip

All airports shown here are depicted
in proportion to one another
in a north-facing position

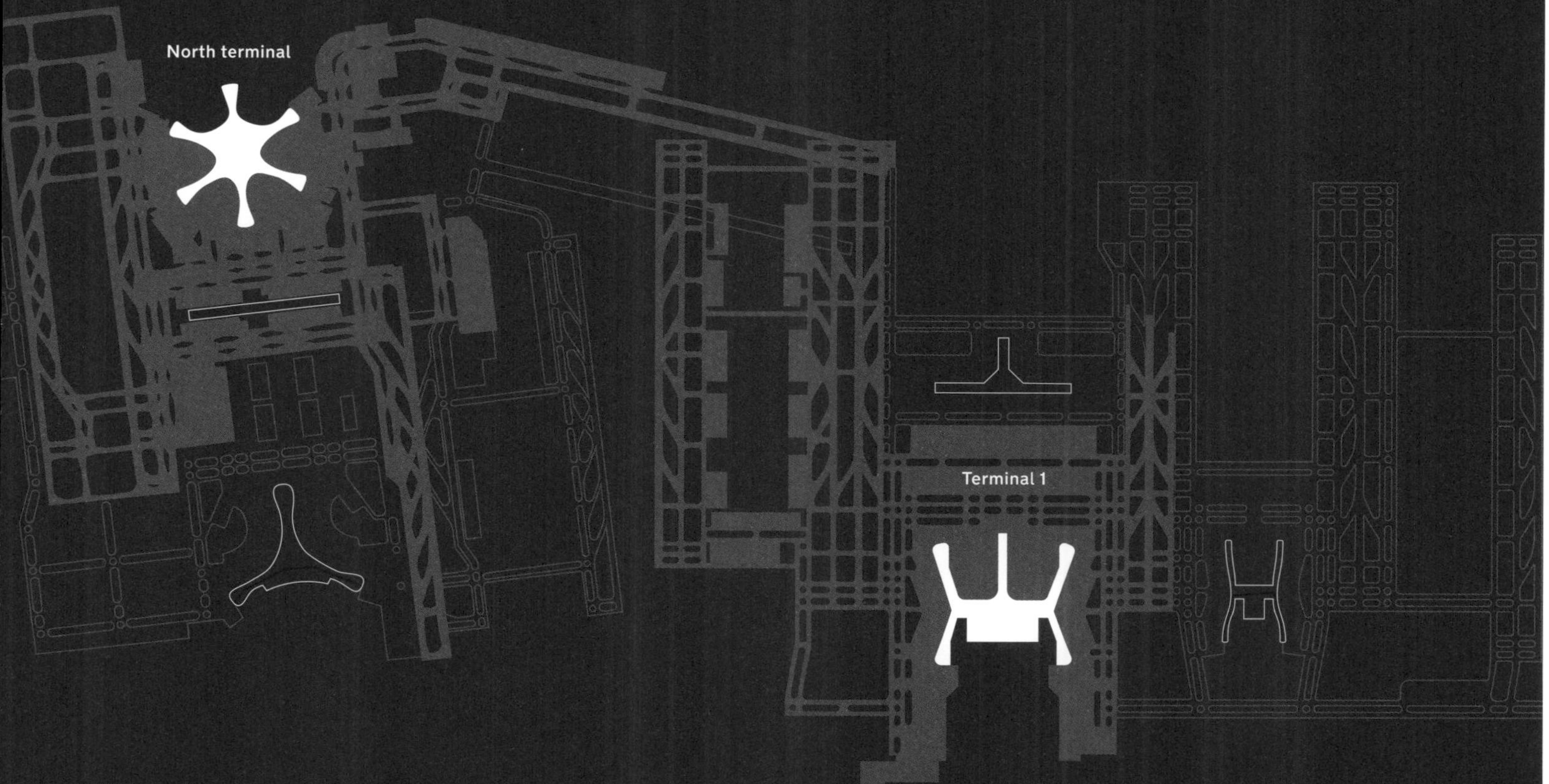

PKX
Beijing Daxing International Airport
Opened 2019
Pax 2023: 39.4 million
Planned final expansion stage: 130 million

North terminal

fig. 11

IST
Istanbul Airport
Pax 04/2019 until 12/2019: 52 million
Pax 2023: 76.2 million
Planned final expansion stage: 200 million

Terminal 1

fig. 12

Giant airports

The large-hub airports that have been recently completed or are currently under construction are all situated between parallel runways. These master plans usually envisage either adjacent piers or a doubling or tripling of the building itself. Unlike the abovementioned examples, the planners in these cases have anticipated the potential rapid growth and accounted for additions in their current plans.

BKK Suvarnabhumi International Airport opened in 2006 and is the second international airport in Bangkok. The airport sections are spread out over eight floors in the main terminal building, from the underground train station all the way up to the observation deck. One of the main characteristics of the wayfinding system is its depiction of paths through the different levels and the location of destination points amongst the levels. Two cross-shaped pier areas, each with a concourse A to G, are connected to the terminal. The original master plan—the subject of much recent scrutiny—envisages a doubling of the airport space through simply mirroring the main building, and constructting two linear satellite buildings to connect the two structures.

↗ see fig. 9 p. 32

HKG Hong Kong International Airport, completed 1998, not only has piers adjacent to the main terminal, the Master Plan 2030 also envisages a three-runway system with two additional mirrored Y-shaped piers. In order to achieve this, planners will have to reclaim and develop additional land to build on. The distribution of passengers arriving from the city will take place in the existing terminal. Travellers will be transported via a people mover from the current terminal to the new Y-shaped piers.

↗ see fig. 10 p. 32

PKX Beijing Daxing International Airport opened in 2019 and is designed to function as a major international hub. Unlike rows of piers or a series of satellite buildings, the direct connection of the piers with the central building allows passengers to reach even the most distant gates in less than eight minutes. The compact, star-shaped layout is also designed to keep the

↗ see fig. 11 p. 33

process of passenger check-in and handling quick and centrally located. The planners envisage an expansion involving the adjacent pier and an additional building with triangular piers between double parallel runways.

1 **HKG** Land has been reclaimed for the Hong Kong International Airport Chek Lap Kok. According to the Master Plan 2030, more land will be reclaimed for a third runway and new terminals, tripling the Y-shape of Terminal 1.

↗ see fig. 12 p. 33

IST The previous Istanbul Airport Atatürk, reached full capacity many years ago. Expansion was limited but politically undesirable. The decision was made to build a new airport 58 kilometres northwest of downtown Istanbul. The airport operator Istanbul Grand Airport (iGA) replaced the old airport in its entirety with the new Istanbul Airport. It began partial operations in 2018. Five piers are directly connected with Terminal 1 via a large concourse. Each building section has no more than 2.5 storeys, leading to a relatively simple pax flow. The master plan envisages a second, somewhat smaller terminal in the same layout, plus a satellite terminal that connects to the two other terminals via a rail link.

There are many reasons why airports develop in different directions over time. A country's geopolitical or economic aspiration may require specific changes, as do economic necessity or exponential growth in passenger capacity. Technical innovations such as updated check-in and handling procedures or new security-related innovations also require changes to existing infrastructure. An airport is a structure in perpetual evolution, constantly adapting and undergoing quantitative and qualitative changes. So too is its instruction manual—the wayfinding system!

B

BER
HKG
LAX

We took an intensive look at three airports, on the basis of which we would like to illustrate and compare some historical, political and geographical factors. These factors influenced the growth of these airports. All three of them are major airports today, one in Europe, one in Asia and one in the US.

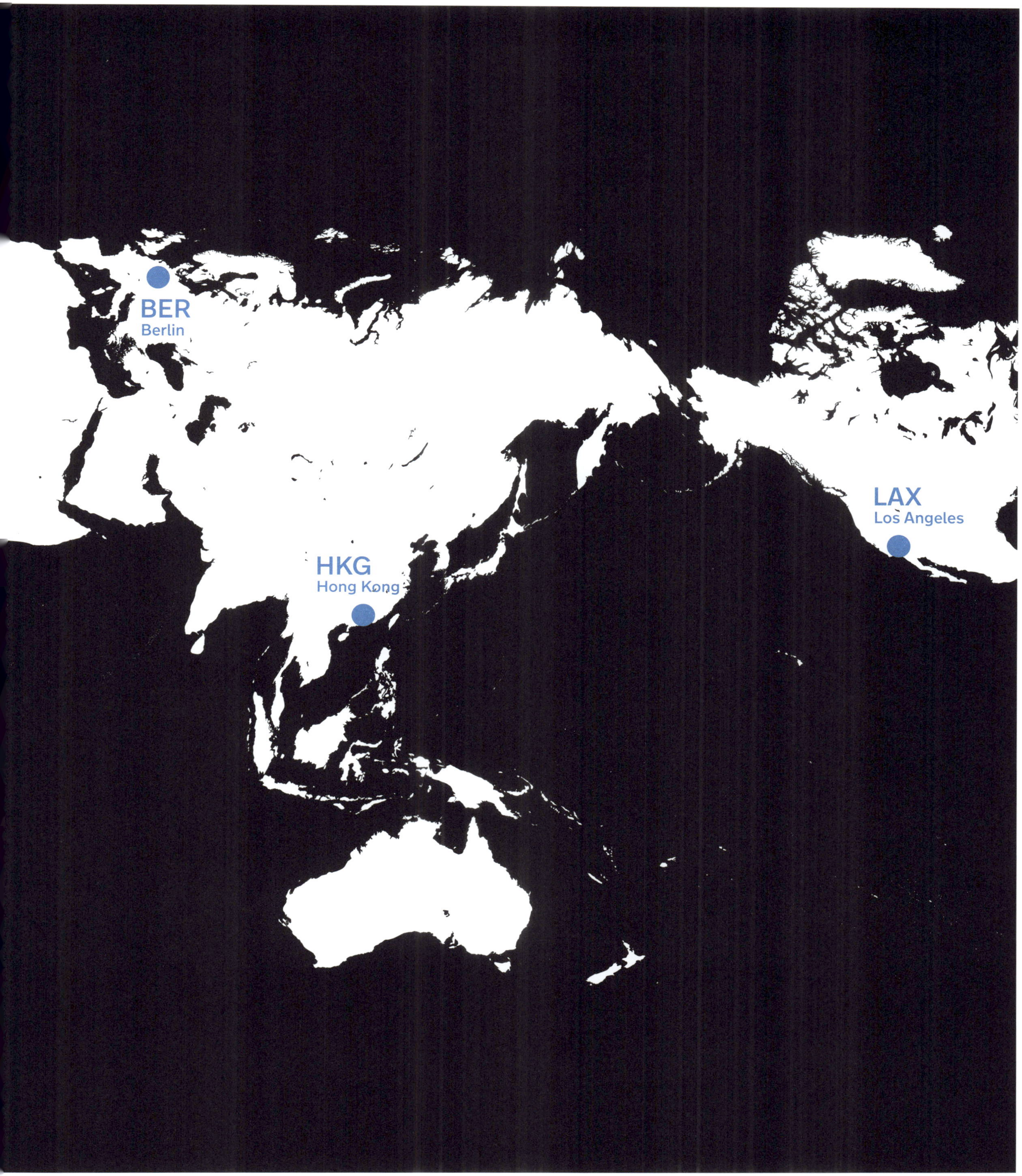
BER
Berlin
HKG
Hong Kong
LAX
Los Angeles

BER—HKG—LAX 1920s and 1930s

The close proximity of the airport to the city centre is one of the key determining factors for its future development.

THF The decision to locate the airport just four kilometres from the city centre had enormous consequences for the development of Berlin's Tempelhof Airport. The airfield was originally used as military parade ground and later for balloon flight testing. In 1923, it was repurposed for passenger and freight aircraft. During its first year of operation, Tempelhof registered 100 aircraft departures and arrivals, a total of 150 passengers and 1,300 kilograms of freight processed. Initially this was a provisional airport, but thanks to its convenient central location, it didn't take long for it to grow. Following a preliminary construction phase where aircraft hangars, a searchlight tower, radio tower and check-in hall were erected, the second construction phase between 1926 and 1929 oversaw the construction of the main building. Air traffic in Berlin Tempelhof Airport grew exponentially into the 1930s.

By 1936, the airport handled over 200,000 passengers annually and with up to ten departures and arrivals per hour, it surpassed the capacity of Paris, Amsterdam or London.

HKG From 1843 to 1997, Hong Kong was a crown colony of Great Britain strategically located at the eastern delta of the Pearl River. A flight school founded in 1924 in Kowloon Bay became the basis for its first airport, Kai Tak. Even at that time it was necessary for the colonial government to reclaim land due to Hong Kong's notoriously rock and hilly terrain to permit the seamless landing of biplanes. Today, Kowloon is the most populous urban area in Hong Kong but at the time the airport was first built, it was approximately seven kilometres from the city centre. In 1936, an airport building was constructed to process the first domestic flights.

City centre

Airport location

City area

LAX In contrast to Tempelhof and Kai Tak airports, in 1928 the city of Los Angeles selected a rural area called Mines Field 25 kilometres southwest of the city centre on the shores of the Pacific Ocean for its new airport location. The runways were still unpaved and the airport was fondly referred to as a wind-blown bean and barley field "out in the country". In 1929 the first two simple structures were erected at Mines Field as flying competitions became grew in popularity. In 1930 it was officially inaugurated as the Los Angeles Municipal Airport and from then on, the city of Los Angeles situated on the remote West Coast of the country, was connected by air with the rest of the United States.

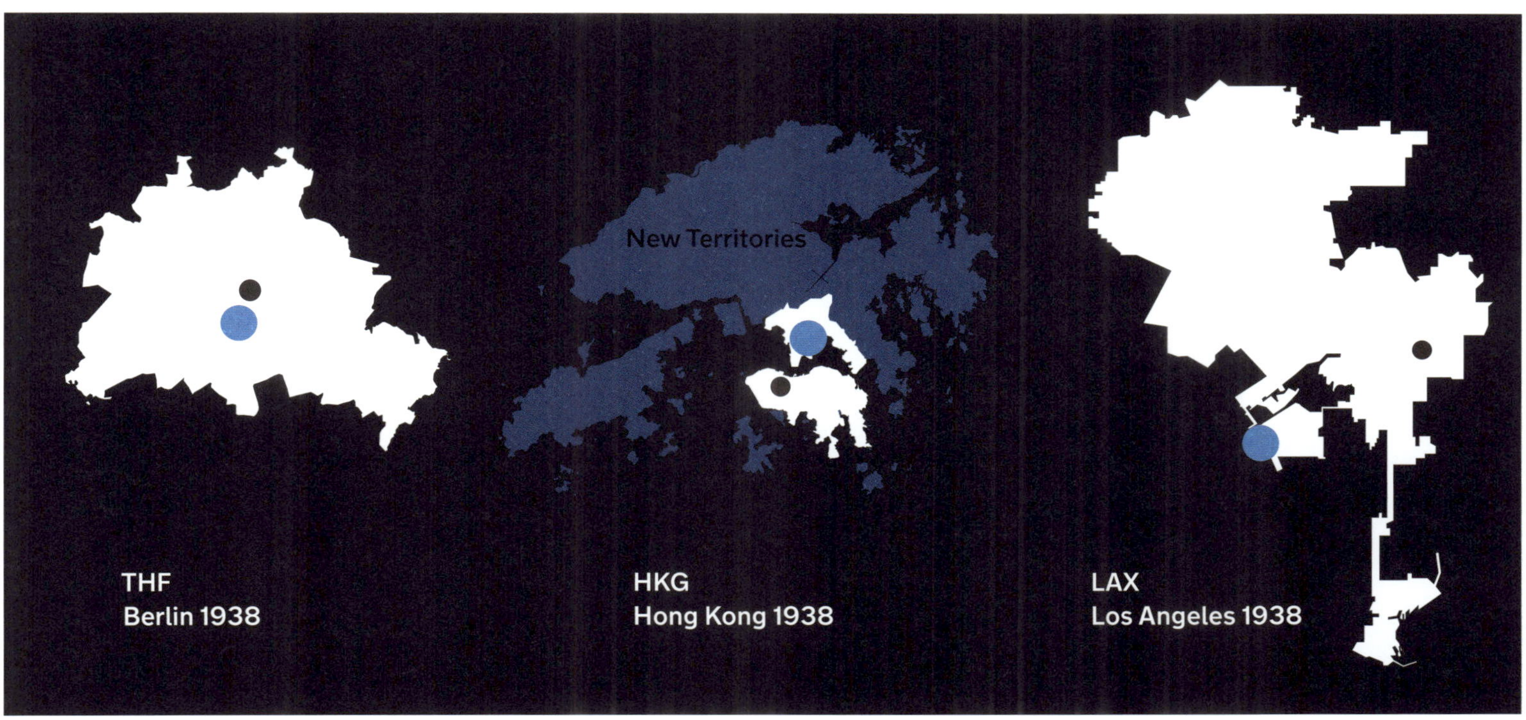

1 **THF** 1926—View of the interior of the Berlin Tempelhof Airport

2 **HKG** 1924—Flight school in the Bay of Kowloon

3 **LAX** 1928—The Mines Field airfield

BER—HKG—LAX 1940s and 1950s

World War II brought epochal changes to airports and air transport. Airports became part of strategic infrastructure and the military use of airports became central to their functionality.

THF In 1935, just six years after the main terminal building had been erected, the Nazi regime commissioned the German architect Ernst Sagebiel (who also did the design for the airports in Stuttgart and Munich shortly thereafter) to construct a massive terminal complex in the typical monumental architectural style of this period. In 1941, the Nazis inaugurated the gigantic complex despite the fact that the construction had been halted due to the onset of the Second World War. For approximately two years, the complex was the largest building structure in the world. Thanks to its strategic significance, the Allies spared the airport during the bombing of Berlin.

From June 1948 until May 1949, the city of West Berlin, situated in the middle of Soviet-controlled East Germany, relied entirely on the Tempelhof Airport for all of its supplies while the Soviets blockaded all road and rail transport to the Allied-controlled western half of the city. As the sole transport hub for the supply of food, fuel and virtually all essential goods for the city of West Berlin, there were times when aircraft took off and landed at Tempelhof every 90 seconds. Only in the 1950s did Tempelhof once again resume civilian air transport for West Berlin and construction of the new building was finally completed. During the Cold War period, West Berlin was upheld as a strategic outpost by West Germany and the Western alliance of the United States, the UK and France. Its population underwent a long period of stagnation.

SXF In the divided city of Berlin, East Berlin was the capital of East Germany and a major hub within the Soviet-controlled Eastern Bloc of Europe. In 1946, the Soviet Air Force moved its East German headquarters from the Berlin locality of Johannisthal to the suburban municipality of Schönefeld just south of East Berlin's city limits in the state of Brandenburg. In the same year, the Soviet airline Aeroflot began flight operations to Berlin, and in 1947 the Soviet Military Command ordered the construction of a civilian airport. Due to its location outside the borders of the city, the East German airline Interflug was permitted to take off and land at Berlin Schönefeld Airport, whereas at Berlin Tempelhof Airport and later Berlin Tegel Airport, which served West Berlin, West German airlines were not permitted to operate due to the stipulations of the Allied occupation. Until the reunification of Germany in 1990, Schönefeld Airport served as the central airport of the German Democratic Republic with connections throughout the Eastern Bloc.

HKG Kai Tak was developed into a coastal airbase for the Royal Navy during the Second World War. Despite its strategic importance, well into the 1950s it exuded the atmosphere of a quiet suburban airport surrounded by water and farmland close to the sleepy town of Kowloon. But during the three years and eight months that Japanese forces occupied Hong Kong, Kai Tak expanded rapidly and was converted into a civil airport. In the years following the Second World War when the Chinese revolution was in full swing, the city's population swelled with over a million refugees from the mainland, many of whom settled in and around Kowloon. The authorities completed construction of a 2,194-metre long runway that protruded into Kowloon Bay.

LAX In the 1940s, the City of Los Angeles had developed plans to expand its modest airfield into a major US airport, and in 1941, it was renamed Los Angeles Airport. But its 25-kilometre distance from the city centre initially posed a challenge to attracting major air traffic flows. The grand development plans were halted during the Second World War when the airport became a manufacturing base for military fighter jets. This was the golden age for airports where they came to symbolise a Zeitgeist of cosmopolitanism and technical advancement. Actors and other celebrities were routinely photographed descending stairs from an aircraft. However, after WWII, the aerospace industry became a major economic factor for the city of Los Angeles and this also had a positive effect on the growth of the airport and its acceptance amongst the residents of the city. From 1946 onwards, all major American civilian airlines operated out of Los Angeles Airport. In the year 1950 it was officially named Los Angeles International Airport.

Overleaf

1 **THF** 1948—The airlift at Berlin Tempelhof Airport

2 **HKG** 1946—Kai Tak Airfield Hong Kong

3 **LAX** 1956—Sign indicating the gates

1

2

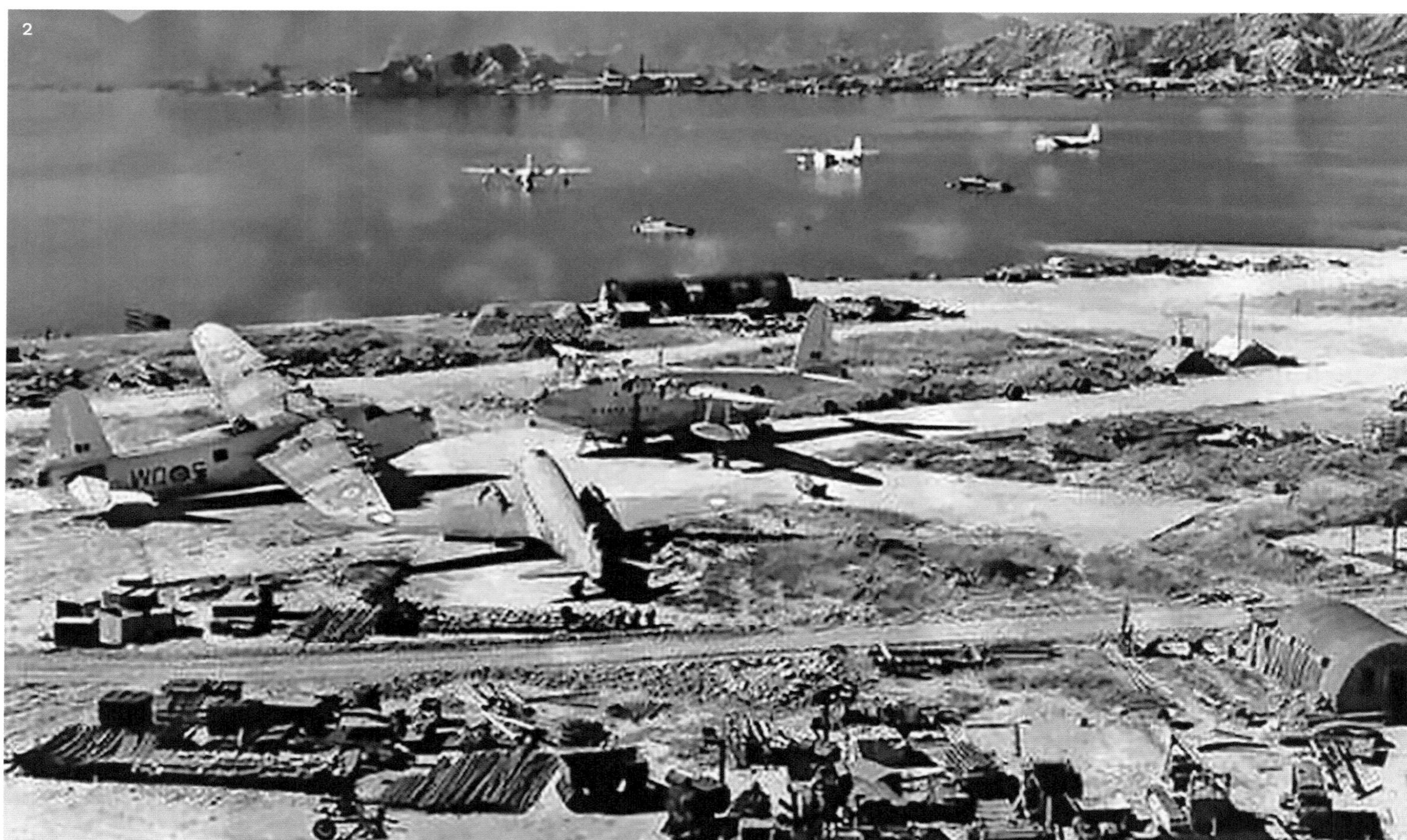

UNITED
DC-7
UNITED
TO PLANES
GATES 22 TO 31 Incl.

BER—HKG—LAX 1960s and 1970s

Civilian air traffic underwent rapid expansion as a result of the rising economic boom of the 1960s and 70s, when jet aircraft were mass produced for civilian aviation.↗

THF Though the division of Berlin into East and West left West Berlin with a stagnating population, air travel to the West grew far more rapidly than expected. Air travel to West Berlin was the only way to reach the city without monitoring in the form of passport and goods inspection by the Soviet-controlled East German authorities. The iconic main hall of Berlin Tempelhof Airport was therefore inaugurated in 1962. A glance inside reveals its clear and concise organisation. Passengers were checked in and processed on the right and left of the Grand Hall and from the far end, they were led to their aircrafts. Arrival and baggage claim were processed here as well. Successively the military sections of the airport gave way to civilian usage. However, despite the primary focus on civilian flight, in 1970 the airport reached its full capacity. From 1975 to 1981 the airport was gradually phased out for civilian air traffic.

TXL To cope with growing demand for air traffic to West Berlin and due to the fact that larger jets were not able to operate in Tempelhof, the city set about planning for its new circumstances, and in 1974 the new Berlin Tegel Airport was opened. It was designed by the young architects Meinhard von Gerkan, Volkwin Marg and Klaus Nickels.

SXF In East Berlin, into the 1970s known as the "Zentralflughafen Berlin-Schönefeld" (Central Airport Berlin Schönefeld), this airport went through several development phases.

HKG In the 1960s, Hong Kong's population swelled to over three million inhabitants. The mainland refugees that inhabited the area around Kai Tak Airport lived in makeshift dwellings constructed out of spare wood and sheet metal. The city government embarked upon a massive public housing programme and erected huge apartment complexes in the immediate vicinity of the airport. By the 1960s, Kai Tak Airport found itself in the middle of the expanding city. In 1962, the airport operators opened the new terminal building and in 1970 and 1975, they had to extend the runways further until it came to one large finger of reclaimed land in the middle of the bay. Planes started and landed surrounded by water and the airport became infamous as one of the most challenging places in the world to land a jet airliner.

LAX The 1960s were a decade marked by significant airport expansion. The city constructed a new terminal complex. Small terminal buildings, also called ticketing buildings, each had a satellite building on the ramp, which could be reached from the ticket area via a tunnel. The ground plans of the satellites were all planned very similarly in a pill shape. The terminal area as well as the iconic, futuristic looking theme building were designed by the Los Angeles-based architects of Pereira & Luckman. The numbers of airlines that flew into Los Angeles increased exponentially each year due in part to the increased spread of airmail. In the 1960s, the city grew in size and the distance between its limits and the airport began to shrink. Complaints over the airport's remote location were now a thing of the past. In 1974, the flagship aircraft of the 20th century, the Concorde, landed at LAX for the first time. In 1979 the era of wide-bodied aircraft was heralded in.

↗ Jet Age
The invention of the jet, an aircraft with turbine engines, launched the so-called Jet Age and ushered in a key phase of aviation history and accompanying social change.

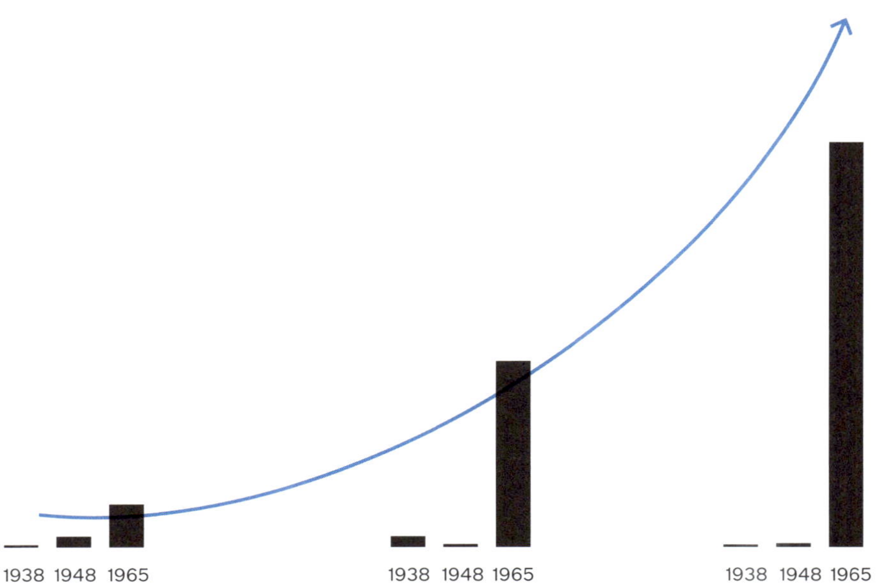

HKG 1965
930,851 thousand pax

THF 1965
3.7 million pax

LAX 1965
8.1 million pax

1

1 **THF** 1963—The large main hall at Berlin Tempelhof Airport. The check-in signage already with internal illumination.

2 **TXL** End of 1970s—The access road to Berlin Tegel Airport. The traffic signs with black writing on a white background.

2

Abflug-Ankunft
Departures-Arrivals
Flug-
Information
BERLIN-TEGEL
KLÖCKNER-STAHL
AEG-TELEFUNKEN
TAXI

2

5
CATHAY PACIFIC AIRWAYS
6
CATHAY PACIFIC AIRWAYS
CATHAY PACIFIC AIRWAYS
CATHAY PACIFIC AIRWAYS
AIR FRANCE

3

5

1 **SXF** 1960s—Check-in at Central Airport Berlin Schönefeld. Signs in three languages: German, Russian and English.

2 **HKG** 1962—Kai Tak Airport with the check-in counters for Cathay Pacific Airways, founded in Hong Kong in 1946.

3—5 **LAX** 1963—Los Angeles International Airport. The wayfinding featured four languages: English, French, Spanish and Japanese, all in black font on a white background. Red and green arrows indicated the direction.

BER—HKG—LAX 1980s and 1990s

By the 1960s and 1970s, each of the three cities had a similar population but vastly different land availability. The 1980s and 1990s were marked by huge challenges, in particularly for Hong Kong, which struggled with uncontrolled population growth. The divided city of Berlin was processing passengers at three different airports. Hong Kong opted to open a new, larger airport. And Los Angeles International Airport entered a new phase when the city won its bid to host the Olympic Games 1984.

THF Berlin Tempelhof Airport resumed civilian air traffic for business travel and airlines with smaller aircraft in their fleets. At 2,116 metres, its runway was just long enough to accommodate the standard, narrow-bodied aircraft often used for domestic and European short hauls. Initially, passengers were no longer handled in the main hall. This was only reopened after the reunification of Germany in 1990.

TXL In 1988 the airport was named Berlin Tegel "Otto Lilienthal" Airport after the German aviation pioneer Otto Lilienthal. With the reunification of Germany on 3 October 1990, the city of Berlin was no longer administered by the four occupying powers, and restrictions to air traffic to Berlin finally ended. For the first time, Berlin Tegel Airport could process aircraft operated by German airlines. Passenger numbers at Berlin Tegel Airport rose sharply.

SXF Berlin Schönefeld Airport, with its network of destinations in the Eastern Bloc, remained the GDR's central airport until the fall of the Berlin Wall. From the 1960s until the reunification (1989/90), the airport was also interesting for the population of West Berlin, because many destinations in Eastern Europe, such as Budapest or Prague, were accessible from here. Later destinations in Western Europe (with the exception of Western Germany) were added at a far lower ticket price than from Tempelhof or Tegel in West Berlin.

HKG Kai Tak Airport soon reached capacity and no further expansion was geographically possible. Also, the noise pollution stemming from the airport became a strain for the rapidly expanding residential areas. The Hong Kong government began surveying locations for a new airport. The small island of Chek Lap Kok, located just north of Lantau Island, was chosen as a location. The island was previously up to 100 metres high; it was excavated to a height of seven metres above sea level and the resulting material was dumped into the sea. On 6 July 1998, the terminal building at Kai Tak Airport was officially closed and subsequently demolished for rezoning. After undergoing a massive development effort that oversaw the construction and fortification of the runway seven metres above sea level, the authorities opened the new Hong Kong International Airport, Chek Lap Kok, that same year.

LAX Into the 1990s, the city of Los Angeles updated both the domestic and international terminals, originally built in the 1960s, during several construction phases. The modernisation was carried out not only because of increasing passenger and cargo numbers, but also because of the Olympic Games taking place in the city. The Tom Bradley International Terminal was inaugurated in 1984 to welcome athletes and guests to the Olympic Games that same year. The Theme Building, from which you have a good panoramic view of the airport, was declared a historical and cultural monument of Los Angeles in 1992. Improving road access to the second level of the building was a key element of this construction phase, which doubled curb space in front of the terminals. As the city had grown closer and closer to the airport, aircraft noise had become a nuisance for local residents. Various concepts for noise reduction were introduced.

1 **LAX** 1984—Major events, such as the Olympic Summer Games, have a tendency to trigger the expansion of terminals and the optimisation of airport operations, as it is essential that the handling of athletes and spectators arriving from all over the world function as smoothly as possible.

Reisebüro HANSA

2

1 **TXL** 1980s —The pictograms are important elements of communication on the signs at Berlin Tegel Airport. Information is displayed on yellow and green sign faces.

2 **HKG** 1996 —At Kai Tak Airport, the wayfinding in the new terminal was bilingual in English and Chinese and featured black font on a yellow sign face.

1

2

1 **THF** 1996—The size of Berlin Tempelhof Airport can be clearly seen from the airfield.

2 **HKG** 1989—Photo taken from an adjacent residential area in the flight path of Kai Tak Airport.

1

1 **LAX** 1980s—Theme Building, opened in 1961

2 **LAX** 1984—Century Boulevard

BER—HKG—LAX 2000s and 2020s

In the years since the Second World War, when were the skies in Europe, India or China ever as empty as they were in spring of 2020? As the world had to cope with the effects of Covid-19, in 2020 departures and landings around the world have been reduced to a minimum and contrails in the sky had become a rarity. Airports that serve as hubs for global connections and as conduits for globalisation are particularly vulnerable to lockdowns.

In the short history of commercial flight, there have been very few moments like this one where the basic assumptions upon which strategies for international air travel were constructed are suddenly called into question.

BER In 2008, the city government of Berlin closed Berlin Tempelhof Airport. In 2010, the airfield was repurposed into a public space affectionately referred to as "Tempelhofer Feld". Today it is a beloved park and sporting area. Berlin is one of the largest airport locations in Germany with years of exponential passenger growth. The city of Berlin began expanding the Berlin Schönefeld Airport site in 2006 to build the new Berlin Brandenburg Airport BER designed by the German architects von Gerkan, Marg and Partners. In 2020, the airport opened and the airport in Tegel closed. The new BER complex includes three terminal buildings, the operational buildings, as well as service and cargo areas. It is estimated that all terminals together will have a capacity of approximately 47 million passengers per year.

Immediately upon entering the BER airport complex, visitors are welcomed into a completely new Berlin airport experience. The wayfinding system utilises the red colour tone—a key component of the new corporate identity. It features a font and pictogram family designed specifically for this airport. This, along with the product design, transport the unique identity of the entire Berlin Brandenburg Airport complex both indoor and outdoor.

HKG Chek Lap Kok, designed by the British architects Foster and Partners, has evolved into one of the most important airports in Asia. It is connected to the city of Hong Kong with a high-speed airport railway system that can transport passengers from the city centre to the airport in 24 minutes. Baggage can be checked in before entering the train in the city centre. In the coming years, the city of Hong Kong will be unveiling further expansions as well as an additional terminal to allow the airport to process between 90 and 100 million passengers. According to the master plan Airport City 2030, the future site will encompass the extended airport as well as a 25-hectare Sky City to include exhibition space, office parks, hotels and retail space just next to the Asia-World Expo site for use by both for Hong Kong residents and international travellers. The wayfinding system today incorporates a blue background and white font. A third colour yellow was introduced as a information highlight. The fourth colour red encodes service information. The former Kai Tak Airport site was converted into a terminal for cruise ships in 2013.

LAX The central airport complex consists of nine passenger terminals arranged around a U-shaped two-level road connection. The airport operators are currently updating the complex to include a "people mover", a driverless electric train system to facilitate connections between terminals, public transport hubs and car rental services. The intention is to reduce the volume of automobile traffic at the airport and create a more seamless visitor experience. Currently more than 50 per cent of passengers arrive at the airport with their own vehicles. At peak times, the figure is around 6,000 vehicles per hour. The Theme Building, whose viewing platform was closed for security reasons after the attacks of 11 September 2001, is still centrally located between numerous car parks and is now open again. On the site is a memorial to the victims of the 11 September 2001 attacks, as three of the four hijacked aircrafts were originally intended for LAX. The terminals are assigned to individual airlines responsible for operating them. The wayfinding system therefore varies between terminals to correspond to the corporate design of each airline.

Overleaf

1 **BER** 2020—Berlin Brandenburg Airport, Terminal 1. At gate A33 in pier south.

2 **HKG** 2020—Hong Kong International Airport, Terminal 1 with its building sections flooded with light by daytime.

A33

10/36
閘口 Gates 1-4
閘口 Gates 5-9
閘口 Gates 10-36
閘口 Gates 40-80
閘口 Gates 201-230
閘口 Gates 501-530

1

1 The former Kai Tak Airport site in 2019—after its repurposing as a terminal for cruise ships. In the background the breathtaking view of the Hong Kong skyline.

2 **LAX** 2004—The gateway and its pylons were first lit in August 2000 to welcome the Democratic National Convention.

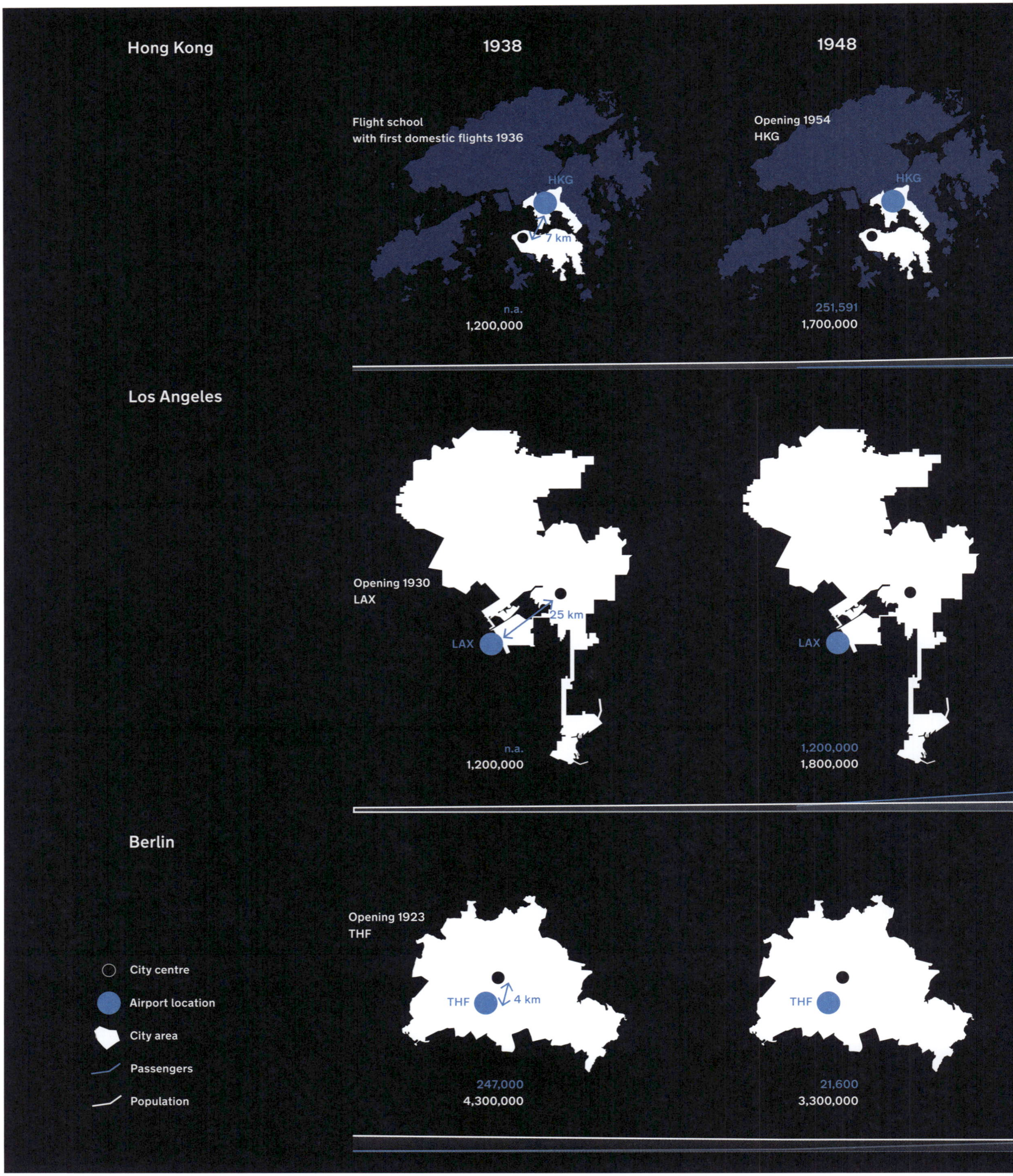
Hong Kong
1938
1948
Flight school
with first domestic flights 1936
HKG
7 km
Opening 1954
HKG
HKG
n.a.
1,200,000
251,591
1,700,000
Los Angeles
Opening 1930
LAX
25 km
LAX
LAX
n.a.
1,200,000
1,200,000
1,800,000
Berlin
Opening 1923
THF
THF
4 km
THF
247,000
4,300,000
21,600
3,300,000
City centre
Airport location
City area
Passengers
Population

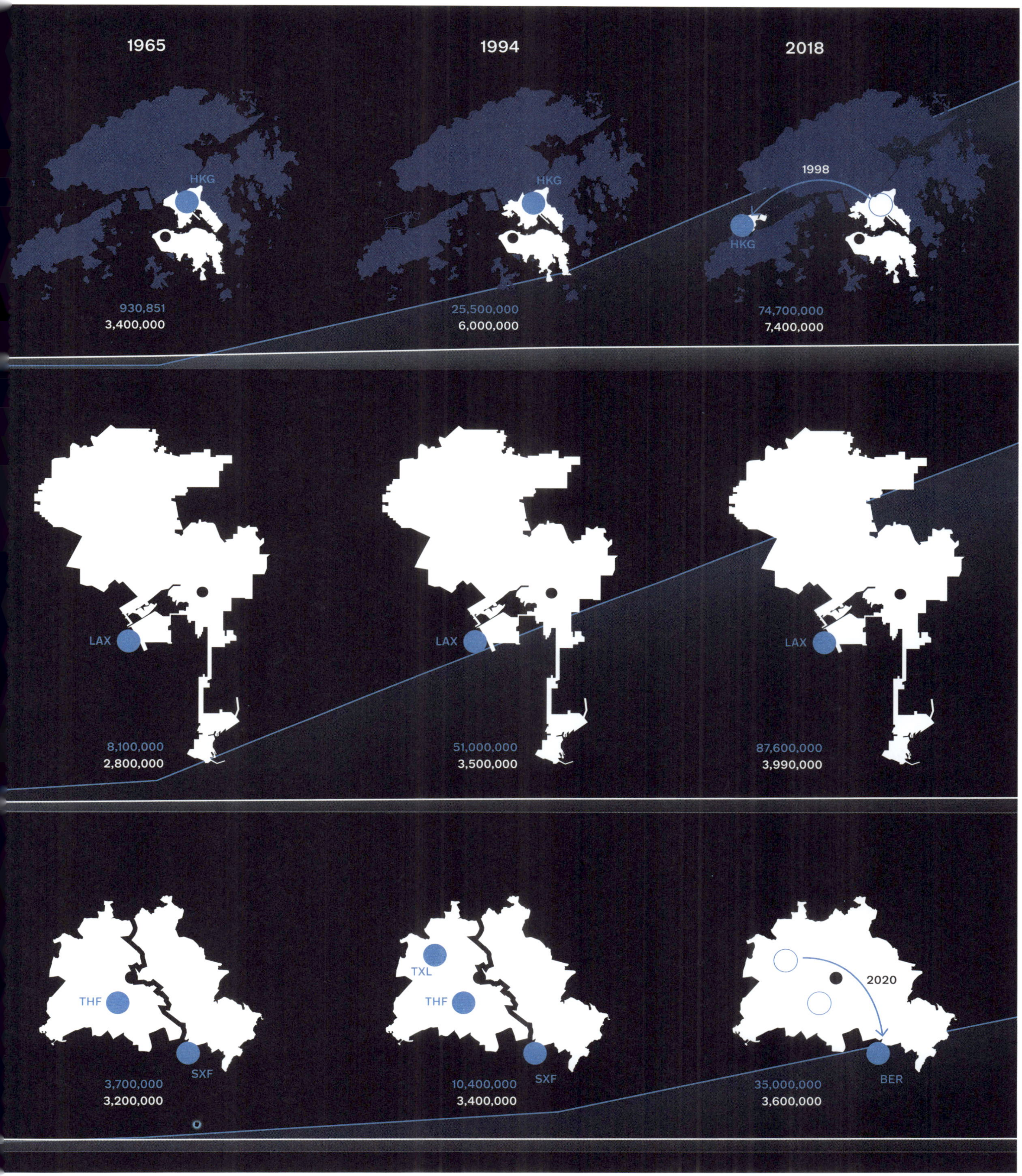
1965
1994
2018
HKG
930,851
3,400,000
HKG
25,500,000
6,000,000
1998
HKG
74,700,000
7,400,000
LAX
8,100,000
2,800,000
LAX
51,000,000
3,500,000
LAX
87,600,000
3,990,000
THF
SXF
3,700,000
3,200,000
TXL
THF
SXF
10,400,000
3,400,000
2020
BER
35,000,000
3,600,000

C

Visions

The birth of aviation prompted the human imagination to soar, often inspiring grand visions of the future. These sometimes fantastical ideas envisaged what airports might look like in years to come and how they could be most successfully embedded in cities.

The history of commercial airlines began in Tampa Bay, Florida, where the first planes began taking off and landing according to a fixed flight schedule in 1914. After World War I, the first airlines in Europe also began flying on a regular basis, albeit with a relatively low number of passengers. Mobility via the skies has always connected cities, countries and continents, and to this day it functions as a bountiful projection space for our dreams and visions of the future. Indeed, one of humanity's most important targets at the moment is the goal of achieving carbon neutrality by 2050.

1 At the Cities of the Future conference in London in 1910, French architect and urban planner Eugène Hénard presented his vision of the future, in which airborne mobility plays a key role.

2 In 1946, real-estate mogul William Zeckendorf proposed an airport which would have stretched a whopping 144 blocks from 24th to 71st streets and from Ninth Avenue to the Hudson River in New York City. This rendering re-imagines his plan in 2020.

3 The CentAirStation is a multi-storey airport concept for the city developed by scientists from Bauhaus Luftfahrt and design students from Glasgow School of Art in 2016.

4 The development of New Urban Air Mobility; this image shows a Volocopter flying over a densely populated area of New York City.

5 The Hardt Hyperloop is set to play a major role in Amsterdam Airport Schiphol AMS becoming the envisioned sustainable multi-modal hub.

1

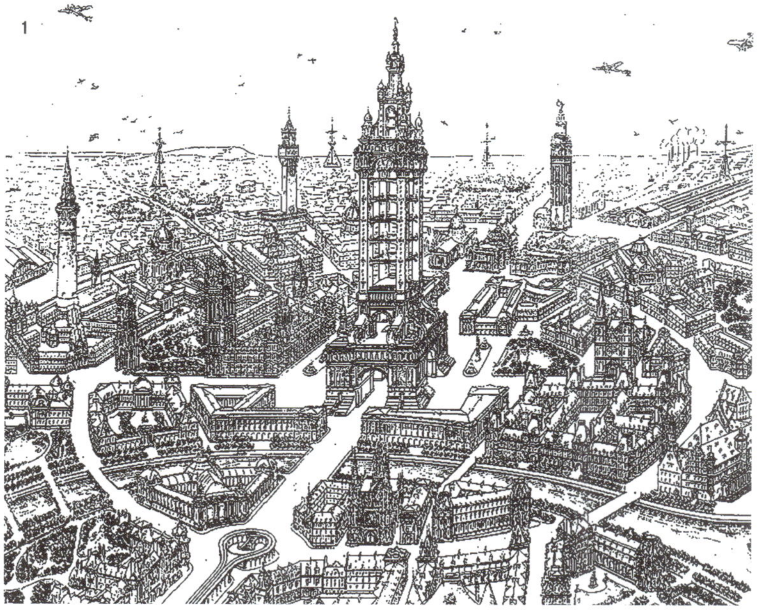

2

3

4

TAXI

5

Brussels 21:40–22:10
Frankfurt 21:15–22:00
Paris 21:05–21:55
HARDT
1000 km/h
To Schiphol
Average energy usage

Zero emissions

Mobility fosters social connections and enables better access to goods, services and cultural activities. Achieving a sustainable transformation of air, inland and maritime transport is crucial as they form the very core of our socio-economic fabric. Efficiency, speed, connectivity and accessibility are the main priorities for all forms of mobility, whether via air, land or waterways. But are these priorities compatible with sustainability? The UN estimates that two-thirds of the world's population will be living in cities by the year 2050. We must therefore transform our current, already overstressed mobility systems to meet the expectations of an urbanised world and the imperative of climate change. According to the EU sustainable development agenda for the next decades, mobility will require a full overhaul. Airports will have to find strategies to adapt and be a part of the solution to decarbonise transport.

Urgent challenge, unique opportunity

In December 2015, the European Commission adopted an Aviation Strategy for Europe as part of the European Green Deal, a milestone initiative to boost Europe's economy, strengthen its industrial base and reinforce its global leadership position. The idea behind the Aviation Strategy is to foster a strong and outward-looking aviation sector that will not only benefit businesses, but also European citizens by offering more connections to the rest of the world at lower prices. It forms part of the Commission's commitment to tackling climate and environmental-related challenges, which the EU sees as a generation-defining task. Indeed, with each passing year, our atmosphere is warming, the climate is changing, an increasing number of species are being lost, and forests and oceans are being polluted and destroyed. The Aviation Strategy is a response to these challenges and reflects the goal of achieving zero net emissions of greenhouse gases by 2050.

Sustainable development in air transport

Sustainability and an improved environmental impact are central issues for the aviation industry today. Air travel accounts for roughly five per cent of global warming. Beside the CO_2 emissions (approximately two-thirds of the aviation industry's environmental impact) there are other aspects, such as Nitrogen oxide, water vapour, fine dust, contrails and changes in cirrus clouds that have an additional warming effect. Not to mention further impacts such as noise pollution.

In the European Union the transport sector accounts for a quarter of greenhouse gas emissions. Civil aviation accounts for around 14 per cent of the emissions in this sector. This is a significant source of fossil fuel emissions. Unfortunately, the exponential growth of the industry in recent years has effectively nullified many of the smaller advances that were made during the same time period. Fundamental changes are required to get to zero emissions by 2035 to 2050. For the industry to achieve a true transformation, it will have to become more sustainable and improve its economic and social impact while reducing its carbon footprint.

Germany's main environmental agency—the Umweltbundesamt—has developed eight modules as guidelines for the aviation industry to reduce its full impact in two phases, the first by 2030 and the second by 2050. These modules are coordinated and interlinked, and only when all of these components function in concert with one another will air traffic be able to meet the goals of climate, environmental and health protection by the year 2050. The modules cover measures relating to airports, changes airlines can implement and technical innovations in the construction of aircraft. And they include efforts that each individual can undertake. Below we outline these modules as they relate to each of the stakeholders.

Module 1: Making the aviation infrastructure sustainable
Module 2: Relocating short-haul flights to rail
Module 3: Minimising climate-relevant emissions
Module 4: Reducing noise—protection of the population
Module 5: Charging external environmental costs to polluters
Module 6: Ensuring clean air
Module 7: Using resources efficiently
Module 8: Flying less

Airports

Airports increasingly see themselves as part of the solution to the climate problem and are maintaining transparency about their efforts to improve resource efficiency. The environmental impact of their operations is under stronger scrutiny and they are beginning to use collaborative platforms to develop and share best practices. Airports are joining together to create standards and certifications to measure and compare strategies with the ultimate goal of motivating one another to keep moving forward.

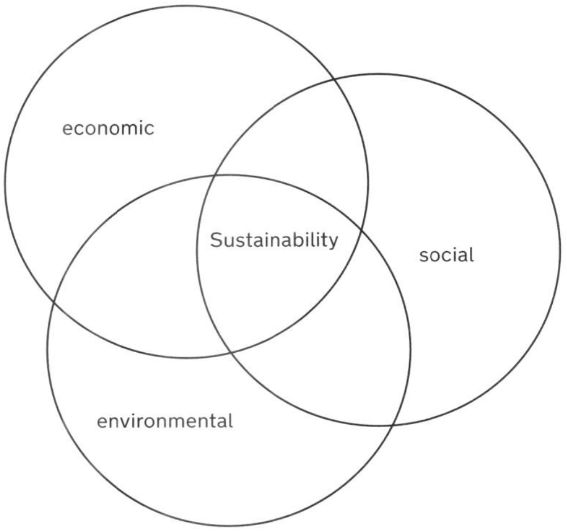

Sustainability covers various fields: economic, social and—the most challenging—environmental factors.

Awareness of the ecological challenges is increasing. Copenhagen Airport CPH, for example, is taking part in an international research project to improve air quality and aircraft construction which could lead to innovations in fuel efficiency. Heathrow Airport LHR has openly and publicly addressed the subject on its homepage by displaying “We need to talk about the elephant in the airport”. Hamburg Airport is the first airport in Germany to join the international network for future hydrogen hubs to establish reliable infrastructure for hydrogen-powered flight.

Cooperation is increasing. The airports in Cologne Bonn CGN and Düsseldorf Airport DUS are cooperating with a start-up to connect cities in the German state of North Rhine-Westphalia via air taxi. Yet another goal is to have electromobility play a larger role on the ground; indeed, ground transport and service vehicles fleets at airports can be fully electrified.

In the future, airports will require extensive connections to local rail networks through dedicated train stations to reduce feeder flights for international connections, and instead encourage intermodal traffic. Effective information design and wayfinding will be central to guaranteeing all visitors smooth shifts between modes of transport. This would require intelligent concepts that create simple interfaces between the modes. Airports could become key junctions in the European rail transport networks.

Amsterdam Airport AMS has developed a distant future scenario which would see the installation of a so-called Hyperloop at Schiphol Airport. The Hyperloop is a system where passengers are placed in protected capsules and then propelled at hypersonic speeds through a system of tubes free of air resistance. This would require the construction of an extensive high-tech network of tunnels throughout Europe. But it would result in a significant reduction in travel over high-speed trains.

As a very effective approach, the locations of airports would have to be rethought. Airport sites could be chosen based on new priorities to allow for better connections to surface transport. Smaller, regional airports could be phased out. Alternatively a smaller network might provide good service if well connected to a high-speed rail network. Some socially compatible form of “degrowth” or other transformative steps appear inevitable.

Airlines

Ideally, ticketing processes should enable and foster intermodal travel. Many airlines offer their customers combined flight-and-train-tickets. With these service passengers can travel easy and safely from train stations to airports and back again. High-speed trains such as France’s TGV and Germany’s ICE have already begun to improve travel times to provide a more sustainable alternative to short-haul flights. Some airlines offer so-called CO_2 compensation payments at the time of booking. They provide this service via external partners.

Aircrafts

The goal is to construct the lightest possible aircraft using materials that have a sustainable product cycle. While aircraft technology and aerodynamics have improved over the course of the past several years, the aircrafts themselves have a very long service life. The Covid-19 crisis has provided an opportunity for airlines to phase out older models in favour of newer, more fuel-efficient aircraft.

Low and zero-emissions technologies—whether batteries, fuel cells, hydrogen or hybrid concepts—will be decisive in reducing the environmental impact of aviation. Currently, a number of different technologies are being developed to make flying as clean and quiet as possible. Norway is actively participating in the technological development of eAviation. The Norwegian airport operator Avinor has set itself the goal of making all air traffic in the country electric by the year 2040. Norway's geography and sparsely dis-bursed population are not ideal for rail and road transportation. Electrically powered aircraft could be a viable alternative for short hauls.

Hydrogen-powered aircraft would be another technological option. Hydrogen has a number of advantages over bio-fuels, synthetic materials and electric propulsion. So far it is not clear which technology will prevail in the race to reduce aviation emissions. One promising option is the use of sustainable, renewable, synthetic fuels (PtL—Power to Liquid) converted from electricity produced by renewable sources is another option. Solutions for alternative energy sources are in high demand. Researchers are also looking into bio-fuels that can be generated from organic waste.

Unfortunately, many of these innovative solutions have been in development for decades without any clear breakthroughs. It is our hope that they will very soon move beyond the status technical visions to become viable realities. Are technology myths stalling aviation climate policy?

Passengers

Until then, one of the changes that we as travellers can implement immediately is simply to fly less. The crisis associated with the Covid-19 pandemic has shown that many business trips can be replaced through video conferencing. Of course, the current pandemic-related situation cannot be the solution to the climate challenge; however, it has shown many people and companies that telepresence can be just as effective as real-time presence.

For private travel, it is up to all of us to carefully consider vacation planning and long-distance travel. The experiences we have as private travellers are irreplaceable. If we must travel, we can compensate for the increase in CO_2. Several companies currently offer effective compensation schemes.

Legislation and regulation

Flight route planning can be updated to reduce flight emissions. The German Federal Environmental Agency—the Umweltbundesamt—is considering blocking airspace that is particularly sensitive to emissions and/or charging transit fees. In any case, the level of awareness among the general public over the industry's struggle with its climate footprint is growing. Introducing a legal and regulatory framework that ensures a fair burden share would be a step in the right direction and improve acceptance of air travel and save fuel even in the short term.

Air travel should coexist rather than compete with rail travel. And for this reason, air travel should not receive any taxation privileges that rail does not have. The international community needs to agree on efficient and globally binding climate protection mechanisms. This will affect both the operations at airports as well as the management of aircraft fleets and fuelling.

Wayfinding and orientation

As the transport sector transforms, wayfinding systems too will change fundamentally and become smarter and more dynamic. In addition to communicating across language barriers, they will become more flexible and able to react to a dynamic environment. Wayfinding will be mobile and personalised, which will facilitate barrier-free and simple communication.

Digital and static elements can be designed to create a seamless experience. Dynamic displays can be switched spontaneously. On the one hand, wayfinding will be dynamic, digital and fleeting; on the other, information graphics will be integrated into the built environment and have a landmark function. Human beings are accustomed to things that are tangible and that they can touch. The challenge for airport wayfinding designers is to fulfil all of these needs by creating a user-friendly environment in which travellers can navigate independently and without any stress. Passengers requiring assistance, can receive it at any time. Holograms are interesting tools and flexible tools for giving an individual passenger a personalised exchange.

Although wayfinding systems are small in size and material compared to the dimensions of the airport, the careful choice of material is no less important than it is for larger more prominent objects. For example, on static signage, the adhesive film applied to the panel should be removed and the panel itself should be reused. The right choice of materials is one way to achieve sustainability in design. Energy efficiency can be improved by using LEDs that consume less energy than fluorescent tubes. Dimmable lights adapt to the brightness of the surroundings can also save energy. In fact, we are already seeing energy-saving alternative technologies such as electronic paper being used in office buildings. Airports too should take advantage of these opportunities, even at a larger scale.

Climate impact of different modes of transport
Graphic based on UBA Austria 2019, data 2017, all emissions in g CO_2/passenger km

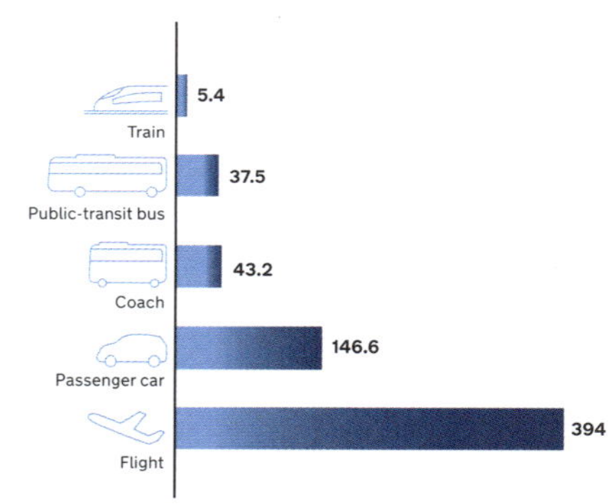

Cirrus clouds caused by contrails
The formation of contrails and the resulting climate-damaging cirrus clouds can be reduced if transatlantic aircraft no longer fly in stratospheres above ten kilometres. Graphic based on: Die Zeit No 41, 2019 (source: World Bank, Bundesumweltbank, International Council on Clean Transportation, International Civil Aviation Organization, Meteorological Applications)

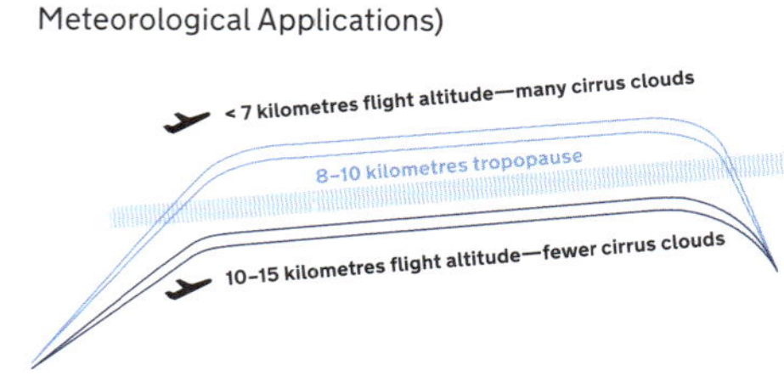

Flight routes optimisation
The EU's REACT4C research programme found that CO_2 emissions on transatlantic flights could be reduced by a quarter if the route from London to New York was placed further south, and from New York to London further north.
Graphic based on: Die Zeit No 41, 2019 (source: World Bank, Bundesumweltbank, International Council on Clean Transportation, International Civil Aviation Organization, Meteorological Applications)

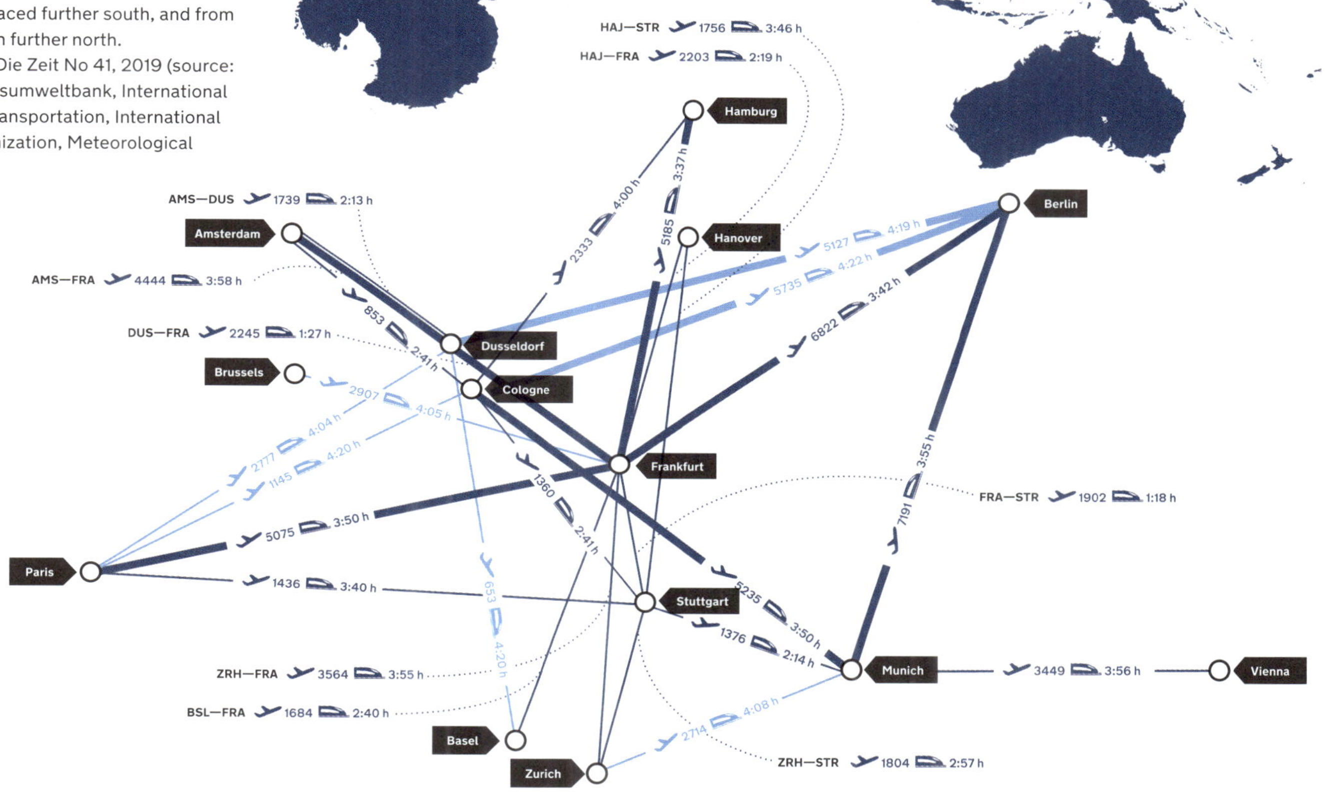

CO_2 emissions (worldwide)
Source: International Energy Agency (IEA), data 2016

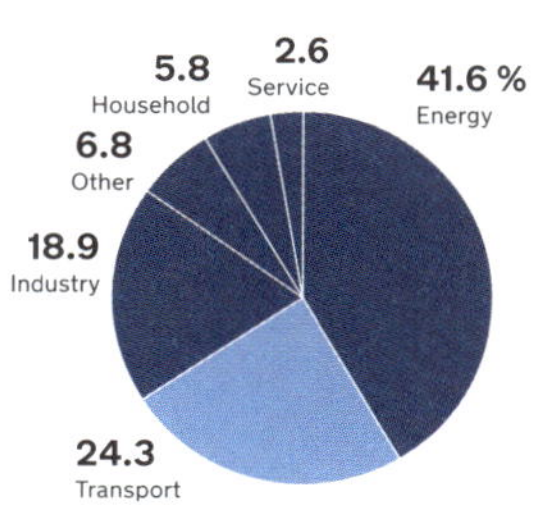

Transport sector (EU)
Source: Statistical Pocketbook 2019, data 2017

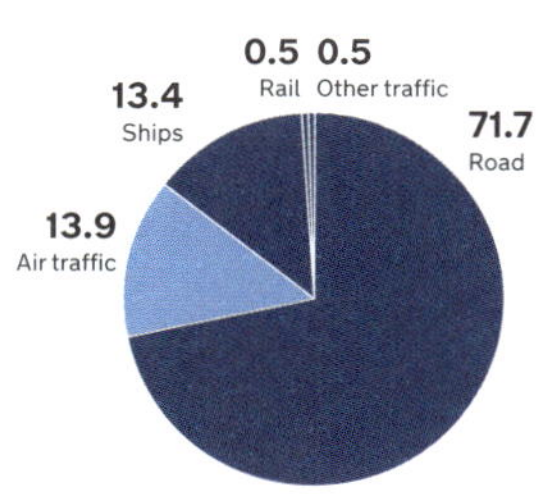

CO_2 emissions commercial aviation
Source: International Council on Clean Transportation (ICCT), data 2018, ourworldindata.org

Reachable by train within four hours
Transfer to rail for domestic and cross-border short-haul flights within Germany's eight busiest airports
— within four hours
— in more than four hours
number of flights (one direction take-offs) per year
travel time by train
— < 4000 flights
— > 4000 flights
Graphic based on BUND 2015

76

Identity

2

77

Opening dates of the world's busiest airports

The top half of this page shows the sites of today's major international airports (2019) and uses a colour scheme to indicate the timeframe in which they were opened to commercial air traffic. The bottom line: the identity of an airport is heavily influenced by its date of construction.

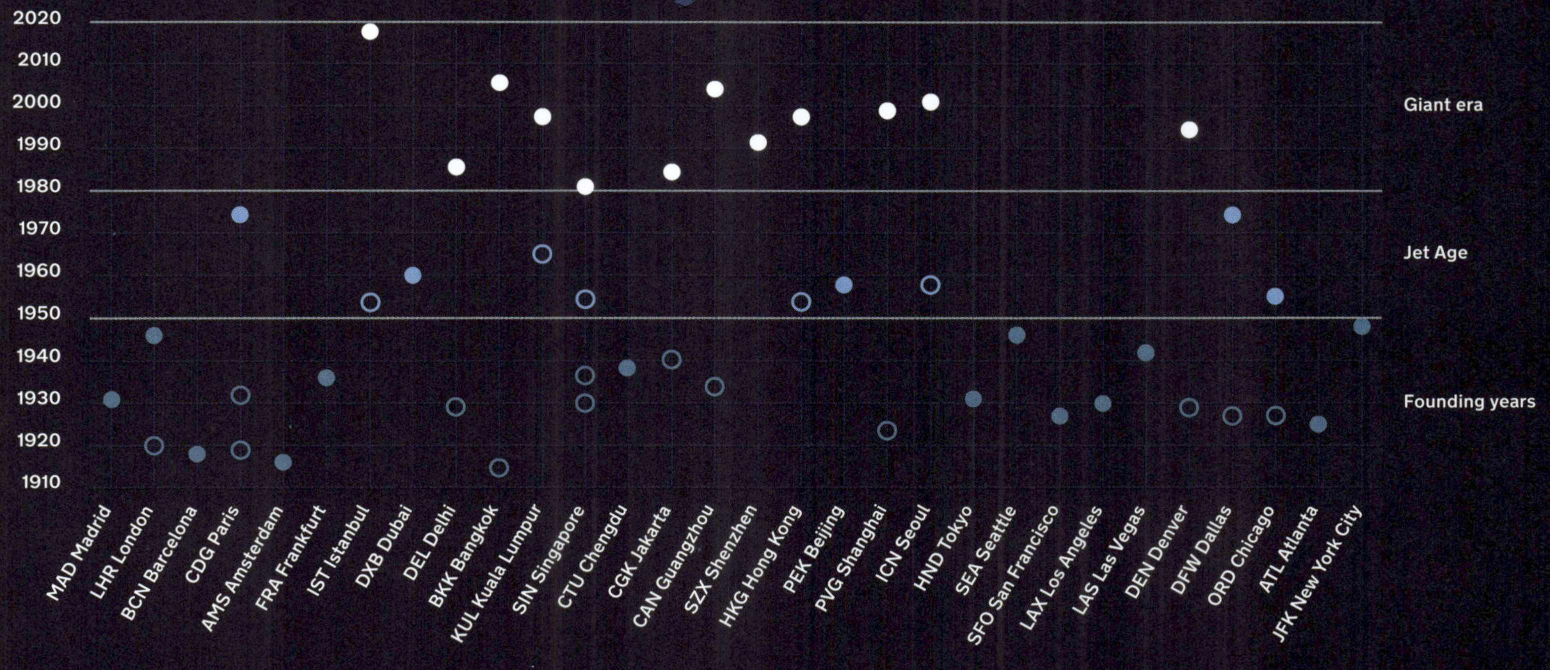

78

Airports as expressions of spirit

79

Airports are outstanding examples of national architectural traditions and have always been considered structures that represent a place and cultivate its image in the world. It is here that a country receives and bids farewell to its guests. In the past years we have witnessed an unprecedented growth in airport superlatives "bigger, faster, more spectacular". It feels like every year, the latest "largest airport ever" opens its doors. This is not just the result of the international expansion in air travel despite the growing threat of climate change. It is also a result of the enormous competition amongst international airport hubs and the pressure to generate revenues at any cost. Airports are the built expression of perpetual growth. This has led to growing passenger volumes, grander visions for growth and ever more spectacular architectural forms dedicated to the business of mobility. Reasonably predictable scenarios such as a global pandemic or climate change were somehow not factored into these grand plans.

Change is coming however. Our perspective towards these cathedrals of mobility and the meaning of representation may change too.

While these wondrous buildings and their massive scale leave us awestruck, we are awestruck too by the forces that led to their commissioning. What political and economic visions are at work and what impact will these visions have on our planet and our society?

D

Architecture

Airports are often the first buildings travellers enter when visiting a new city or country. Airport operators therefore go to great lengths to create a memorable environment that will give passengers a warm welcome, a smooth user experience and a lasting positive impression, while also tapping into the purchasing power they possess. The visual presentation of an airport plays a key role in improving the quality of the visitor experience. Indeed, many of today's state-of-the-art airport complexes feature impressive architecture, inviting interior design, entertainment options, wellness services, shopping areas and, most recently, indoor "garden" or "natural" spaces. In this chapter, we examine airport architecture and the layout of the airport, including its shape, roof and structure, as well as new paths in interior design, all of which influence our work as information designers.

One of the world's most innovative airport structures was the TWA Flight Center at John F. Kennedy International Airport JFK in New York ↗1, a building that has long since become an icon of airport architecture. Since we have always been fascinated by the terminal and its history, it is a logical place to start before we turn to more contemporary airports:

The TWA Flight Center, designed by Finnish-American architect, designer and sculptor Eero Saarinen ↗2, opened in 1962 and closed—after 40 years of use and a long period of vacancy—in 2001. A classic "futuristic" building of the 20th century, it had been unable to meet the requirements of a modern functional passenger terminal for many years. A public outcry saved it from demolition and it was lovingly restored and transformed into a hotel and conference centre in 2019. Unlike most airport buildings, from the moment it opened, it was celebrated as an iconic architectural heritage site.

The TWA Flight Center is more a monument to the architect's and airline's intention to create a building to embody the 1960s futuristic vision of air and later space travel than it is an adherent to the form-follows-function postulate of Mies van der Rohe's Classical Modernist school of architecture. The TWA Flight Center was not simply designed to bring passengers to their flights, its very structure feels as if it is about to lift off with spread wings and take flight. To this day, this architectural vision has not lost any of its utopian inspirational charm. At the time, of course, the architects were confident in the scientific principle behind the building's eccentric form. Their field studies of comparable airports and Grand Central Station in New York had demonstrated that passengers moved not in linear patterns but along curved paths. This was their empirical rationale for the rounded forms of the Flight Center building.

The building's flowing lines are also reflected in the organic shapes of the signage. The sculptural boards displaying the arrivals and departures are particularly impressive. Engineering and information design unite here to form corporate architectural icons that place the progress that air travel represents at the core of the TWA brand.

↗1 John F. Kennedy International Airport in New York had originally been planned as a set of seven distinct terminals, of which the TWA Flight Center was one. They were boldly termed the "Seven Wonders". Each architect vied to create the most pre-eminent of the seven structures.

↗2 Eero Saarinen's building was inaugurated on 28 May 1962 and features a reinforced concrete shell consisting of four segments that reach outwards from a single central point in the interior. The concrete moulded "wings" extend far out to the right and left. Under these concrete wings, passengers walked through conduits to the respective satellite buildings, known as Flight Wing One and Flight Wing Two. Today, JFK's new Terminal 5 designed by Gensler architects is built on the spot where these satellite buildings once stood.

Overleaf

1 **JFK** John F. Kennedy International Airport. In the TWA Flight Center. View of the central departure display, the building's flowing lines are reflected in the organic shapes of the signage.

2 **BOM** Chhatrapati Shivaji International Airport, Mumbai, with the alphabetically coded check-in areas.

3 **PKX** Beijing Daxing International Airport. Standing signposts as landmarks indicating the change of level via stairs and escalators. Information counters circle around the descending roof.

4 **LED** Pulkovo Airport in St Petersburg. Directions to the gates are applied directly to the light interior walls.

5 **SZX** Shenzhen Bao'an International Airport. In the check-in hall, signs float from the ceiling and standing signs pointing to escape routes rise from the floor.

1

DEPARTURES
LOCAL
TIME
MATION

2

3

4

5

Metaphor—Shape

Starfish

PKX Beijing's Daxing International Airport opened in 2019 and became the city's second largest airport after the Capital International Airport. Zaha Hadid Architects' design was inspired by the traditional Chinese town planning compounds for streets and courtyards, known in Beijing as hutongs. In the Chinese capital in particular, these areas are characterised by interconnecting spaces organised around an inner courtyard.

The terminal building features an open, multi-storey concourse that mimics the traditional Hutong. Passengers traverse the hall to reach the structure's five piers as well as the connecting building to the trains, busses, hotels, offices and the Airport City. From above, the structure's star shape is discernible with six arms that emanate outwards from the core of the building. Zaha Hadid likened the building to a starfish and further accentuated the resemblance by adding a shiny red metallic rooftop structure that extends over the entire building complex.

The sheer height of this colossal complex as well as its shimmering materials and the extravagant lines of its cover panelling are truly awe inspiring to behold. Indeed, one feels very small in its presence.

Grand escalators and glass elevator towers connect the core building's multiple levels and function as a type of passage and stairwell through the structure. Sculptural double-steles reinforce the building's polymorphic appearance and act as signposts directing travellers to different floor levels.

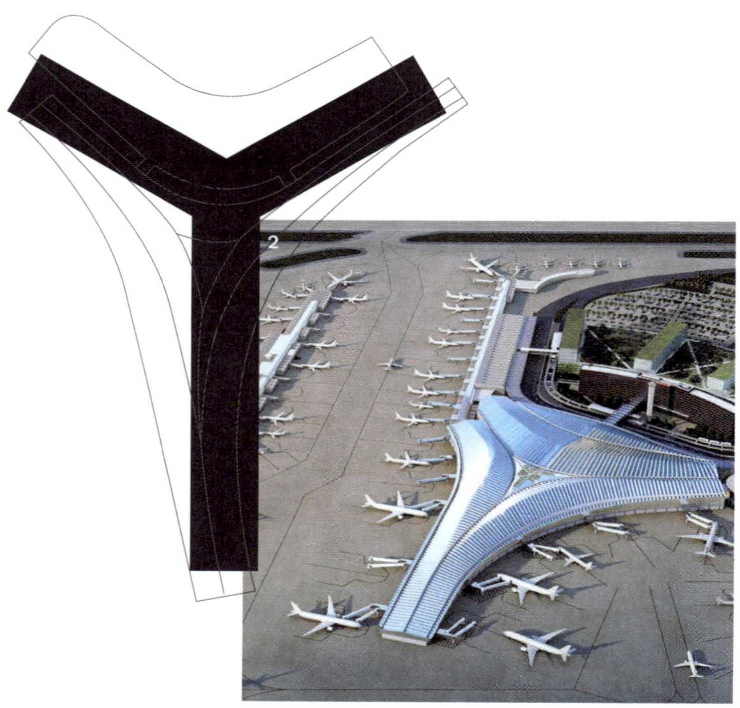

Chicago River

ORD The O'Hare International Airport groundbreaking ceremony is set for 2023. The design for the airport's new Terminal 2 has the distinct shape of the letter "Y"—an inspiration drawn from the confluence of the northern and southern arms of the Chicago River. This shape is a key element in Chicago's official city marketing and corporate identity. The roof of the forthcoming terminal is also supported by slender Y-shaped columns.

Studio ORD with lead design architect Studio Gang were commissioned for this comprehensive expansion of O'Hare International Airport.

The building's wayfinding system has yet to be premiered. Will planners continue the wayfinding concept in use at O'Hare for several years or can we expect an airport-wide relaunch? And will the "Y" play a role?

Manta ray

SZX With the completion of Terminal 3 in 2013, the annual passenger capacity at Shenzhen Bao'an International Airport was expanded to over 40 million. According to Fuksas, the Italian architects of the terminal, the concept behind the airport's design evokes the shape of a manta ray: "A fish that breathes and changes its own shape, undergoes variations, turns into a bird to celebrate the emotion and fantasy of a flight. The structure of T3—an approximately 1.5-kilometre long tunnel—seems to be modelled by the wind and is reminiscent of the image of an organic-shaped sculpture."

Natural light reaches the interior of the building through the double-layered "skin" that diffuses it creating glistening effects. The wayfinding system features signposts that hang from the double-layered ceiling and large floor applications.

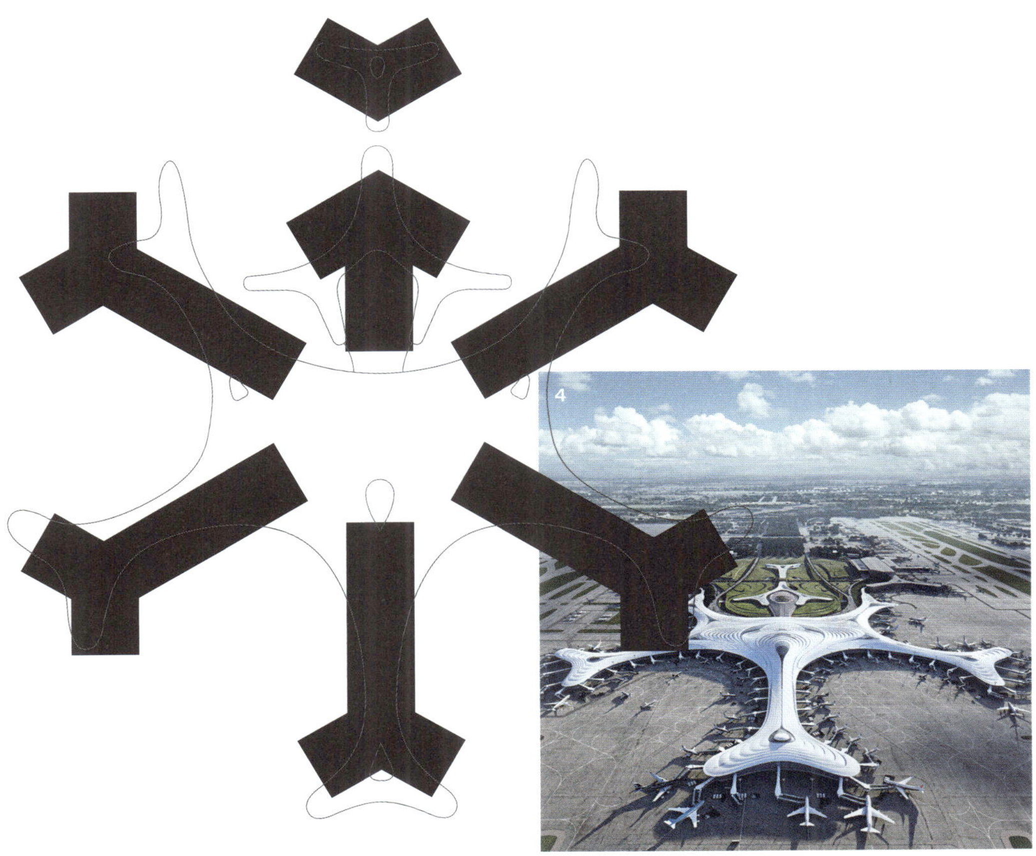

Snowflake

HRB Still in the design phase: the snowflake-shaped terminal designed by MAD Architects. The new Terminal 3 at Harbin Taiping International Airport takes on the shape of an oversized snowflake floating just above earth. The region around Harbin is prone to heavy snowfall, hence the association. The design is also inspired by the gentle slopes of China's vast northern plains.

The design of the airport's interior and wayfinding system has yet to be revealed to the public.

Metaphor—Roof

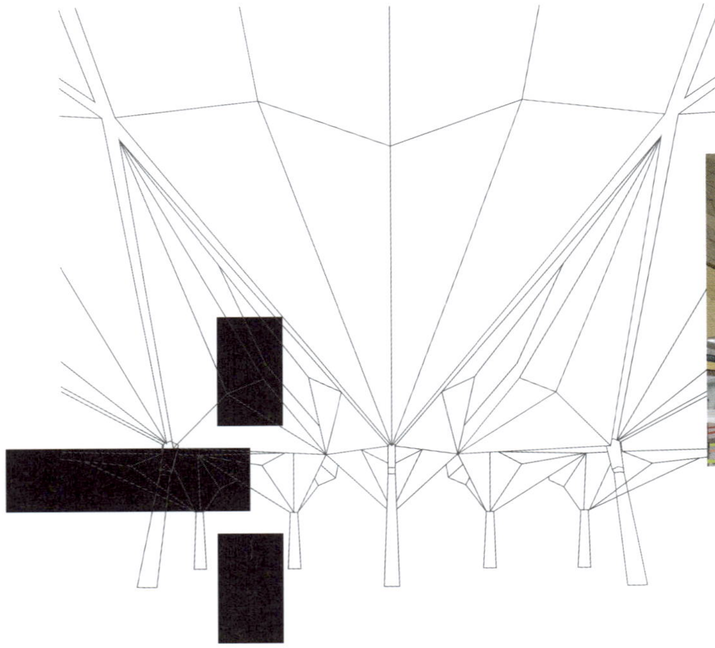

Golden rooftops

LED Pulkovo Airport in St Petersburg—"The airport where arrivals are just as important as departures." Designed by British architects Grimshaw and Partners, Terminal 1 was opened in December 2013. Here, too, the architects drew several parallels to the local urban planning tradition. The faceted geometry of the underside of the terminal roof recalls the city's rooftops. The surfaces evoke the crystalline patterns of ice crystals and snowflakes. The warm patina of the shiny gold surfaces is a reference to the golden domes and towers of St Petersburg. The roof as a direct reference to the city's skyline. According to the architects, it is a building about form and space.

However, at Pulkovo Airport, there is no signage hanging from the imposing ceiling. At the request of the architect, the ceiling will continue to remain untouched by the wayfinding system. All wayfinding information is communicated using standup display boards. The set of pictograms developed for the airport is just as unique as its ceiling.

1

Bazaar

IST The international design team responsible for the architectural concept at Istanbul Airport comprises Grimshaw Architects, Haptic Architects, Nordic Architects and Scott Brownrigg. Their design draws upon architectural references from the storied city it serves. Vaulted ceilings evoke the high and open ceilings of Istanbul's bazaars. It is an architectural citation to remind us that modern airports are built for more than just taking off and arriving.

Considerable effort was also put into the wayfinding system for this representative construction. The multifaceted signage family is also notable for its well-conceived information design.

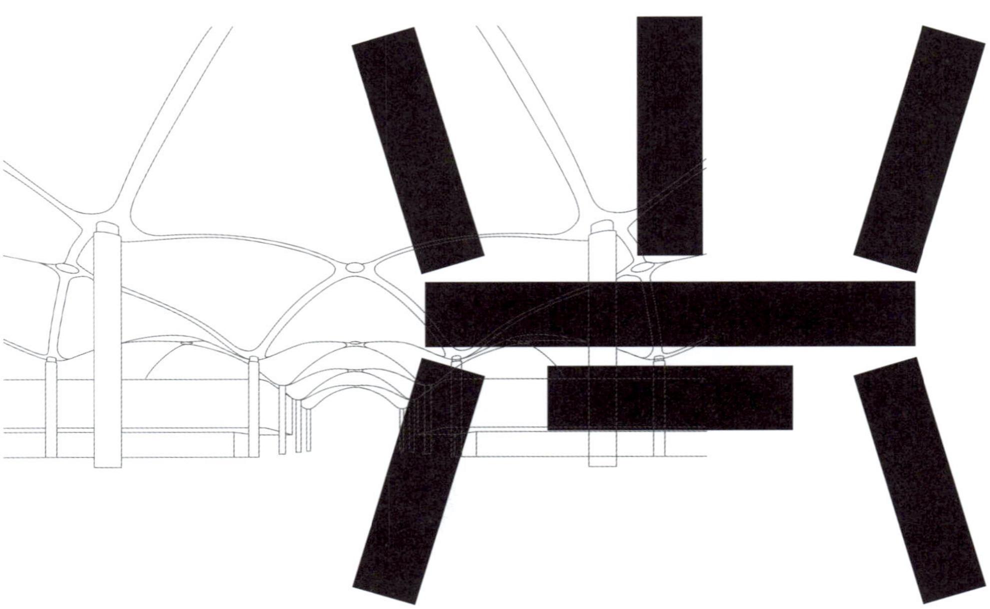

2

Metaphor—Structure

Arctic Ocean

HFT The design of the small Arctic Ocean Airport near Hammerfest in Norway also seeks to capture the spirit of its surroundings and express it in architecture and materials. In this case, the design draws upon natural elements, such as light and water. According to Haptic Architects, the shape of the roof is the key element of their design. It serves as a metaphor for the spectacular Norwegian landscape.

The building is still in the draft stage and its wayfinding system has not yet been made public. We are very much looking forward to learning how the designers have embodied the spirit of the location in the wayfinding system.

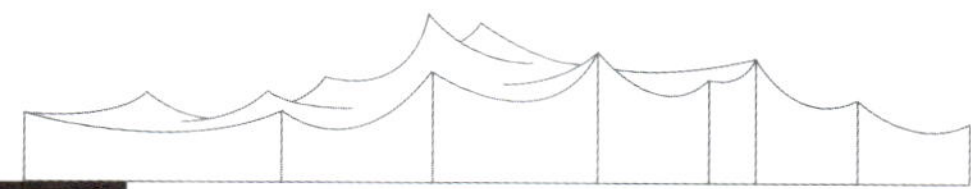

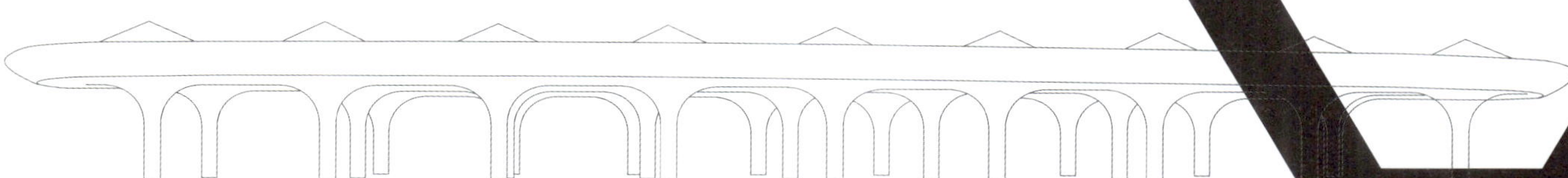

2

Pavilion

BOM For their work on Terminal 2 at Chhatrapati Shivaji International Airport in Mumbai, the US architects Skidmore, Owings & Merrill (SOM) sought to evoke the shape of traditional Indian pavilions. The architects integrated traditional Indian patterns and textures into multiple dimensions of their design. Opened in 2014, the terminal reflects the high standards of its operators in an elegant mix of modernity and tradition, from the coffered columns and rooftop in the main building to the complex Jali window shades that filter out the light in the corridors.

The airport's new visual identity was an integral component of its modernisation process. The stylised shape of a peacock feather—a sacred symbol in the Hindu religion—is a recurring theme in the building. It is a component of the logo and woven into the building's surfaces. In the wayfinding system, the feather is integrated into each sign and the illuminated frame.

Integrated design

As we discussed above, in public buildings, architecture and wayfinding systems are closely intertwined through a myriad of service and contact points. They also have a mutual influence on one another; while the architecture makes it possible to enter a space, the wayfinding systems make it possible for visitors to navigate it. For us, it is only logical that architecture and wayfinding systems be conceived and developed in tandem. This is particularly important in redesign projects for existing buildings, where changes in visitor flows have made it necessary to update the wayfinding system. Of course, one can always superimpose a wayfinding grid onto a completed structure. But this is not an option for airports which develop detailed concepts for passenger flow. In this case, pax flow and wayfinding systems must be designed by integrated design teams. These teams not only ensure the ideal technical set up, they also work to achieve functional design synergies.

Integrating ready-made wayfinding systems into buildings with highly customised architecture was common practice in many places. However, it inevitably leads to a sense of unease, not only amongst architects. In contrast integrated design is the structural integration of wayfinding into the architectural concept from the very beginning. An example is customised flush-fitted signs in panel walls designed specifically for the building in question. This allows the wayfinding system to be calibrated into the architectural grid and then mounted in pre-determined spaces. Product design, surfaces, materials and colours can be selected in a collaborative process and supply cables for electrical connections can be integrated into the planning. In our experience, integrated design yields a unified product language or a unique architectural corporate design for the project.

Here we would like to examine some outstanding examples of integrated wayfinding systems in airport buildings. Information that requires visibility from a long distance can be extended across the length of a wall, either painted or backlit. Key destinations can be marked using sculpted or 3D-forms lettering, numbers and characters. Whether as landmarks or even suspended freely in the air, they create a pleasing contrast to the sign typology.

1 **IST** Istanbul Airport
2 **BOM** Chhatrapati Shivaji International Airport
3 **BER** Berlin Brandenburg Airport
4 **LHR** Heathrow Airport
5 **BER** Berlin Brandenburg Airport
6 **FRA** Frankfurt Airport
7 **DOH** Hamad International Airport
8 **IST** Istanbul Airport
9 **SIN** Singapore Changi Airport
10 **SZX** Shenzhen Bao'an International Airport
11 **PKX** Beijing Daxing International Airport
12 **BOM** Chhatrapati Shivaji International Airport
13 **OSL** Oslo Gardermoen Airport
14 **LHR** Heathrow Airport
15 **FRA** Frankfurt Airport

New paths

Airport terminals include many purely functional areas, such as check-in, security check and baggage claim areas. Though planners do strive to improve the visitor experience in these areas, their high traffic requires that they maintain maximum functionality. In general, however, many airport design teams are deviating from traditional concepts for the interiors and implementing more open interior scenarios rather falling back upon the tried and tested solutions and the conventional furnishings of the past.

In the early years of passenger air travel, terminals were very luxurious spaces to reflect the exclusivity of air travel. With the dawn of the Jet Age, innovative design teams began rendering airport buildings into iconic structures that served as calling cards for their home countries. As air travel became accessible for larger subsections of the population and with the emergence of low-cost air carriers, the trend shifted towards more cost efficiency and processing large numbers of passengers. Very little attention was paid to the quality of the space. While luxurious interiors, such as First Class Lounges and Premium areas, were built to cater to an upscale clientele, more airport space was reserved for the large halls to accommodate masses of low-cost carrier passengers.

There are many examples to illustrate how simple furnishings can both look good and be fun. At Tokyo's Narita International Airport NRT Terminal 3, designed by Nikken Sekkei + Royohin Keikaku, the wayfinding features large-scale graphic banners and signs applied directly on the walls. Floor markings resembling a sport pitch act as a cross reference to the Olympic Games set to take place in Japan in 2021. They create a new and playful experience of the space and an amusing element of surprise.

1 **NRT** A racecourse at Narita International Airport, Tokyo. This low-cost carrier installed the tartan track markings to mimic a sport pitch.

2 **IST** The new Istanbul Airport features spacious lounge areas without traditional seating.

1

2

Casual

Imaginative interiors, casual waiting areas and even environmentally-friendly furnishings await the air travellers of today. Interior concepts have begun reinterpreting our set notions of an airport with warm and inviting environments. The benches of Green Furniture Concept in Malmö Airport MMX could just as easily be installed in a hip downtown neighbourhood. They are arranged in a circle around an abstract tree to provide a comforting resting spot in an otherwise foreign environment.

Privacy, atmosphere

The constantly evolving traveller usage scenarios have also led to the emergence of new furnishing concepts, such as sleeping pods and napcabs. These allow passengers to retreat into tiny spaces which they have all to themselves. Some airports offer other micro-spaces, such as business meeting capsules and nursing containers which can be booked in advance. They allow airports to give travellers a degree of privacy amidst the bustle of the airport.

Landscape airport

Another interesting trend in newer terminals is the integration of plants and indoor gardens. Natural environments exert a calming effect on travellers and positively influence their sense of wellbeing. The design team for the new Global Terminal at Chicago O'Hare International Airport is Studio ORD, a collaboration between lead design architect Studio Gang, Solomon Cordwell Buenz, Corgan, Milhouse Engineering & Construction, Inc. and STLarchitects. They have created a green island, called the Central Green in the middle of the terminal, like a park in a city centre. It functions as a landmark within the complex where passengers take a moment to orient themselves. The star-shaped opening of the roof, called the Oculus, allows natural light to flow into the terminal.

1 **OSL** Wood and a modern style characterise the interior concept at Oslo Gardermoen Airport. It is an example of typical Scandinavian design. The colours of the wayfinding system correspond to the materials used in the terminal.

2 New airport concepts like these sleeping pods offer passengers a quiet and private space and improve their overall quality of stay.

3 **MMX** Organic designs found in nature: lighting trees and sustainable furniture at Malmö Airport.

Overleaf

4 **ORD** Planning for the future— the building is designed to meet a high LEED standard for green building certification. A large green oasis in the middle of the new Terminal in O'Hare International Airport.

5 **SGN** Concept of Long Thanh International Airport in Dong Nai Province, Vietnam designed by HEERIM ARCHITECTS & PLANNERS CO., LTD.: a lotus shape, symbolising the elegance, strength and warm culture of Vietnam including a green planted departure area.

6 **SIN** There are half a million plants and trees at Terminal 4 of the Singapore Changi Airport, giving passengers a soothing and natural welcome in all areas, particularly in the baggage claim area.

1

2

3

1

2

3

Places

Airport shopping

On the airside, airports have long been successful retail centres. Eager consumers meet lavishly designed sales areas with attractive offers. During the so-called Golden Hour, when the stress level has dropped after passing security and before boarding, passengers like to spend time shopping or exploring the international brand retail areas. Some are interested in local products that they can conveniently purchase as a memento of their visit. Airports are adapting their retail to an international clientele because their economic success as a venture depends on it. In areas frequented by wealthy travellers, one will often find shops selling premium products.

Good visitor orientation is the precondition for a relaxed shopping experience. When passengers are aware of their walking times to gate and trust the wayfinding system to get them there, they are more inclined to shop. Central wait areas and departure lounges allow passengers to use catering services or retail options until just before boarding.

Special issues

Specific passenger needs and new issues like hygiene measures are getting increasingly important in the airport environment. Airports have become sensitive to the need for universal design and barrier-free mobility. In 2008, in compliance with a regulation issued by the European Parliament, all European airports began offering assistance services for passengers with reduced mobility—a response not only to aging populations but also to the needs of other demographics who require support while travelling. Individual airports and transnational initiatives are offering special mobility services and assistance concepts at airports. Persons with Reduced Mobility (PRMs) or guests with limited cognitive capacity are often provided with designated service areas in an effort to improve their airport experience.

1 **AMS** The sanitising service spot at Amsterdam's Schiphol Airport has gained in importance in the Covid-19 era.

2 **PMI** Palma de Mallorca Airport. Meeting points are designed to welcome all passengers with reduced mobility at Aena-operated airports. A well-conceived interior design will clearly designate these areas, and the wayfinding system will ensure that they are easily locatable.

3 **LGW** Gatwick Airport, London aims to be an accessible airport, giving everybody an equal opportunity to fly. Information on Special Assistance Services are integrated into the information chains online as well as on-site. To be effective, the Special Assistance Services concept must be embedded into the colour scheme, the pictogram set and the interior design.

1

Sanitising Service
HEMA

2

aena
sin barreras
sense barreres
aena
sin barreras
sense barreres

3

Special
assistance

E

Colour

An airport is an environment full of sensory impressions: multiple information streams, shopping options, audio announcements. In this whirlwind of sights, sounds and colours, visitors need to be able to find, read and process the information contained in the wayfinding system. Colour schemes can help influence whether the wayfinding system stands out from or fades into the hustle and bustle of the airport. The right choice of colour can help a business traveller in a hurry, holidaymakers on a stroll and employees and delivery staff find their destination safely and effectively all at the same time.

The choice of colour is amongst the most influential and perhaps also the most emotional design components along with the typeface and the set of pictograms in an airport wayfinding system. It also plays a key role in transporting the identity of the airport.

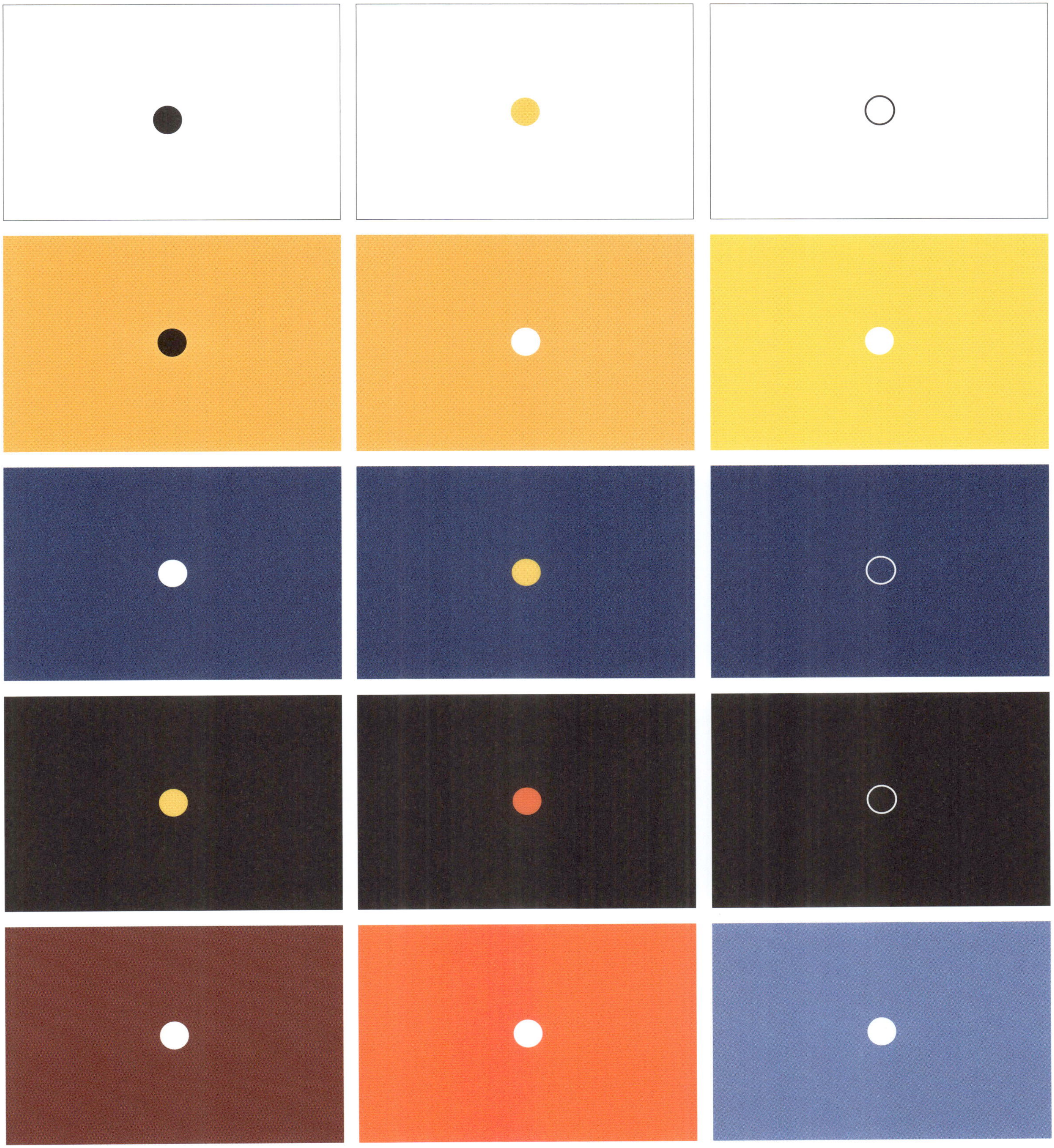

Emotional

Colours invoke an emotional reaction. We intuitively perceive certain colours as cold or warm, exciting or calming. Colours are amongst the first words in a child's vocabulary and amongst the first words we learn to read and write in school. Colour associations can vary strongly between cultures and geographies. In Europe black is the colour of mourning. In Asia it is white. International air traffic has managed to achieve a certain consensus in the perception of colours.

How strongly visitors perceive colour in an airport wayfinding system depends on various factors such as the luminosity of the colour in question, the overall building lighting concept and the colour contrasts in the interior environment.

Advertising, security announcements and information all compete for passengers' attention at the airport. The most important information for the purpose of wayfinding therefore, must be clearly identifiable in colour. Colour can be a tool to establish a hierarchy of information with the most important information clearly highlighted in strong tones.

Colour contrast is also decisive in achieving good legibility. This can be the contrast between foreground, in the form of pictogram and text, and background, in the form of the colour of the sign surface. But the contrast between the sign colour and its surroundings is also decisive.

Light also has a huge influence on our experience of colours. Every airport has to contend with very different lighting situations in one complex. Some areas are flooded with daylight, others rely on artificial light. There are large bright rooms as well as long dark corridors. Some gate areas enjoy direct sunlight while windowless duty free areas are full of captivating advertising displays. Colours contrast differently in each of these different settings. To ensure legibility in all lighting situations, wayfinding system designers employ techniques to keep information consistently visible, including external illumination, internal illumination and increasingly LCD display systems.

1

2

3

4
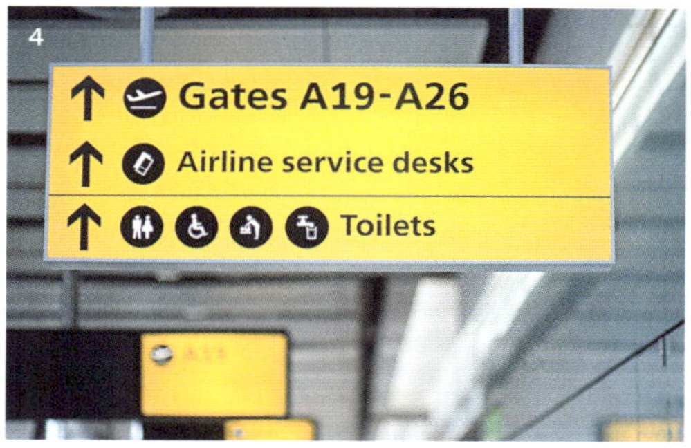

5

6

7

8

9

10

11

12

13

14

15

1 **BKK** Suvarnabhumi International Airport
4 **LHR** Heathrow Airport
7 **FRA** Frankfurt Airport
10 **OSL** Oslo Gardermoen Airport
13 **BER** Berlin Brandenburg Airport

2 **HND** Tokyo Haneda International Airport
5 **AMS** Amsterdam Airport Schiphol
8 **RAK** Marrakesh Menara Airport
11 **AMM** Queen Alia International Airport
14 **MVD** Carrasco International Airport

3 **ADL** Adelaide Airport
6 **CAI** Cairo International Airport
9 **PEK** Beijing Capital International Airport
12 **STR** Stuttgart Airport
15 **MUC** Munich Airport

In situations with direct sunlight or backlighting, the luminous intensity is adjusted for better visibility in a very bright environment. Most airport signage is internally illuminated to deliver consistent legibility and to provide a strong light-dark contrast.

Wayfinding signage increasingly uses self-luminous LCD technology. The luminosity can be adjusted to the environment to achieve a consistent contrast on signs throughout the complex. Analogue externally illuminated signage is the most difficult to control and is therefore rarely used at large airports. LCD displays deliver an even luminance and cast no shadows in contrast to internal illuminated signs. For messaging changes, displays require less maintenance because there is no need for the manual replacement of films. Also, displays have become far more affordable and flexible. Until recently, screen sizes were limited to just a few formats. Today, there are a multitude of options including narrow oblong formats that resemble traditional ceiling signs integrated seamlessly into the existing wayfinding system typology. Displays have the added advantage that the information can be changed and adapted easily. LCD technology does shed luminosity over time and colour quality also declines. The combination of internally illuminated analogue signs and LCD displays with identical information structure and colour provides seamless orientation in the best case scenario. If well executed, passenger will not notice whether the information is displayed on analogue or digital media.

White

In the early days of flight travel, an airport was comprised of just one building and functions could easily be indicated and seen at a glance. Indeed, the first signs were painted directly on the walls. These were later replaced by sign bodies. The information on the sign face protected behind glass became more valuable. These early signs were generally white with black lettering.

As global air travel grew, airports were required to accommodate ever more functions in addition to passenger services. These included air traffic control facilities, airline offices, customs processing and meteorological services. The airport buildings, at some point, included viewing terraces and car parks as individual mobility proliferated. Soon airlines began operating their own terminals as an extension of their corporate design, with the signs. All these developments added complexity to the airport structure and suddenly there were multiple destinations that required some form of wayfinding. Soon, the first internal illuminated signs appeared.

In the 1920s and 30s, the first neon advertising displays were displayed in cities and sign makers were keen to install them in airports too. But even then it was clear that airport signs couldn't look like advertising and they had to include much more information. In the 1940s and 50s, a new generation of sign technology emerged: moulded plastic with silk-screen printing on the sign face, internally illuminated. A few years later, silkscreen printing was replaced by thin self-adhesive plotted film.

1 **THF** Berlin Tempelhof Airport (closed in 2008)
→ opened in 1923, photo 1926

2 **LBG** Paris Le Bourget Airport
→ opened in 1919, photo 2013

3 **MUC** Munich-Riem Airport (closed in 1992)
→ opened in 1936, photo 1960

4 **JFK** John F. Kennedy International Airport, New York, TWA Flight Center Terminal 5 (closed 2001)
→ opened in 1962, photo approx. 1972

5 **LAX** Los Angeles International Airport
→ opened in 1962, movie 1963

6 **SHA** Shanghai Hongqiao International Airport, Terminal 1
→ opened in 1923, reopened in 1964, photo 2002

7 **LAX** Los Angeles International Airport, Terminal 7
→ opened in 1962, photo before 1967

Rauchen verboten.
DEUTSCHE LUFT HANSA
Fluggäste
Zoll

2

DEPART

3

Zollgepäck-Ausgabe
Customs Baggage Claim

TICKET LOBBY

5

ELEVATOR ASCENSEUR
ASCENSOR エレベーター

6

登机口
Gate
4.3.2.1A.1B

7

SELF SERVICE
BAGGAGE CLAIM
BAGGAGE
FROM FLIGHT

Yellow

On 7 December 1944, the international community held a Convention on International Civil Aviation in Chicago. Fifty-two countries went on to sign the convention as air travel for commercial purposes began to proliferate around the world. At the Chicago Convention the International Civic Aviation Association (ICAO) was established to standardise civil aviation internationally and in particular develop passenger safety standards. From the 1940s and 50s onwards, the ICAO published a series of guidelines for airport signs as well as runway markings and taxiways for aircraft including the familiar "follow me" signs. For this signage, the ICAO recommended yellow on black. Yellow provided an excellent contrast to the dark taxiway. A white and black combination would have been less suitable as it wouldn't have offered sufficient contrast in dark or winter conditions.

Once the yellow and black contrast had proven itself in the outside area, it found its way into the interiors of the terminal buildings. By the end of the 1960s, the German Airports Association (ADV) had set yellow and black as a standard for passenger wayfinding inside the buildings and established norms and standards for signs at German airports—the first national association in Europe to do so. It had been empirically established that black writing on a yellow background provided the best legibility and that the colour yellow possessed the best luminosity of all the spectral colours. The second colour for the sign background, varied amongst the airports between green and white, as to be seen on page 111 photos number 5 to 8. In Germany, the recommendation was followed inter alia by Cologne Bonn Airport, Berlin Tegel Airport, Berlin Tempelhof Airport, Hannover Airport and Munich-Riem Airport. Helvetica was defined as the standard typeface along with a uniform set of pictograms.

Our analysis shows that many international airports at the time followed this guidance because it promised safety and was well recognisable for passengers, whether they landed in New Delhi, Rome or Sydney. This idea of standardising airport wayfinding systems predated globalisation by many decades. Today, the internet makes it possible for us to research our destinations in advance and travellers today expect to experience local identity at the point of landing.

Of the 15 airports in the analysis that originally used the colour yellow for their wayfinding systems, 12 have now chosen to use other colours today.

At the end of the 1960s, the signage at Heathrow Airport, London LHR featured black lettering on a yellow background. During the planning phases for Terminal 5, which opened in 2008, the operators discussed a redesign of the wayfinding system whereby a new typeface and a new colour scheme would be introduced. However, after some deliberation and analyses of passenger behaviour and perception, they opted to stick with the black on yellow colour scheme. Of course, making the switch would have been costly had it encompassed the whole airport complex with four existing terminals along with the fifth about to open. But authorities learned from their market research that the colour yellow was strongly associated with Heathrow Airport and had been learned by passengers. Had just the new

Terminal 5 been given a new colour, the wider airport wayfinding system would have been inconsistent. The authorities opted to replace the font over time starting with Terminal 5. This was less noticeable than changing the colour. Today, the yellow wayfinding system at Heathrow Airport is considered iconic for its unmistakable background colour.

The same is true for the wayfinding system at Amsterdam Airport Schiphol AMS. Its signage dates back to the late 1960s and features Dutch information in black lettering and English in white lettering on a yellow sign face as you can see on page 157. When the wayfinding system was updated in the 1990s by design agency Mijksenaar, these strong elements were retained. The yellow colour of the sign face was also kept. The Dutch language was dropped and the English unilingual text was set in black on the Schiphol yellow sign face. The legibility was improved by switching to the Frutiger typeface. Pictograms were also introduced. The wayfinding system drew on a critical analysis and was set up with the aim of rationalising and safeguarding the airport's functions. It is very consistent in its application. The colour yellow today provides the typical Schiphol identity.

1 **TXL** Berlin Tegel Airport. Yellow sign faces and green sign faces with pictograms on a white square field with rounded corners.

2 **LHR** Heathrow Airport, London. Yellow plus the additional rail blue for trains.

3 **LHR** Heathrow Airport, London. Yellow plus the additional purple for flight connections.

4 **AMS** Amsterdam Airport Schiphol. Yellow as the primary colour for arrivals and departures. The colours dark grey for facilities, light grey for instructions and blue for transportation, retail and catering industry.

Blue

In keeping with changing global architecture trends, airport terminal buildings around the world were increasingly constructed with brighter steel and glass. These materials have come to symbolise the technical advancement of flight travel. As these materials became the standard around the world, airports began implementing wayfinding systems that use blue sign faces with white lettering. Blue has additional advantages for this type of infrastructure. Flight travel evokes blue skies and it is often chosen as a corporate colour for many companies in the industry. It is also a national colour in many countries with major airport operations such as the United States, France and the UK.

As architectural style became more technological, signage no longer had the task of attracting attention at all costs. Instead, it needed to complement the striking technical interiors of the terminal building. Blue is the modern signage colour that conveys technological advancement and safety.

China has the most expansive and the youngest air transport infrastructure in the world. Most Chinese airports are less than 30 years old. The vast majority of them have chosen to use blue sign faces with lettering and pictograms in white. In this context, blue signals the opening of China to the world as a modern country aspiring to a bright future. Blue also reflects China's self-confidence and stands in sharp contrast to the yellow of the 1960s and 70s in the West.

Beijing Capital International Airport PEK is located 29 kilometres northeast of downtown Beijing and is the second busiest airport in Asia welcoming passengers from all over the world. Planning for the airport was elaborate and reflected the prestige associated with flight infrastructure as a gateway to China. In Beijing, the iconic Terminal 3 was designed by the British architect Norman Foster in time for the Olympic Games 2008. From above, it resembles a dragon. The interior architecture was designed with the same effort and attention to detail as the overall architecture. This is particularly true of the colour concept for the interior. All materials and shapes are held in the traditional Chinese colours red and yellow—even the gate seating is red. The sole exception is the blue wayfinding system that navigates passengers throughout the complex. The approach was to follow the national Chinese trend and not design a wayfinding system specifically for the building's layout.

Black, grey

Increasingly dark or black sign faces are becoming the international convention for airport wayfinding. This elegant and reduced approach has become possible thanks to new innovative technologies for signage that have vastly improved visibility and readability in this colour combination. A black wayfinding system with clear backlit information in white can be a calming presence and provide a welcome contrast to the bustling visual surroundings of a modern airport. This is the opposite approach to the logic of the yellow sign with black lettering of years past. Many airports are currently revising their wayfinding system to introduce a dark background sign face, often with yellow information—basically the inversion of the dominant colour scheme in the 1960s.

However, in the 1960s, there was already a trend towards dark sign faces with white information—particularly in the United States. Architects designed all aspects of airports interiors—including signage—to conform to one overarching architectural concept. Eero Saarinen's work on Baltimore-Washington International Airport BWI, is one example of this, as you can see on page 154. His team designed all elements within the terminal building including each sign. They featured information set in white typeface on an elegant black sign face. The letters were in all capitals but the signs were not backlit. Jane Davis Doggett's work for George Bush Intercontinental Airport, Houston IAH and Baltimore-Washington International Airport BWI on pages 162 and 175 are further examples of this design style.

Now that airports are evolving into architectural monoliths, the dark sign faces for wayfinding are undergoing a renaissance. With their own architectural language, incredible building size and passenger numbers, airports are once again the expression of political statements. They depict dragons, stars or snowflakes and they achieve identity through their external form. The wayfinding systems are expected to blend in, be restrained and not too conspicuous.

In place of the uniform blue signs still found in many Chinese airports, Beijing Daxing International Airport PKX, which opened in 2019, opted for dark grey signs with information set in white-yellow. Shanghai Hongqiao International Airport SHA, which began civic aviation in 1923, continued to use a white wayfinding system until 2014. Today, it has a similar colour concept to Beijing Daxing.

In 2014, Chhatrapati Shivaji International Airport in Mumbai BOM, introduced an updated black wayfinding system in the new Terminal 2. The airport logo is in the form of a peacock feather. Each black sign is framed by a pattern of abstract miniature peacock feathers which ornamentally frame and illuminate it and lend the signage an air of elegance.

3

4

5

1 **PEK** Same blue sign face all over China in the 2000s era. At the Beijing Capital International Airport T3 as well.

2 **WUH** At Wuhan Tianhe International Airport blue signs in the year 2005.

3 **PKX** Beijing Daxing International Airport, dark grey and the colour yellow as the accent colour for pictograms.

4 **SHA** Shanghai Hongqiao International Airport, dark grey and the colour green as the accent colour for pictograms.

5 **BOM** White typeface on a black background at Chhatrapati Shivaji International Airport, Mumbai.

1 **LHR** Graphic reproduction of a sign at Heathrow Airport, London.

YELLOW STILL IN USE ↓

YELLOW REPLACED IN THE RECENT YEARS ↓

2 **LHR** Heathrow Airport—ongoing
5 **MUC** Munich-Riem Airport—until 1992
8 **TXL** Berlin Tegel Airport—until 2020
11 **LED** Pulkovo Airport—until 2013
14 **AGA** Agadir-Al Massira Airport—until about 2015

3 **GRU** São Paulo/Guarulhos Intl. Airport—ongoing
6 **CGN** Cologne Bonn Airport—until 2000
9 **DEL** Indira Gandhi International Airport—until 2003
12 **AMM** Queen Alia International Airport—until 2013
15 **CDG** Charles de Gaulle Airport—until 1994

4 **SVO** Sheremetyevo International Airport—ongoing
7 **HAJ** Hannover Airport—until 2020
10 **VIE** Vienna International Airport—until 2012
13 **GVA** Geneva Airport—until about 2014
16 **HKG** Kai Tak Airport—until 1998

1 **HGH** Graphic reproduction of a sign at Hangzhou Xiaoshan International Airport, Terminal A.

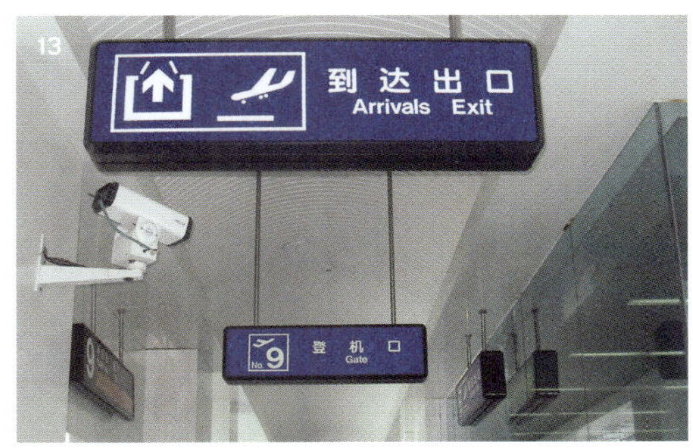

2 **HEL** Helsinki Airport 2018
5 **BOM** Chhatrapati Shivaji International, T1 2015
8 **CGN** Cologne Bonn Airport 2008
11 **IST** Istanbul Airport 2019
14 **NKG** Nanjing Lukou International Airport 2006

3 **FRA** Frankfurt Airport 2020
6 **PRG** Vaclav Havel Airport 2019
9 **ORD** O'Hare International Airport 2020
12 **CTU** Chengdu Shuangliu International Airport 2006
15 **PVG** Shanghai Pudong International Airport 2002

4 **GVA** Geneva Airport 2018
7 **RAK** Marrakesh Menara Airport 2015
10 **DUS** Düsseldorf Airport 2017
13 **KMG** Kunming Changshui International Airport 2002
16 **DXB** Dubai International Airport 2013

1

1 **BOM** Graphic reproduction of a sign at Chhatrapati Shivaji International Airport, Mumbai in Terminal 2.

2

3

4

5
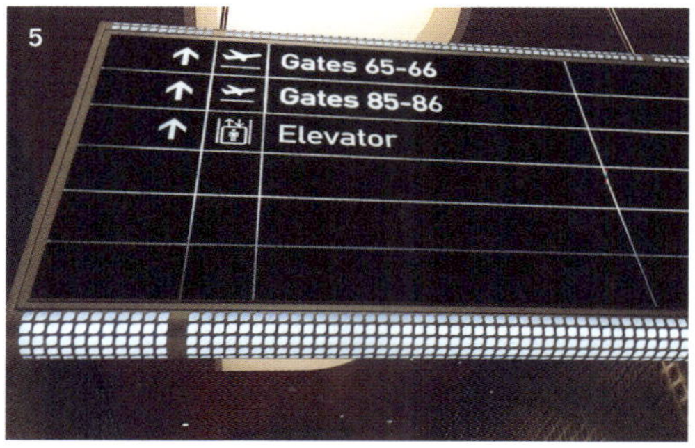

6

7

8

9

10

11

12

13

14

15

16

2 **ZRH** Zurich Airport 2010
5 **BOM** Chhatrapati Shivaji International T2, 2019
8 **OSL** Oslo Gardermoen Airport 2018
11 **SIN** Singapore Changi Airport 2019
14 **LIS** Lisbon Airport 2019

3 **VIE** Vienna International Airport 2018
6 **TPA** Tampa International Airport 2018
9 **AMM** Queen Alia International Airport 2018
12 **VCE** Venice Marco Polo Airport 2018
15 **HND** Tokyo Haneda Intl. Airport Terminal 1, 2020

4 **MUC** Munich Airport 2016
7 **STR** Stuttgart Airport 2013
10 **DUB** Dublin Airport 2014
13 **HAN** Noi Bai International Airport 2010
16 **MAA** Chennai International Airport 2014

1 **MAD** Graphic reproduction of a sign at Adolfo Suárez Madrid-Barajas Airport, Terminal 4.

2

2 **MAD** Terminal 4, departure gates.

1 **MUC** Graphic reproduction of a sign at Munich Airport, Terminal 1.

2

2 **MUC** Terminal 1 at Munich Airport, departure gates.

1 **BER** Graphic reproduction of a sign at Berlin Brandenburg Airport, Terminal 1.

2 **BER** Terminal 1, view into the check-in hall at Berlin Brandenburg Airport.

1 **MVD** Graphic reproduction of a sign at Carrasco International Airport.

2 **MVD** Driveway at Carrasco International Airport.

Airport operator

International conventions in wayfinding are the result of much more than just official international guidelines and years of experience in handling passenger journeys. They are also influenced by the standard practices of large airport operators. Many implement the same wayfinding system in all airports they operate internationally. For example, all Spanish airports are operated by the same company, Airport Operator Aena (Aeropuertos Españoles y Navegación Aérea). They implement the same wayfinding system in all their airports.

The Aena wayfinding system is a standard that codifies information along a colour hierarchy on a dark grey background. Yellow is used for the most crucial information such as departures, connecting flights and arrivals. It is also used to indicate special needs assistance for PRMs (persons with reduced mobility) and onward transport options such as train, bus, metro and parking. Terminal services such as toilets, lifts, shops, lounges and restaurants appear in blue. At large airports with several terminals, each terminal building is assigned a colour red, yellow or green. The gates within the terminals are also assigned a colour, up to about 13 colours are available.

Each airport uses the same information structure, independently of the architectural layout, floor plan, building size or number of building sections. The result is a colourful and unique identity for Spanish airports.

1

Striking colours

The colour palette for airport wayfinding systems has expanded over the years as a result of new technical developments. Film manufacturers now provide a wide range of colours and digital printing technology has been game changing. In addition, the cost of printing has come down and designers are free to use customised colour tones and combinations on one surface area.

MUC Munich Airport

In 1992 Munich Airport MUC moved to a new location about 28 kilometres outside of the city centre in the community of Erdinger Moos. The architectural concept for the new Franz Josef Strauß Airport was a complete departure from the previous airport in the Munich borough of Riem. The operators relaunched the corporate design for the new airport to correspond with the architectural concept for the interiors and exteriors of the terminal buildings. The colour concept for the wayfinding system was inspired by the official colours of Bavaria, blue and white. The signage at the previous airport in Riem complied with the ADV standard yellow.

"Munich Airport, opens to the sky and the light" written in "M Flughafen Munich 1992", the three-volume slipcase for the opening of the airport, described the aim of Hans-Busso von Busse architects. The Terminal 1 building is highly technical, modern and flooded with light. The central architectural concept for the building is that the constructive elements and the building skeleton are prominently visible throughout the complex. This guiding

2

3

principle was then adopted to the product design for the wayfinding system. Framed in white, each sign sets a prominent blue accent in a hue mixed exclusively for this airport.

The text is backlit in white on the basic colour. This unique blue tone adds to the atmospheric quality of the building which is quite unique in the world of airports. Later on, the colour orange was introduced to the signs to indicate retail and service areas in the Munich Airport Centre. Terminal 2 opened in 2003 and is co-owned and operated by the airport operating company and the German airline Lufthansa. This terminal features dark grey as the base colour for the wayfinding system. The dimensions and proportions of the signs in particular in Terminal 1 are based on the 1.20 m x 1.20 m architectural grid. This gives the wayfinding system a uniform typology.

BER Berlin Brandenburg Airport

1990 was the year of German reunification. The city of Berlin was also reunited and soon to regain its status as the capital city of Germany. The city set out to build a new and modern airport to serve the whole metropolitan area as well as its surrounding region Brandenburg. Our firm Moniteurs was awarded the commission to design the wayfinding system for the new Berlin Brandenburg Airport BER by the architects gmp von Gerkan, Marg and Partners. From the beginning, it was clear to us that the concept would be a departure from the yellow signage of the 1970s installed at the three existing Berlin airports Tempelhof, Tegel and Schönefeld. The identity of this future airport serving the dynamic metropolis that Berlin has become, had to be new. From the official colours of the city state of Berlin and the federal state of Brandenburg, we created a unique signage red to reflect the bold and dynamic new identity that the city and the region had taken on since reunification.

Upon reaching the BER airport complex, one is immersed in design of the Berlin Brandenburg Airport. The elements of the corporate design—the red, the custom pictograms, the font and the product design—are visible from the outside grounds and throughout the airport complex. Red is the first element visible to the approaching visitor. Closer proximity reveals that all flight-related information is set in this warm red tone, whereas service information is set on dark grey signage that corresponds to the architecture.

The guiding principle for the information design and wayfinding system is the translation of the clear geometric structures of the architecture into lines. The pine forests of Berlin and Brandenburg with their straight trunks form a linear pattern that defines Berlin's architectural history. It is a reference of the columned entrance hall of Karl Friedrich Schinkel's Altes Museum. It appears in the strict architectural grid of Mies van der Rohe's Neue Nationalgalerie. This linear motif was the inspiration for the architects of this airport. It is reflected in the airport's curbside structure with its columned canopy. The terminal building echoes the building tradition of the German capital region. The signage also takes up the linear motif and mixes red grey and white lines in a hierarchy of information all set on internally illuminated signs. The red sign face is printed in a pleasant glow without glaring. The white information elements are bright and well contrasted to guarantee good legibility.

4

LAND BRANDENBURG

Berlin

1 **MAD** At Adolfo Suárez Madrid-Barajas Airport all gates A, B, C, D, E etc. are colour-coded.

2 **MUC** Munich Airport's Terminal 1 wayfinding system is inspired by the national colours of Bavaria, white and blue.

3 **MUC** The colour blue for the wayfinding at Munich Airport is a special mixed unique blue. Slightly warmer than the Bavarian blue.

4 **BER** The state colour of Berlin and Brandenburg, a strong, pure red.

5 **BER** The BER signage red of Berlin Brandenburg Airport is reminiscent of the red of the state colour of Berlin and Brandenburg, but has a stronger contrast value and is clearly distinguishable from the red tone used as a warning colour.

MVD Carrasco International Airport

The Carrasco International Airport MVD is located a few kilometres east of Montevideo, Uruguay. On 5 October 2009 the operators opened the new terminal building designed by the Uruguayan-American architect Rafael Viñoly. The warm orange of the Uruguayan sun plays a central role in the airport's corporate design and as a distinct accent in the airport wayfinding system. The destination points and arrows are indicated in orange fields on a white background. The white provides a cooling contrast to the hot orange sun.

1

2

NRT Narita International Airport, Terminal 3

Narita International Airport NRT is Japan's second largest airport and handles most international flights to and from Tokyo. Here the colour of he wayfinding system is used in a completely different way than usual.

In the new low-cost and energy-saving terminal, digital displays and passenger treadmills are almost completely eliminated. Instead, a wayfinding system consisting of blue and red running tracks, reminiscent of a sport stadium show the way. The blue paths symbolise the sky and lead to departure, the red ones stand for earth and thus mark the arrival area. All necessary information, such as the distance to the nearest terminal, exits, baggage claim, etc., was sprayed directly onto the tracks in white. The ceiling signs with their black sign face and white information fit well into the overall structure at the usual information and viewing height.

The important role of colours

A well-designed wayfinding system that uses a colour scheme carefully chosen for the building in question will be extremely effective in navigating passengers throughout the airport. If the colour hierarchies are clear and contrasts high, travellers will instinctually locate the information they seek quickly. With clear and readable signage, passengers and visitors feel secure in the complex. Colour enhances clarity and readability and helps communicate the airport's identity.

1 **MVD** The sun symbol, as the airport logo at Carrasco International Airport, derived from the Uruguayan flag.

2 **MVD** The colour orange at Carrasco International Airport as an accent colour on the white sign. Parking for disabled people and pregnant women.

3 **NRT** The view into a corridor of Terminal 3 of Narita International Airport, Tokyo. The intuitive wayfinding system on the floor, clearly colour-coded, encourages sporty walking. No one can make a wrong turn here.

F

Typography

Type and typography play pivotal roles in transporting an airport's individual identity. There are currently just over 60 major airport hubs worldwide. Competition amongst these airports for passengers, airlines and service providers is becoming increasingly fierce. As a result, they invest significantly in their user experience. Reliable orientation is key to a successful customer journey and wellbeing. Indeed, the (type)face welcomes each visitor. Let's embark on a journey through the evolution of the typography of the modern airport from the 1950s until today.

6 x Frutiger, 2 x Helvetica, 1 x Myriad, 1 x Franklin Gothic, 1 x Clearview, 1 x The Sans

Half of the twelve largest airports in the world in 2023 have chosen to use Frutiger or similar typefaces for their wayfinding systems. This grid illustrates how type identity has been neglected in the hyper-globalised aviation industry.

1 **ATL** Hartsfield-Jackson Atlanta International Airport
→ Frutiger et al.
4 **LHR** Heathrow Airport
→ Frutiger
7 **IST** Istanbul International Airport
→ Myriad (similar to Frutiger)
10 **DEL** Indira Gandhi International Airport
→ Franklin Gothic

1 **DXB** Dubai International Airport
→ Frutiger et al.
5 **HND** Tokyo Haneda International Airport
→ Frutiger (english)
8 **LAX** Los Angeles International Airport
→ Helvetica
11 **CDG** Charles de Gaulle Airport
→ Frutiger

3 **DFW** Dallas Fort Worth International Airport
→ Clearview ADA
6 **DEN** Denver International Airport
→ The Sans
9 **ORD** O'Hare International Airport
→ Helvetica
12 **CAN** Guangzhou Baiyun International Airport
→ Frutiger

Typographic globalisation

Frutiger is one of the most popular typefaces for airport wayfinding systems. This becomes strikingly clear as we examine the world's largest airports and the rankings for the world's top airports. What are the reasons for this uniformity in choice? Each airport could have selected a typeface rooted in the society, culture and design tradition of its location and reflect the individuality of the airport. To a great extent, the history of wayfinding and typography is still visible at global airports. In this chapter, we examine the boom period of 13 different airports across a century and around the globe. We follow the evolution of transport design and its most prevalent typefaces.

In the early days, typefaces were not digitally available. Architects and designers often drew their own designs. They realised the need for effective wayfinding and appropriate fonts which are suitable in an environment and easy to read. Deviating from tested and proven ones that deliver good functionality is a challenge. But innovation and identity considerations will affect font choices in the future. Choosing a typeface is a challenging task. Designers have to take many aspects into account, such as multiple languages, displayin information in large and small size, digital communication channels and not least the need to express brand identity.

World legacy: Frutiger

London-based consultancy Skytrax launched the World Airport Awards to recognise and rank the top airports in terms of exemplary performance and quality of stay. The signage system and good orientation are important criteria. The award is based on extensive traveller surveys and has become the industry standard. Overall, airports from the Asia-Pacific region have dominated the World's Best Airport rankings since 2012 and consistently occupy first place. Passenger growth there was extremely high. These growth levels require an constantly improving and effective wayfinding. Two Japanese airports hold top spots in the ranking as a result of their excellent preparation for the Olympic Games 2021. Five European airports, Charles de Gaulle Airport CDG, Munich Airport MUC, Zurich Airport ZRH, Istanbul International Airport IST and Airport of Roma Fiumicino FCO have gained their spots in the top twelve ranking. They have caught up in terms of digitalisation and prepared for handling a huge amount of international visitors.

Six of the twelve airports use Frutiger in their wayfinding systems. The main reasons for Frutiger's wide use as an airport font lie in its ability to deliver high-level reading comfort. It appears to be the perfect typographic choice because of its wide acceptance and universal pervasiveness. It is easily combined with the characters of various languages and letterforms, as seen in Asian and Arab airports. On the other hand, airports could choose more specific fonts with the same quality of legibility to underline their identity and express their unique appearance.

The World's Top Airports for 2024 as voted by air travellers around the world in the 2023/2024 World Airport Survey.

1 **DOH** Hamad International Airport
→ Nitti Grotesk (English), Frutiger (Arabic)

2 **SIN** Singapore Changi Airport
→ Frutiger (English, Malay) et al.

3 **ICN** Incheon International Airport
→ Frutiger (English) et al.

4 **HND** Tokyo Haneda International Airport
→ Frutiger (English) et al.

5 **NRT** Tokyo Narita
→ Frutiger (English) et al.

6 **CDG** Charles de Gaulle Airport
→ Frutiger

7 **DXB** Dubai International Airport
→ Frutiger et al.

8 **MUC** Munich Airport
→ Univers (by Frutiger)

9 **ZRH** Zurich Airport
→ Custom Font (similar to Akzidenz Grotesk)

10 **IST** Istanbul International Airport
→ Myriad (similar to Frutiger)

11 **HKG** Hong Kong International Airport
→ Helvetica (English) et al.

12 **FCO** Airport of Roma Fiumicino
→ Frutiger et al.

1958—London LGW

London in the mid-1950s. Air travel is new and exclusive to the moneyed classes. It exudes jet set glamour—a veritable cocktail of society, fashion, money and jet planes. In 1958, after undergoing a major construction phase, London Gatwick Airport LGW was reopened with a new terminal and became the first airport in the world with a direct train connection to the city. More than a year prior to the reopening, a team of designers led by Jock Kinneir set about developing a stringent wayfinding system for Gatwick Airport. Kinneir studied print graphics in the 1930s. He taught part-time at the Chelsea School of Art in London and worked at the renowned design consultancy Design Research Unit (DRU). DRU were amongst the first designers to combine and apply the skills of architects, graphic designers and product designers in developing design solutions for buildings. Kinneir founded his own design consultancy in 1956. The architects David Allford of Yorke, Rosenberg and Mardall presented him with the unique opportunity to design a wayfinding system for the new airport London Gatwick LGW from the ground up. Kinneir hired his talented student from the Chelsea School of Art, Margaret Calvert, and set about work on the design concept including materials, layout, colour scheme and typography.

Legibility as a key criterion for design

After having thoroughly researched existing fonts, they felt that none of them were appropriate for application in an airport wayfinding system. Kinneir then began to design a unique font for Gatwick signage. The open forms improved legibility and the fluidity of the typeface while allowing much space in between letters. Jock Kinneir had learned from Edward Johnston—the designer of the typeface and signage for the London Underground in the early 20th century—how to improve the legibility of a typeface. The curl of the lower case letter "l", for example, distinguishes it more clearly from an "I". Calvert used mock-ups on the construction site to study the effectiveness of the typography and improve legibility. The team paid particular attention to perfecting

1 Calvert said: “Gatwick was all learning [...]. We established how to get the weight of the letters right and all those kinds of things.”

the spacing between letters to ensure that the information was easy to read from a distance. Kinneir and Calvert developed a sophisticated technique to best space individual letter combinations exactly as defined. When cutting each letter individually from a foil and applying it to the carrier, a lining system helped to adjust them in the right distances.

The wayfinding system is monolingual and therefore does not require any differentiation between languages. Kinneir and Calvert obsessed over the details of the signage. To aid legibility, they set words in upper and lower cases. Sign-messages were aligned to the left or the right of the sign in order to intuitively indicate the direction in which they could be found. Pictograms were used very sparingly only for the terms Departure Gate and Toilets.

The wayfinding system at Gatwick Airport was hugely successful and embraced by the UK Ministry of Transport. Between 1959 and 1963 the font was further developed and later became to typeface called Transport. Collaborating with Jock Kinneir, Calvert went on to define design standards for road signage throughout Great Britain. In 2009, Transport was updated and digitalised by Henrik Kubel in collaboration with Margaret Calvert. It now goes by the name New Transport, a homage to its origins, excellent legibility and unique form. We have chosen it as the typeface for this book. For us, it signifies the perfect combination of function and identity, which makes it the ideal font with which to present our text.

1 The airport was very well linked to the city by road and rail. Arriving passengers were guided to the station and reached London quick and easily. In the 1960s, some shops were located in the centre of the hall.

2 Margaret Calvert's hand-drawn version of the New Transport font in 2012. The characters are similar to the font for Gatwick Airport in the early sixties by Jock Kinneir, later to be used as Transport for the British Road signage.

3 Original artwork, lower case letters, 1957–64

1

BRITISH UNITED
RESERVATIONS
W.H.SMITH & SON
Flight arrivals
Flight departures
Toilets and shops
Arrivals information
Way out
Car park
Trains

2

agij

3

abcde
fghijk
lmnop
qrstu
vwxyz

1961—Paris ORY

France in the Jet Age: The massive growth in passenger numbers as a result of the boom in jet travel in the 1950s transformed the small airfield in the Paris suburb of Orly into a new modern airport. A terminal was built that featured modern gates and gangways and the airport boasted a large parking lot for better car and bus connections to Paris. In 1952, Air France moved its operations to Orly because the modest Paris Le Bourget Airport had quickly become too small.

The Orly South Terminal opened in 1961. It corresponded to a new typology of buildings constructed on an innovative steel skeleton structure. In 1971, the Orly West Terminal opened to further expand capacity. ↗

Frutiger became the standard bearer

Charles Peignot was General Director in the third generation of the renowned Paris Foundry Deberny & Peignot, where the young Swiss typeface designer Adrian Frutiger was an employee. Deberny & Peignot were commissioned to develop a signage system for the Orly South Terminal and Frutiger was enlisted for the typeface design. He drew a custom font, the Alphabet Orly, in a narrow and wide version for the airport signage that combined aspects of the fonts Peignot (named after his employer the designer Charles Peignot) and Univers. Letters were set in upper cases. The signage was bilingual; French with English text in cursive letters. Colour-coding was introduced for the different points of destination: blue for departure, red for arrival. The background colours also varied depending on the position of the sign. However, the colour concept soon became too complex.

The quality of the physical signs was inconsistent as they had been produced by different manufacturers. Frutiger's experience—both positive and negative—with the Orly Airport signage system was a huge influence on his next project, the wayfinding system for Charles de Gaulle Airport CDG. The high quality of CDG signage and typography would become an international standard in airport wayfinding.

↗ After a century of operations, the designation of the historic terminals at Orly Airport ORY changed in March 2019 when a new building was erected to join Orly South and Orly West to create four zones. The former Orly West Terminal is now ORLY 1 and ORLY 2. The new junction building in the centre of the complex is ORLY 3 and the former Orly South is now ORLY 4.

1 Paris Orly with signage by Charles Peignot and a font by Adrian Frutiger.

1961—London LHR

Heathrow Airport LHR was planned during the Second World War and opened shortly thereafter in 1946 as London Airport. For ten years, the airport consisted only of a few runways and tents. It was not given the name London Heathrow until 1966. In 1951, when passenger numbers had grown to over 700,000 per year, the British architect Sir Frederick Gibberd was commissioned to design the first permanent structures. In 1955, Queen Elizabeth II officially opened a control tower as well as the Central Terminal Area. The passenger terminal initially called the Europa Building was later renamed simply Terminal 2. Herbert Spencer was commissioned to design a signage system. Spencer was a cartographer, typographer, photographer and professor of graphic design at the Central School of Arts and Crafts. His works were inspired by abstract painting, architecture and 20th-century poetry. He designed the signage system to embody the "modern" with its use of strong colour contrasts, geometric shapes with an arrow composed using a triangle and a rectangle.

Wayfinding design roots in arts and culture

When London's Heathrow Airport opened the Oceanic Building (today Terminal 3) for long-haul flights in 1961, London had become one of the most important hubs in the world. The terminal included a heliport on the roof to enable direct access to central London. Politicians, celebrities and managers all landed at Heathrow. Hollywood stars were photographed landing here. It was simply "the place to be". The airport had become a catwalk and its design underwent closer scrutiny. As the passenger numbers increased, so too did the demands on the airport signage. In 1960, the British graphic designer and later co-founder of the design consultancy Pentagram, Colin Forbes, was commissioned to develop signage for the Oceanic Building.

1 An elegant design that abstains from the use of pictograms. The wayfinding signage in the Oceanic Building, which was designed by Colin Forbes in 1961 for long-haul flights, uses a typeface by Matthew Carter.

Forbes had been a student of Herbert Spencer. The signage system was black on white, with some secondary information displayed in white on black. The font was to be the central element of the signage system, and Forbes entrusted the young British type designer Matthew Carter with its design. For the signage at Heathrow's Oceanic Terminal, Carter designed a new font, the Airport Alphabet based on Akzidenz Grotesk or Standard, as it was known in Great Britain at the time. The font featured long middle lengths and short descenders in order to display as much information as possible on the signs. This new font was remarkably similar to Helvetica, which was unknown to Forbes and Carter at the time. Had they been familiar with Helvetica, they later stated, they would have been happy to use it.

As the airport developed and passenger numbers increased, Forbes' signage in Heathrow gradually gave way to a next wayfinding system. Renowned designers such as Terance Conran had been commissioned to design the interiors and commercial and retail areas. Airport interiors were now state of the art, exclusive and contemporary. The airport operator British Airport Authority (BAA) commissioned Jock Kinneir and Margaret Calvert to build on their experience at Gatwick Airport and develop a wayfinding system and a design manual to include detailed typographic guidelines for Heathrow Airport. The designers chose a font they had originally designed for the National Health hospitals and later British and Danish rail systems. Design concepts for transport infrastructure are very closely linked and requirements are often the same: large crowds of people must be able to navigate seamlessly through a building or complex that is foreign to them. Information must be legible and easy to understand. Yet transport design is also a product of its time. It reflects the design perception and technological standards of the period in which it was implemented.

In the mid-1990s, the BAA Bembo became the typeface for Heathrow's wayfinding system. Bembo is an adaptation of the classic Monotype font Bembo cut by Stanley Morison who based it on the 15th-century French Renaissance font Antiqua. With its bibliophile character, it was a popular and widely used font in Great Britain at the time. Several years prior to the Heathrow relaunch, the British Airport Authority had adopted Bembo as its corporate font. One of the most common considerations in choosing the font in a wayfinding system is whether it should be consistent with the airport corporate font or whether the brand can tolerate additional fonts.

In 2008, the Heathrow operators adopted a new font, Frutiger, for its signage to coincide with the opening of Terminal 5. Initially they had considered a full overhaul of the wayfinding concept for the new terminal. An extensive study on the legibility of Bembo revealed that a more humanistic linear antiqua font such as Frutiger would be more effective for wayfinding. Experts have questioned the validity of the study, but Frutiger undoubtedly arrived in Heathrow. The wayfinding system features a customised version of the typeface which is also used for the airport's corporate design.

1 Airport Alphabet designed by Matthew Carter in 1960; a distinctive feature is the very short descenders, which in multi-line sign layouts ensure that descenders and ascenders do not collide. This helps accommodate more information into a small space.

Overleaf

2 Heathrow Airport LHR Terminal 1 waiting area in 1969

3 British Airport Authority (BAA) Signage Manual, lettering, symbols and pictograms, colours—individual chapters for the basic elements that characterise the visual language of a signage system.

4 British Rail Alphabet designed by Margaret Calvert and Jock Kinneir (Kinneir Calvert Associates) in the early 1960s; appeared first as constituent part of an integral signing system for the United Kingdom's National Health hospitals, later in British and Danish rail systems and finally in all BAA airports.

5 Pioneering, internally illuminated signage at Heathrow, black lettering on yellow background, early 1970s. Lettering designed by Margaret Calvert and Jock Kinneir (Kinneir Calvert Associates).

1
ABCDEFGHI
JKLMNOPQR
STUVWXYZ
1234567890
abcdefghij
klmnopqrs
tuvwxyz

2
destination
time
flight number
information
EDINBURGH
18:10
BE 5404
NOW BOARDING GA
BLACKPOOL
HULL/TEES-SIDE
18:35
OU 027
MANCHESTER
18:35
BE 4106
NOW BOARDING GA
DUBLIN
18:40
BE 871
JERSEY
18:45
BE 3058
ABERDEEN
18:50
BE 5528
TEES-SIDE
18:55
OU 049
GLASGOW
19:00
BE 5058
JERSEY
19:05
BE 3058A
GLASGOW
19:30
BE 5060
Flight departures for United Kingdom

destination time flight number information
7 LEEDS/BRADFORD 19:20 BK 416
CHESTER/LPL 19:30 CS 4856
NEWCASTLE 19:50 BK 460
sle of Man, Channel Islands, Republic of Ireland only
THE TIMES

3

Terminal 1
20x (A)
14x (legend area)
Flight
departures
5x (D)
Lettering
Symbols and pictograms
Colours

4
abcdefghijkl
cdego
mnopqrstuvw
acdegos
bceop acdegos bceop acdegos
xyz ABCDEFG
bceop cdego acdegos
HIJKLMNOPQ
eo
5 x tile ht.
RSTUVWXYZ
ruwy aeo
aeo
aeo
ceo
aeo
1234567890
4
£&/()’-,.-
word space

Transfer
passengers

Arrivals
Baggage
reclaim

1962—New York JFK/TWA

The Trans World Airline (TWA) Flight Center was designed by Eero Saarinen and served as TWA's terminal at John F. Kennedy International Airport JFK in New York from its opening in 1962 until 2001. It was constructed during a period where airport operators envisioned terminal buildings as being appropriated to individual airlines.

Signage as an element of interior design

Each element of the TWA Terminal was designed and constructed to reflect the airline's brand including the signage system and the interiors. Swaths of the TWA red tone were visible throughout the structure and some lettering was set in bold italics. The architects at Saarinnen Associates designed the signage as a key element of the interior design. At the same time the office was working on the airport design for the Washington Dulles International Airport IAD. However, the concepts differ significantly. In the TWA Terminal, many of the signposts are oval-shaped to correspond to the main destination board and the swooping curves and special flow of the building's form.
The components of the signage system were designed with great attention to detail. The architects drew different fonts, for directional signs, for flight information and for signage in the lounge areas. The TWA Terminal is an iconic building of the Jet Age. Today it serves as a hotel. The John F. Kennedy International Airport JFK is using the typeface Frutiger for its wayfinding system for a long time. With the new Port Authority Wayfinding Manual it will be replaced by Helvetica in the future.

1 View of the main hall of the TWA terminal building, Terminal 5, John F. Kennedy International Airport (Idlewild Airport) in 1968. Oval “sign UFOs” lead the passengers to their gates.

Overleaf

2 Lettering styles depend on the information displayed. Signs are designed to be an essential component of the interior design.

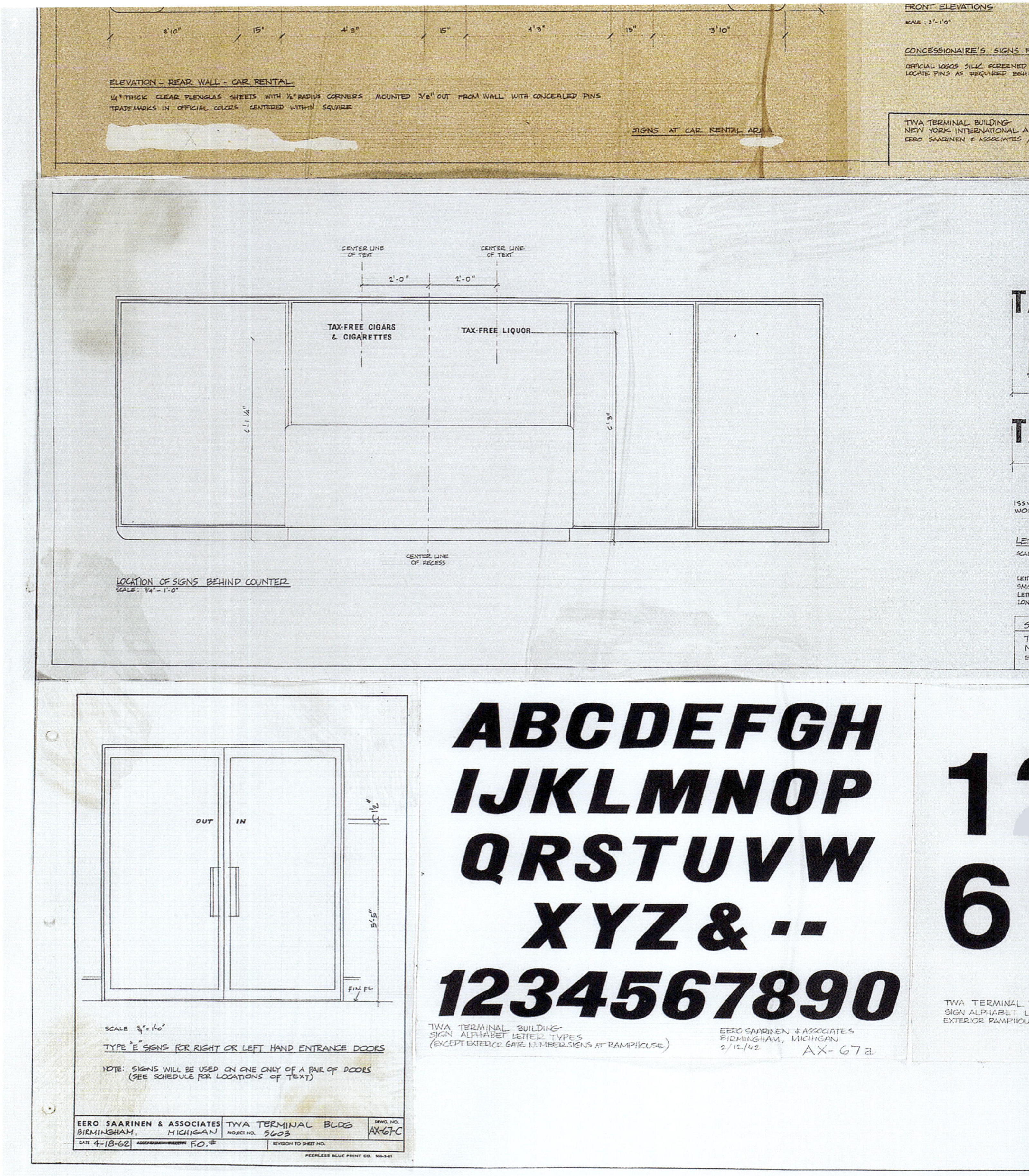
FRONT ELEVATIONS
CONCESSIONAIRE'S SIGNS
ELEVATION - REAR WALL - CAR RENTAL
SIGNS AT CAR RENTAL AREA
TWA TERMINAL BUILDING
NEW YORK INTERNATIONAL AIRPORT
EERO SAARINEN & ASSOCIATES
CENTER LINE OF TEXT
TAX-FREE CIGARS & CIGARETTES
TAX-FREE LIQUOR
CENTER LINE OF RECESS
LOCATION OF SIGNS BEHIND COUNTER
OUT
IN
TYPE "E" SIGNS FOR RIGHT OR LEFT HAND ENTRANCE DOORS
NOTE: SIGNS WILL BE USED ON ONE ONLY OF A PAIR OF DOORS (SEE SCHEDULE FOR LOCATIONS OF TEXT)
EERO SAARINEN & ASSOCIATES
BIRMINGHAM, MICHIGAN
TWA TERMINAL BLDG
5603
AX-67-C
4-18-62
ABCDEFGH
IJKLMNOP
QRSTUVW
XYZ & - -
1234567890
TWA TERMINAL BUILDING
SIGN ALPHABET LETTER TYPES
(EXCEPT EXTERIOR GATE NUMBER SIGNS AT RAMPHOUSE)
EERO SAARINEN & ASSOCIATES
BIRMINGHAM, MICHIGAN
AX-67a

SIDE ELEVATIONS
RENTAL AREA
AX-67-D
ISSUED TO GSWK, TWA, ROZAS, PRICE FOR CONSTRUCTION 5-10-62
ISSUED TO TWA (D. MCCARTHY) FOR APPROVAL – 5-1-62
-FREE CIGARS
CIGARETTES
-FREE LIQUOR
FOR TAX-FREE LIQUOR & TOBACCO COUNTER
AX-67-E
FRONT ELEVATION – SIGN FACE & HOUSING (HOUSING N.I.C.)
GATE NUMBER SIGN FACES
STEEL FRAME BY OTHERS
NEOPRENE STRIPS BOTH SIDES
SECTION THRU FRAME
NOTES:
FOR SIGN INFORMATION ONLY
ISSUED ON FIELD ORDER 1-9-62
GATE NUMBER SIGN FACES
RAMPHOUSE #1
TWA UNIT TERMINAL BUILDING
NEW YORK INTERNATIONAL AIRPORT
EERO SAARINEN & ASSOCIATES, ARCHITECTS
1/20/62
DWG AX-66
2345
7890
EERO SAARINEN & ASSOCIATES
BIRMINGHAM MICHIGAN
2/12/62
AX-67 b
NOTE: AX-64 IS VOID
AX-66 INFORMATION IS SHOWN ON SHEET NO. 130
AS BUILT RECORD SET JULY, 12, 1963
AS BUILT DRWGS. AX-64 – AX-67E
TRANS WORLD AIRLINES
UNIT TERMINAL BUILDING
NEW YORK INTERNATIONAL AIRPORT
EERO SAARINEN AND ASSOCIATES
ARCHITECTS
HAMDEN, CONNECTICUT
152

1962—Washington IAD

The early 1960s in the United States were a hopeful time. The young John F. Kennedy with his wife Jacqueline by his side was running for President as "Jack and Jackie". On 20 January 1961, JFK was sworn in as the 35th President of the United States. Jackie Kennedy was a fashion icon with her pillbox hat and sunglasses. In 1962, President Kennedy opened the new Washington Dulles International Airport, designed by the Finnish-American architect Eero Saarinen. It is one of the iconic structures of the Jet Age. Saarinen developed an innovative concept for handling passengers: so-called Mobile Lounges brought travellers from the terminal building directly to the aircraft.

Type in the space age

Airport signage was an integral part of the architect's planning scope. The system featured long strips on which all information was set in capitals—regardless of whether it was relevant to flights or indicated commercial areas. The typeface was drawn by Eero Saarinen. Both letters and numbers are geometrically formed to appear highly technological. After all, the Americans were planning to fly to the moon by the end of the decade.

Typography was not yet digital so templates for the signs were drawn by hand—often as a slight modification of existing fonts. Architects like Carlo Scarpa, Richard Neutra and Mies van der Rohe routinely drew fonts for their buildings. In 2003, the font design studio House Industries commissioned the typographer Christian Schwarz to develop a digitally compatible version of the font using Saarinen's original plans for use in Washington Dulles International Airport. Because this font is an integral part of the airport identity, it is currently being used to set specific information in the building. Frutiger is used as prior font for the wayfinding system.

1 The architect Eero Saarinen designed a geometric, futuristic font for his building, which is still in use in the terminal today and an integral element of the brand identity.

1

1

FOREIGN CURRENCY
DEPARTS

2

SNACK BAR
COFFEE SHOP
RESTAURANT
LOUNGE
RESTROOMS

3

1 The terminal at Washington Dulles International Airport IAD by Eero Saarinen, opened in 1962 (photo 1979); simple markings on black strips.

2/3 Type specimen by Christian Schwartz

1967—Amsterdam AMS

In the beginning of the Jet Age, a third European hub, in addition to Charles de Gaulle Airport CDG and Heathrow Airport LHR, began operations in the Netherlands: Amsterdam Airport Schiphol AMS. Schiphol heralded in a new generation of passenger-friendly airports using state-of-the-art technology. Travellers arrived at their aircrafts using "fingers".

In the early sixties, the architect Marius Duintjer was commissioned to build a new terminal building. Dutch designer Kho Liang Ie was responsible for the interior design. Kho Liang Ie was born in Indonesia and came to the Netherlands in the late 1940s, where he trained as an interior designer at the Rietveld Academy. He is best known for his furniture designs. The graphic designer Benno Wissing, co-founder of the Dutch firm Total Design, developed the wayfinding system which maintains its excellence to this day. Wissing chose the font Akzidenz Grotesk, with its high centre length and short descenders. This is a critical factor to achieve maximum font sizes for multi-line information. The colour concept features black type for Dutch and white for English information. The yellow background is used for primary and green for secondary targets. With the exception of the gates, all targets were set in lower case lettering.

Wissing's admiration of the minimalist De Stijl artist movement was a strong influence on his signage design. The reduction to just a few design principles and the consistency with which they are implemented throughout the building distinguish the high quality of these designs.

Experience the terminal

Architects, interior designers and graphic designers working together created a perfect interior ambience that lent cool elegance to the emerging jet set lifestyle of the 1960s and heightened the traveller experience. Their work on the project began in 1962, when the first major Jet Age airports opened. Schiphol Terminal was completed in 1967. Early in their deliberations, the multidisciplinary team spent a lot of time at international airports studying

1 The minimal, modern typography for Amsterdam Airport Schiphol AMS became iconic. Flight information is differentiated from non-flight information, services and facilities by colour as well as the two languages, English and Dutch.

1

nrs
gates
A1 /A6
nrs
gates
B21 /B26
nrs
gates
C41 /C47
uitgang en wachtkamer
exit and lounge
nrs
gates
B28 B30 B32
buffets and sh

1

passenger behaviour and flows. They concluded that the key to the success of the new hub would be the connection between architecture, design and people. People make up part of the environment and should feel comfortable in it.

The interior should be completely in neutral shades of grey and brown. The coloured signs, a key component of the design, would be a stark contrast and therefore remain clearly visible from all points within the interior spaces. Liang Ie designed his interiors in modules. Wissing applied the same principles to the wayfinding system. Text and arrows were placed on an imaginary grid and the illuminated sign boxes in different sizes could easily be combined. The basic design principles from the origins of Schiphol continue to influence its identity today. In the new Terminal A, set to open in the coming years, the idea of this first design will still be recognisable. In the publication of their most recent plans, the architects for Terminal A, Kaan Architects write: "The most inspiring architectural and planning DNA at Schiphol is that of De Weger and Duintjer's 1967 Departures Hall, with interior design by Kho Liang Ie Associates, which is characterised by abundant daylight, simplicity of space and an impressive spatiality."

The Dutch design consultancy Mijksenaar further developed the wayfinding system and replaced the Akzidenz Grotesk with Frutiger. Later they updated the colour scheme, reserving the colour green solely for escape route signage and no longer for secondary messages.

2

1 In the wayfinding system, all destinations with the exception of the gates are written in lower case. A popular practice at the time, which shows the proximity of the designer to modern design movements, such as Bauhaus and De Stijl.

2 A dominant graphic element has retained its purpose to this day: the iconic black arrow on a white circle. This element appears throughout the building viewing holes on the walkboarding piers, as a reference to the close connection between architecture and graphic design.

1969—Houston IAH

Houston's George Bush Intercontinental Airport IAH opened in 1969 with two symmetrically arranged terminal buildings, A and B. The rooftops of the terminal buildings featured generous parking areas to accommodate private automobiles, which were the dominant means of transportation to the airport.

Codification by colour and shape

At Houston, the roadways approach signage had to be clearly visible for arriving motorists to guide them to the two separate A and B Terminals. (Eventually there would be additional Terminals C and D.) Graphically coded terminals with a common symbol, and with the letters, A and B, on separate colour fields were visibly striking thanks to the use of a colourful outline symbol representing the terminal building perimeter to frame each of the terminal letters. The signage system was designed by another pioneer in way-finding, Jane Davis Doggett. Her distinguished career began in 1959, when she was commissioned to develop the graphic design programme for the new jetport at Memphis, Tennessee. She was brought into this opportunity by Roy Harrover, an architect friend who was seeking the commission to design the Memphis International Airport MEM.

As a graduate student at the Yale School of Art and Architecture, Doggett studied under the German Bauhaus artist Josef Albers, who was renowned for his theories in the use of colour and for his abstract geometrics and themes of spatial movement of abstract forms. At Yale, Doggett excelled in Albers' course in the interaction of space and colour, later incorporating her findings into her unique wayfinding systems for airports and other mass public facilities. She is a pioneer in her holistic approach to airport wayfinding design, linking the logo and codifying visual elements—letters, numerals and symbols—into one visual concept. Her work on Houston's airport was highly influential in demonstrating the importance of close cooperation between architects, engineers, transportation planners and graphic designers.

1 George Bush Intercontinental Airport IAH at Houston was one of the first multi-terminal airports of the Jet Age. Doggett introduced letter and colour-coding to identify and separate routings to the two Terminals A and B. Road-way approach signage was an integral part of the total concept that extended the letter and colour-coding into the airport interior routings.

1

Airport
Exit
B
A
Crossover
Departing
Flights
Arriving
Flights

1

Take Escalator Down
First Level
Baggage Claim
Ground Transportation
All Exits
Lower Level
Tunnel Train To
Parking Lots
Terminal B For
AERONAVES • AMERICAN
BRANIFF • DELTA
KLM • PAN AMERICAN
All International Flights

Alphabet A for airports

The model for Doggett's Alphabet A was the Standard font from Europe, a readable, sans serif typeface designed for the printed page. She enlarged the printed characters and then adapted the rough-edged artwork and reworked each letterform to emphasise a balanced stroke. In addition, for each condition—exterior roadways signage vs. interior signage—she established alphabet kerning standards, spacing increments between each character, which ensured consistency throughout of message layouts. For roadways signage, for example, she increased spacing between characters to enhance maximum legibility in distance read-out. Her aim was to offer passengers, by foot or by vehicle, instantly clear destination routings.

In the more than 40 airport projects Doggett worked on, the airports were "laboratories" in which she explored the graphic possibilities in the use of symbology, colour and typography. In the rapid expansion of airports throughout the USA, it has not always been possible to preserve original standards of certain facilities in architecture, street furniture, or signage. Many airports in their expansion projects that require new or amended signage did not call in special wayfinding design consultants, but, instead, called commercial sign-makers.

Today the font Clearview is often recommended for airport signage. It is a sans serif typeface, which Doggett considers "not very aesthetically elegant", but meets standards of adequate distance read-out. It was developed by independent researchers. Clearview is familiar to US motorists in that it is commonly used for guide signs on roads in the United States. Labozan Associates is currently planning a new wayfinding concept for all Houston metropolitan area airports.

2

1 A comprehensive concept for the signage at Houston: The information was uniformly arranged in white characters on dark backgrounds, set in Alphabet A. These were initially designed for the Memphis International Airport MEM, which opened in 1961. As the Houston airport had two levels, directions were posted flanking the escalators on two sizable black panels.

2 Alphabet A, designed by Jane Davis Doggett, an adaptation of the Standard typeface, enlarged from type for the printed page and adapted in large sizes to meet the needs of signposting in large-scale environments such as airports.

1971—Zurich ZRH

The wayfinding system at Zurich Airport ZRH dates back to 1971. The third construction phase for Zurich was completed in 1975 transforming the airport into an international hub in Europe. The wayfinding system was developed for the expansion and features a clean and functional graphic style. Its main element was the sans serif font Akzidenz Grotesk, a classic of Swiss typographic tradition and strong visual reference to the airport's very Swiss brand identity. The 1975 design team, led by Ruedi Ruegg for the renowned Swiss design consultancy Müller Brockmann & Co., created a design manual for the Zurich airport "Signaletiknormen des Züricher Flughafen", which is still in use today.

International Style

The system that features black signage with white lettering radiates a cool and timeless elegance though it too is a product of its time. Indeed two other signage systems from this period use similar design elements: the New York Subway and the Milan Underground. Both were created by the well-known designers Massimo Vignelli and Bob Noorda in the late 1960s and are today considered seminal examples of effective wayfinding in public transportation infrastructure. For the New York Subway System, the designers chose a local adaptation of Akzidenz Grotesk, which was replaced by Helvetica in 1989. Karl Gerstner created the Grotesk version used at Zurich Airport ZRH until the current revision in 2020. It differed from the widely popular Akzidenz Grotesk drawn by Günter Gerhard Lange. All are based on familiar typefaces created in the end of the 20th century.

In 2020, the Zurich Airport ZRH implemented a custom font similar to Akzidenz Grotesk. The new typeface has been designed for improved legibility to meet the demands of air travel today.

1 Check-in at Zurich Airport ZRH. Unlike today, in 1975 all letters were set in capitals. The large display panel was still located in the visual axis of the spacious hall. Today, it sits above the central passageway and offers constant updates on the wait times at each security checkpoint.

1

1 PRO PASSAGIER
KABINENGEPÄCK: 1 PRO PASSAGIER
CHECK-IN / ABFERTIGUNG ENREGISTREMENT
50
DEPARTURE
CIGARETTEN
Zürich Airport
PRECISA

1974—Paris CDG

By the beginning of the 1960s, Paris' Orly Airport ORY was bursting at the seams. In January 1964, the French Council of Ministers decided to build a new major airport on the sparsely populated farmland near the village of Roissy-en-France. Charles de Gaulle Airport CDG would become the third major airport in Paris in 1974. The job was awarded to the young French architect Paul Andreu. Andreu pursued a new concept: passengers should enter the UFO-like building directly by car or bus, then descend into the structure via escalators which would lead them to tunnels connecting to the circularly arranged satellites from which they take off.

Not only the spatial concept and the passenger flows in the building were new, Andreu's interdisciplinary working processes were also very new. Like his contemporaries in Amsterdam, he too sought to achieve a holistic design. He organised a series of workshops with architects, designers, psychologists and artists in order to create something groundbreaking in Roissy. The airport even had its own sound, the "Indicatif Roissy" composed by Bernard Parmegiani.

Amongst the experts in Andreu's team was the Swiss font designer Adrian Frutiger. He had enjoyed international renown after releasing the typeface Univers in 1957 and was to take the lead in drawing the typeface for the new signage system. Frutiger had already worked on the Orly Airport and was now determined to develop a font that would deliver perfect legibility for wayfinding. This font should have no historic references. It should integrate into the new language of the architecture and be part of the overall picture. Despite Andreu's admiration of Univers, Frutiger was convinced it would be inappropriate for signage. The signage had to have signal quality and be legible from a distance and while in motion. Open forms would take precedence over geometrical consistency. So Frutiger revisited a sans serif design called Concorde, which he had drawn with André Gürtler seven years previously. For the presentation in Andreu's workshop, Frutiger cut out the words "Départ" and "Departures" in a stronger Concorde from a black piece of cardboard and from a yellow background respectively.

1 Spirit of the 1970s at Charles de Gaulle Airport CDG Terminal 1; sign cubes, commercial boards and seating areas are all individually designed.

Overleaf

2 Terminal 1 at Charles de Gaulle Airport CDG

1

2

1 View into the iconic tubes of Terminal 1 which connects to the satellite buildings.

2 Mock-ups have helped to perfect the comprehensibility of information, left-aligned French/English texts create easy access to the information—pure typography without pictograms, colour-coding of the different hierarchies of information are all measures to optimise effectiveness of signage.

He prepared the same cut-outs in the Univers font. Concorde's superior legibility was apparent for all participants and Paul Andreu was enthusiastic about the idea of a dedicated airport font. After a period of intensive study to optimise character spacing and width in various intensities, Frutiger drew the Alphabet Roissy font for the wayfinding system at the new airport. He studied all the customary international forms and obsessed over the minute details of each letter's design. He paid particular attention to the numbers that appear in airports most frequently in the form of gate numbers. He also was very involved in the production of the signs insisting on precise folio cut-outs to achieve an exact reproduction of each letter and number combination on the signs.

A new era: from Concorde to Roissy to Frutiger

In addition to the typeface, the sign layout is also extremely well planned and structured. French and English signalling texts are left-aligned, but the arrows point alternately in the respective direction in which the target point is located. The colour concept allows for quick differentiation between the two different languages with French applied in white on the yellow shield surfaces and the English ones in black. The interior furnishing is in a distinctive orange. Both colours provide a strong contrast to the colours of the structure and are therefore very visible from all perspectives.

With over 76 million passengers a year in 2019, Charles de Gaulle Airport CDG is one of the largest airports in the world. Several terminal buildings have been added since Terminal 1 first opened in 1974. The original idea was to replicate the Terminal 1 concept as the complex grew. Though this was never implemented, all terminal buildings form a cohesive entity with its signature curved design language. This is also true of the wayfinding system. It went through several relaunches, most prominently by the famous French typographer Jean Widmer, who designed signs with a grey background. Today, it has been reworked in the colour blue and implemented both at Charles de Gaulle Airport CDG and Orly Airport ORY. But Frutiger remains the signage typeface.

In the words of Frutiger himself: "My masterpiece is Univers but my favourite font remains the original Frutiger. It is probably the font that stands in the very middle of the font landscape." His fonts have shaped an entire era.

Letraset
instant lettering
S35365
aaâàäbbbcçd
ddeeêéèëffgg
hhiiiîïjkllllmmm
nnnnooooôöpp
qrrrrsssssttttu
uûüvvwxyzæœ
ABCDEFGHIJK
LMNOPQRSTU
VWXYZÇ&()/;
1234567890*?!
« »
B3586
«Alphabet ROISSY, appartenant exclusivement à l'Aéroport de PARIS»

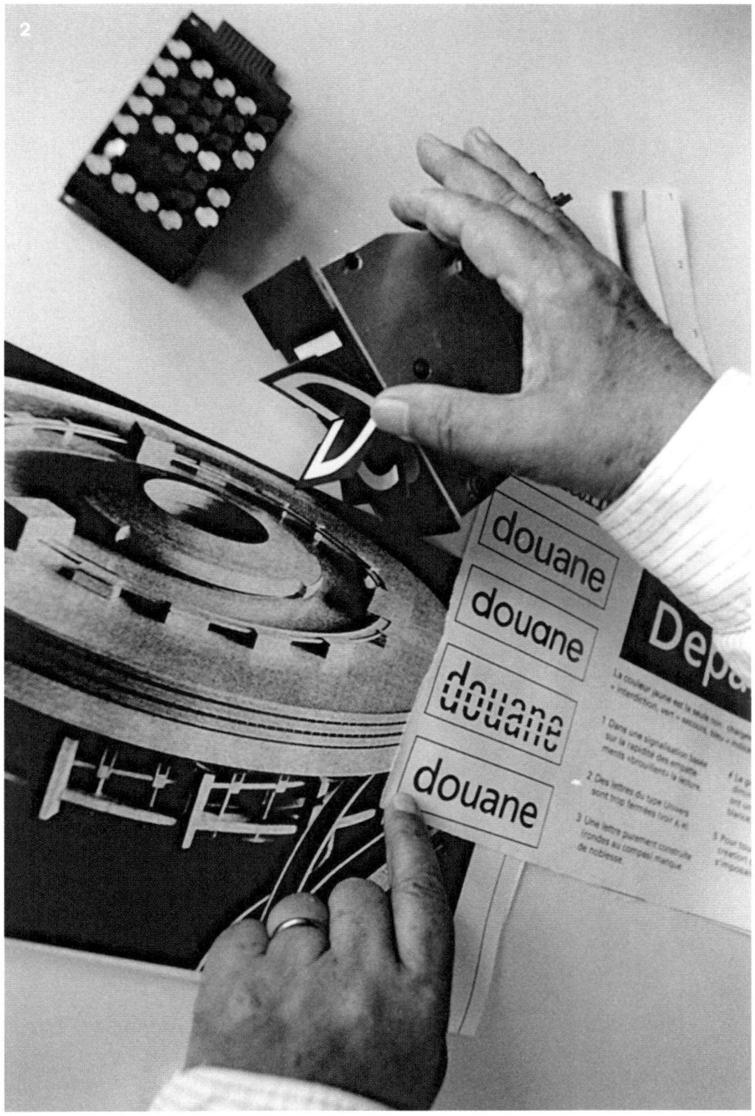

1 When the Charles de Gaulle Airport CDG was inaugurated in March 1974, the wayfinding system set new standards with its Alphabet Roissy (later Frutiger). Layouts were fashioned using Letraset typeface sheets.

2/4 Frutiger was intimately familiar with the technical development of typefaces and technology such as phototypesetting and digital font generation. He was also keenly interested in display technology. For the airport, his colleague Hans-Jürg Hunziker designed a special version of Alphabet Roissy for the drop-sheet displays of the passenger information display systems (FIDS).

3 Typographers from all over the world were anxious to use the new typeface for printed materials. In 1977, D. Stempel AG and Linotype released Frutiger. It quickly became a bestseller and has undergone multiple updates, most recently in 1999 as Frutiger Next by the designer himself.

1980—Baltimore-Washington BWI

The City of Baltimore sold its airport to the Maryland Transport Ministry in 1978. The following year, the airport underwent and completed a thorough overhaul. The update allowed the airport to double the number of concourses in the form of "fingers". In 1980, the airport opened a train station making it the first US destination with directly connecting train lines to the city and to other major points. The new terminal expansion would pose new problems and challenges as passenger numbers swelled. Getting people around the new airport terminal would become more complex, therefore directional signage was given high priority.

As part of the design team, Doggett was brought in by Charles Brickbauer who was the architect commissioned for the airport project, as well as a colleague and fellow classmate from the Yale School of Art and Architecture. Brickbauer designed an outstanding terminal pavilion of exposed steel and glass that spanned the length of the massive airport building, with a high, open ceiling that gave the space a wonderful light and airy feeling. The wayfinding system cleverly utilised the International Nautical Signal Flags—A, Alfa; B, Bravo; C, Charley, etc.—to codify the separate concourses, which Doggett recommended be called "piers".

Gateways with identity

Her graphic gateway theme drew inspiration from Baltimore as a major US shipping port, and the Nautical Signal Flags were a natural source of bold, graphic/colour symbols designed for maximum visibility at sea and constituted an international language. In order to present her concepts for the thematic and wayfinding design systems and demonstrate fully their functional as well as aesthetic values, she had her staff build a detailed scale model of the terminal pavilion.

1 An upright, tall, free-standing signpost was in scale with the high-ceiling ticket lobby. The kiosk was positioned at each pier entry, with the pier-designated big nautical letter symbol on top, which could be viewed on three sides from a great distance away. Airport facility information was displayed on the kiosk at a lower reading level in Doggett's sans serif Alphabet A in capital letters and upper and lower case lettering.

1

PIER A
PIER B
Baggage Claim
Ground Transportation
Parking
DIRECTORY
Upper Level
Lower Level
PIER A

1992—Munich MUC

On a single day in May 1992, Munich's airport MUC moved from its first location close to city centre to its new location outside of the city in Erdinger Moos. The new terminal was a huge contrast to its predecessor—modern, airy and flooded in natural light. The new airport featured a wayfinding system that uniquely captures Munich's identity. The German graphic designer Otl Aicher created the corporate identity for the Olympic Games Munich 1972. It reflected the city's openness and welcoming character. Aicher chose Adrian Frutiger's Univers as the corporate font for the Games. It offered a uniquely systemic structure and 21 line weights—a very geometric font that worked extremely well for the new Munich Airport 20 years later. The font is a key design element of Munich Airport's wayfinding system.

1

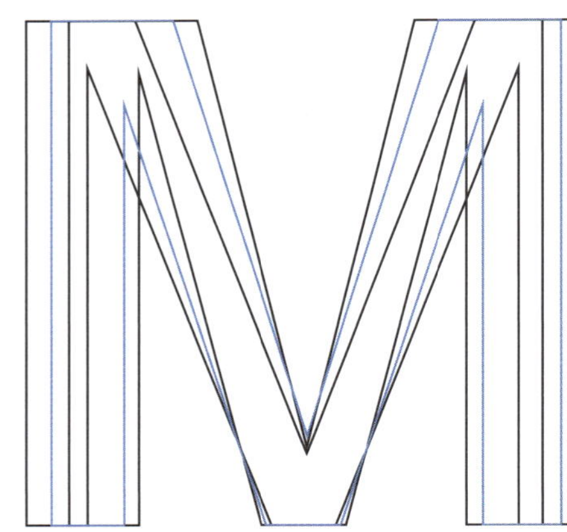

Frutiger's Univers system

The relocation of the airport was preceded by a relaunch of the airport operator's corporate design. In 1982, Otl Aicher, along with the designers Eberhard Strauß and Ursula Wangler, had created a new "cross-object visual appearance" for the airport that anticipated the features of the future MUC wayfinding system: Univers as the lead font and the light blue as the main colour. By deliberately deviating from the ADV signage standard of the former site which dictated the use of Helvetica, Munich Airport opted to form its own unique brand identity and abandoned standardisation efforts within German airports.

In 2020, the Munich Airport operators commissioned Moniteurs with a relaunch of the wayfinding system in Terminal 1. Since its opening in 1992, Munich has evolved into a top international hub and is one of the few European airports that belong to the category 5-Star Airports awarded annually by Skytrax. The operators wanted subtle adjustments to the signage to achieve a uniform look throughout the airport complex. The design team chose to work with a variable font, a new font technology which allows precise adjustment to type parameters.

1 At the time, Univers represented a revolutionary new approach to typeface. One of the basic principles in Frutiger's 1953 font design is its variability along various axes. The variable font version of Univers (shown above) is therefore the next logical development and suitable for the next wayfinding concept.

2 Univers as the wayfinding system font is structured and functional and complements the terminal's overall presentation. In Munich it is still an important part of the airport's visual identity.

2

2017—Singapore SIN

With over 59 million passengers per year in 2023, Singapore Changi Airport SIN is one of the most important hubs in Southeast Asia and a popular destination. With more than 13 million foreign tourists a year Singapore is amongst the most visited cities in the world. This multiethnic city state is also one of the richest countries in the world. The airport has consistently held top spots in the World Best Airports ranking since 2013. It features high-end interiors, tropical gardens and a wide range of leisure activities that provide a welcome contrast to the hectic pace of the airport.

Multilingual typography concept

Originally opened in 1981, the wayfinding system used Helvetica as a lead font. For decades, Singapore had been a British Crown Colony and its signage was influenced by Western models. For example, the signage was initially in English only without any reference to Asian culture. The airport grew exponentially from the construction of Terminal 1 in 1981 until the opening of Terminal 4 in 2017. As the airport went through various phases of renovation and expansion, the wayfinding system, too, has evolved. English is still the main language but the signage now includes the languages most commonly used by Changi Airport passenger: Chinese, Malay and Tamil. Two languages are set in Frutiger. Frutiger is the most widely used font in wayfinding systems in Asia—perhaps due to its compatibility with the flowing letterforms of Asian font. It certainly provides good legibility.

The Singapore Changi Airport SIN follows a holistic approach. The identity is not so explicitly determined by the graphics but by the overall design language of the complex. This is reflected in many details, such as the patterns in the floor coverings, the shape of the self-service kiosks and the interiors.

1/2 Singapore Changi Airport SIN has grown rapidly over the past decades. The typeface in the wayfinding system was changed from Helvetica to Frutiger. To reflect the languages spoken by its passengers, the signs are now multilingual.

1

Check-in Rows 1-7
Departure
Arrival
Cash Machine (ATM)
Shop & Dine
7
6
Departure

2

Arrival Pick-up
(at Basement 1)
候车处
Tempat Pengambilan
車両乗降場
Hotel Booking
酒店预订
Tempahan Hotel
ホテルの予約
City Shuttle &
Limousine
Bas Shuttle dan Limo
Information
Train to City
JEWEL

2020—Berlin Brandenburg BER

The Berlin Brandenburg Airport BER opened in autumn 2020. The character of Berlin and the state surrounding it, Brandenburg, are captured throughout the architecture of the terminal complex. The linear structures are a reference to both the tall pine forests of Brandenburg and Berlin's many iconic architectural structures, such as Mies van der Rohe's Neue Nationalgalerie and Karl Friedrich Schinkel's Altes Museum and other monumental buildings. The font used in the wayfinding system is also unique to Berlin and Brandenburg and exclusively designed for the airport.

The airport was planned by the renowned German architects von Gerkan, Marg and Partners (gmp) and JSK Architects. Moniteurs was commissioned for the wayfinding and established holistic guidelines for the BER airport complex signage at a very early stage. These include a modular sign family, red as the primary colour, a pictogram set and an exclusively designed typeface. It was designed by the Berlin-based typeface designer Alexander Branczyk in collaboration with the font specialist Georg Seifert. It delivers both optimal legibility and a contemporary look. The font features a type width between regular and condensed and four optimally matched weights: light, regular, medium and bold plus italics. Open letterforms and a large x-height make it legible from far away. Its dynamic form is reminiscent of take-offs and landings.

Consistent wayfinding and communication

The Berlin Brandenburg Airport typeface is in use for all applications such as signage, information displays, the airport's website, maps and passenger communication. This illustrates once more the strength of the clear, integrated design concept. The goal was to implement a font that provides optimal legibility and, at the same time, is identity-enhancing.

1 The wayfinding system is applied in a large format directly to the wall in certain terminal areas. Arrows and letters have their own character, as do the numbers. The typeface designers paid special attention to the numbers so they would be easily distinguishable and reflect the conventions of international type design.

B34–35

1

2

1 A special feature of the BER-Sans font is its dynamic form. The “f” opens wide upwards, as if it is about to take off. The “g” and “t” show the opposite, the landing movement. German and English languages are differentiated by two type weights so they are easy to distinguish.

To highlight and code information in the wayfinding system, letters and pictograms have a lined form as an additional font. This enables organising information hierarchies within tonal value, such as the letter “A B C D…” for the gate areas. This solution spans an abstract visual bridge back to the airport architecture.

2 In designing the letters, the type designers incorporated characters typical of Berlin such as the “ß”, the German character representing a double “s” found in Berlin street signs.

3/4 The wayfinding system seamlessly integrates into the building. A line grid, reminiscent of Brandenburg’s tall pine forests, and the linear structures of the terminal serve as a code and differentiate between the various levels of information. It was optimised for different font sizes and is used as an additional font.

3

4

The typefaces

ac

→ Akzidenz Grotesk

The Akzidenz Grotesk had become a popular typeface in the early wayfinding systems. Its origins date back to 1898. Over the years a large number of variations with slightly different details have circulated.

ac

→ Helvetica

The Swiss graphic artist Max Miedinger draw a typeface with the name Neue Haas Grotesk in collaboration with the director of the Haas foundry, Eduard Hoffmann, in the early 1950s. In 1957, it was licensed under the name Helvetica (Latin for Switzerland). Displayed here is the 2019 revisited version Helvetica Now.

ac

→ Transport

The Transport Alphabet was designed by Jock Kinneir in the 1960s. It is still in use for the United Kingdom's motorways and all-purpose roads. The predecessor was the typeface Kinneir and Calvert had worked with for Gatwick Airport LGW in 1958. Shown here is the digitally reworked adaptation, New Transport (2009) by Margaret Calvert and Henrik Kubel.

ac

→ Frutiger

The typeface Frutiger (Frutiger Next, Neue Frutiger) is a later version of the typeface Roissy. Adrian Frutiger designed it for Charles de Gaulle Airport CDG at Paris Roissy which opened in 1974.

Today

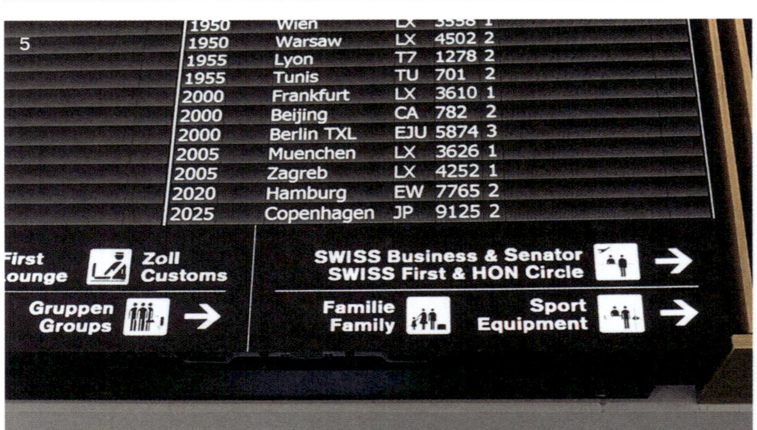

1 **CDG/ORY**—Aéroports de Paris → Frutiger
3 **IAD**—Washington Dulles International Airport → Frutiger
5 **ZRH**—Zurich Airport → custom font similar to Akzidenz Grotesk

2 **LGW**—London Gatwick → Myriad
4 **IAH**—George Bush Intercontinental Airport → Helvetica, et al.
6 **MUC**—Munich Airport → Univers (by Frutiger)

7 **LHR**—Heathrow Airport → Frutiger
9 **BWI**—Baltimore-Washington International Airport → Frutiger, et al.
11 **SIN**— Singapore Changi Airport → Frutiger

8 **JFK**—John F. Kennedy International Airport → Helvetica (will replace Frutiger)
10 **AMS**—Amsterdam Airport Schiphol → Frutiger
12 **BER**—Berlin Brandenburg Airport → BER Signage

G

Pictograms

The thousands of different languages and dialects spoken around the world are a testament to the ingenuity of human communication. The wealth of writing systems across the globe are visual evidence of this diversity and enable the dissemination of language. Spaces frequented by travellers from diverse language communities require a communication system that can be universally understood. The local language cannot always fulfil this function. The combination of English with pictograms has become the default language for international air travel.

Ideally, pictograms are symbols—or combinations of symbols—that transmit spoken and written content in the form of images which are decipherable across cultural and linguistic borders. The wildly ambitious goal of a pictogram is to be universally understood. These symbols are such elementary components of airport wayfinding, that we have dedicated a chapter full of images to examine them and their various iterations in airports around the world.

DOH Doha

Departure

The search for a universal meta-language dates back to the beginning of travel to far-away destinations. How do people communicate without a common language? With sounds and gestures, of course—and with images! With the increasing mobility of people, goods and services, it became essential to establish a common basis for shared truths and rules of behaviour. Traffic signs were the first universally applicable standards to function as international norms and communicate both permitted and prohibited behaviour with graphic symbols. A red dot with a horizontal white line running through it is not universally self-explanatory. People simply have to learn its meaning before they can obtain a driver's license. But there is no "traveller's licence" for international travel. Passengers rely instead on visual symbols drawn from a familiar canon of images, all of which are self-explanatory and frequently repeated around the world. We all strive for a common basis of understanding. Images that traverse cultures have, over time, evolved into symbols and into pictograms are extremely helpful in this process. Pictograms can encapsulate a wide variety of messages: they can be culture specific reflecting the regional and cultural context; they can express an spectrum of emotions and characteristics of the Zeitgeist of the time; and they can communicate universal international norms.

In the 1920s and 30s, the Austrian scientist and philosopher Otto Neurath collaborated with his future wife, the German mathematician and illustrator Marie Neurath (born Reidemeister), and the German graphic artist Gerd Arntz to develop the first pictorial symbols. Their work was driven by the socio-political motivation that scientific information should be accessible to everyone, regardless of their level of education. This trio was united in the conviction that all citizens should be given the means to participate in politics and public life. In contemporary terms, they saw pictograms as tools for democratic participation—information design for all. Starting in 1934, Otto Neurath began referring to his proposal for a simple, picture-based method as Isotype ↗. Neurath's pictorial symbols were informative and could be understood across cultural and language borders.

↗ Isotype (International System of Typographic Picture Education)
According to the Isotype rulebook, it should be possible to capture the symbols with three views. They should be reduced to the bare essentials and without embellishment: "A picture produced according to the rules of the Viennese method shows at first glance the most important features of the object; obvious differences must be immediately apparent. At second glance, it should be possible to see the more important details and at the third glance, what other details there might be. A picture that provides further information at the fourth and fifth glance is, from the standpoint of the Viennese School, to be rejected as pedagogically unsuitable."

ADV

AIGA

BER

CGN

DOH

LED

LHR

MAD

MUC

SIN

The picture of the airplane taking off has become a symbol for departure. The pictogram shows the aircraft at take-off, the last moment when the passenger leaves the ground. Passengers are now highly familiar with the image, and its meaning is easily understood in the context of the airport.

Many airports have formally varied the pictogram for departure, adapting it to the style of the time or to the pictogram family. Its function is to convey a meaning, and through its individual design it brings the respective identity of the pictogram family into the airport.

Standards

With the sharp rise in travel by train, car and air in the first half of the 20th century, it became necessary to standardise sign and pictogram systems at the international level. The International Federation of the National Standardizing Associations (ISA) was founded in 1926 and began instituting standardised pictorial symbols as early as 1932. In 1946, representatives of 25 countries founded the follow-up to ISA, now called the International Organization for Standardization (ISO). The ISO grew to 56 member countries in 1972 and by 1977 comprised 155 technical committees. The technical committee responsible for the standardisation of graphic symbols is known as TC 145. The steering organisation for the TC 145 is the German Institute for Standardisation (DIN). Many of the pictograms used at airports today were developed out of the ISO 7001 Public Information Symbols established in 1980. For example, to depict a lift or elevator, ISO 7001 recommends a sign showing a person in a box pressing a button alongside up-and-down arrows. The designer is responsible for the iteration of the pictogram in the individual location.

In 1968, the working group representing German airports, known as the Arbeitsgemeinschaft Deutscher Verkehrsflughäfen (ADV), published a recommendations manual for the use of pictograms at airports. Their objective was to facilitate passenger navigation by implementing the same pictograms at all airports. As the German graphic artist Herbert W. Kapitzki recounted in his memoir: "The ADV commissioned me to undertake a study of passenger wayfinding pictograms with the goal of developing a unified representational form for airports in Germany and Austria and eventually in all of Europe." Kapitzki went on to collaborate with the designer, artist and semiotician ↗ Martin Krampen on the use of pictograms in wayfinding systems for airports.

In the early 1970s, the American Institute of Graphic Arts (AIGA) cooperated with the US Department of Transportation as well as with the American designers Roger Cook and Don Shanosky to develop a set of 50 pictograms for use at US airports. The first 34 symbols were released in 1974, followed by the next 16 symbols in 1979. Currently these pictograms can be downloaded online without a license.

Over the past decades, the China National Institute of Standardization (CNIS) has continuously updated the Chinese pictogram standard. In such a vast country, where several languages and innumerable dialects are spoken, this is a particularly challenging process. The pictograms were created by a team at Tsinghua University in Beijing under the leadership of Professor He Jie and are used at all airports in China as part of their comprehensive Graphic Symbol Communication System.

↗ Semiotics is the study of signs. It emerged as an independent discipline thanks to the work of the American philosopher Charles Sanders Peirce at the end of the 19th century. In the mid-20th century, the American semiotician and philosopher Charles William Morris, a student of Sanders Peirce, categorised visual signs as functioning on semantic, syntactic (sigmatic) and pragmatic levels.

The recipient interprets the semantic meaning of a sign. In the case of airports, the recipients are travellers. The interpretation is based on a number of factors; sign context, the combination of signs onsite, the recipient's knowledge level and education as well as their cultural and social background.

On the syntactic level, recipients understand a sign based on the formal means with which a sign's content is portrayed. This includes its form, colour, material and line/texture.

The pragmatic level reflects the relationship to the recipient. What is the sign's intention: indicative speaks to the recipient's thought process, imperative speaks to their will, and suggestive corresponds to their feelings.

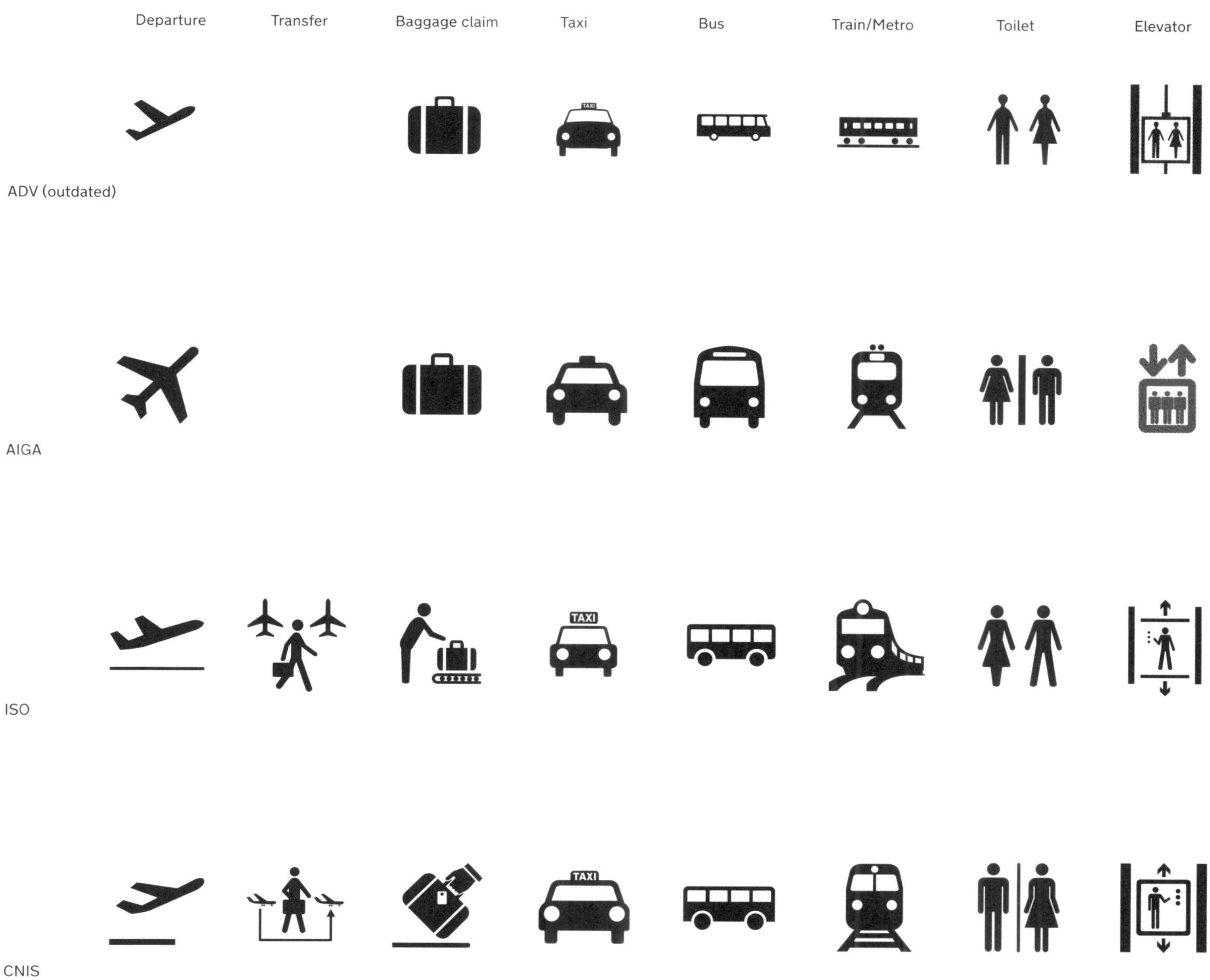

ADV Arbeitsgemeinschaft Deutscher Verkehrsflughäfen
German Airports Association
AIGA American Institute of Graphic Arts
ISO International Organization for Standardization
CNIS China National Institute of Standardization

As one can see, the standards are similar in terms of content and design. Committees constantly review and update them to meet the constantly evolving demands on non-verbal communication.

On the go

Pictograms are indispensable elements in airport wayfinding and are used on almost every sign. They are so useful because they can be quickly understood by people across a wide spectrum of language communities, and because they require very little space on a sign. The information they convey is lengthier than the pictograms themselves. They make it possible to include more information on the same sign space or for information to be featured in a larger format. Large formats guarantee visibility of information from a greater distance. Passenger orientation is more effective the earlier information is introduced. Passengers are led intuitively from sign to sign as they proceed to their destination without having to slow their speed. A complex text-based message, possibly in multiple languages, would require more processing time.

The designers who developed pictogram archetypes for airports over the past several decades built the foundation for today's standards. As designers of wayfinding systems, we have several options with regards to the standards. We can simply adopt them, develop them further, or adapt them to create unique pictogram sets. Unique pictograms can help to visually strengthen the airport's brand positioning. The advancement of the personal computer and creative software programmes for graphic layouts in the 1980s brought about a turning point in the evolution of pictograms. The notion in the late 1960s that all European airports should standardise their pictograms could not take hold because airports were unable to integrate location specific symbols into the wayfinding system.

As long as the Berlin Tegel Airport TXL remained in operation, it continued to use the pictograms recommended by the ADV in 1968. Tegel Airport was opened in 1974 and these pictograms were standard at the time. Despite the fact that the airport operated with state-of-the-art technologies and systems until 2020, the 1970s architecture and pictograms used in the signage gave it a nostalgic feel. Just like languages, visual symbols undergo a constant process of transformation and require regular updates. Standards have to be regularly revisited and reviewed to reflect changes in society and the changing role of airports.

New services and new topics

Decades ago, airports were sites only for arrivals and departures. Today they are multifunctional branded complexes and commercial centres where people meet and where passengers and visitors spend longer periods of time. Good pictogram design can improve the quality of the airport experience and can also convey a unique style, value or atmosphere. If we designers succeed in expressing the spirit of the site by allowing the pictograms to speak an individual language, we not only communicate information, we help impart the site with its own identity.

Today, airports feature far more services, facilities and retail space than they did 30 years ago. At many international airports, the number of pictograms in the pictogram set has grown to over 100 motifs. As new services for passengers emerge, new pictograms are added to the set and quickly learned by visitors. New pictograms are developed according to predefined design parameters and remain part of a visually unified set.

Carry-on luggage

Security check walk-through detector

Print out bag tags

Baggage drop-off

Automated check-in machine

Boarding pass control

Charging station

Social distancing

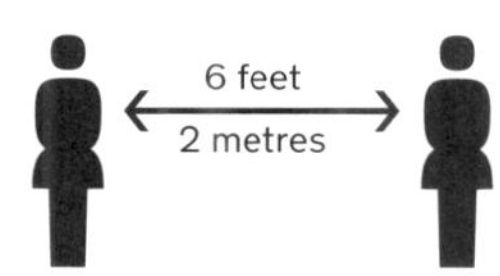

We don’t just check-in our own bags, we also print out our own luggage tags. We check in online and pass through automated boarding pass controls, priority lanes, e-car charging stations and much more. The pictogram set at Berlin Brandenburg Airport BER includes these new services.

Pictograms are a friendly and internationally-established means to communicate social distancing rules in the context of Covid-19. The rules can be integrated naturally into the wayfinding system as graphic elements and are perceived by passengers as simply part of the visual language in the airport.

Development and revision

Airports and train stations are buildings frequented by people from all over the world who need to navigate their way and process information quickly. The same is true of large-scale international events where navigation must function independently of language and culture. In the early 1960s, the Japanese graphic artist Katsumi Masaru led a design team that created the first ever uniform set of pictograms for the Olympic Summer Games Tokyo 1964. Soon thereafter, a German graphic designer named Otl Aicher took things to the next level with his strictly modular pictogram set designed for the Olympic Summer Games Munich 1972. Aicher's design was based on a pattern that allows for a surprising variety. Both he and Masaru set pictogram standards for the future.

While he was developing the pictograms for the Olympic Games in Munich, Aicher and his team were simultaneously working on a pictogram series for the Frankfurt Airport FRA. Twenty years later, the same pictograms were implemented at the Munich Airport MUC that opened in 1992. The pictogram set there is still in use today. It undergoes continuous updates to include new services and reflect new regulations.

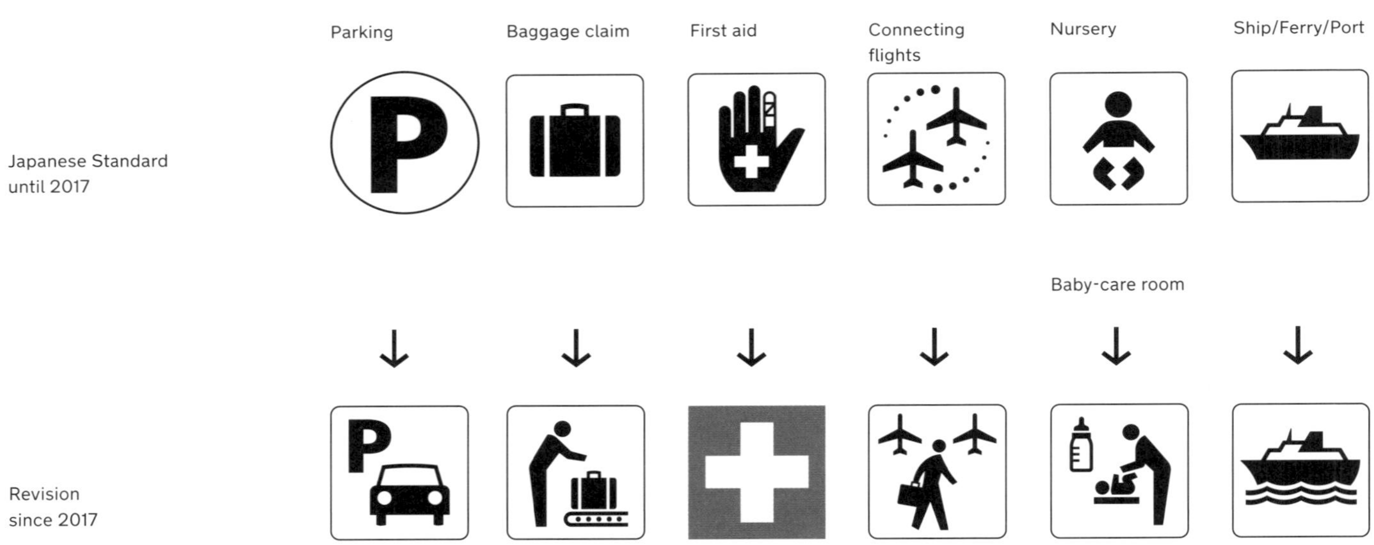

The pictograms at Japan's airports are based on the Japanese Standards Association (JSA). After conducting a series of comprehension tests in focus groups, the symbols were revised in 2017 to the ISO 7001 design for public information.

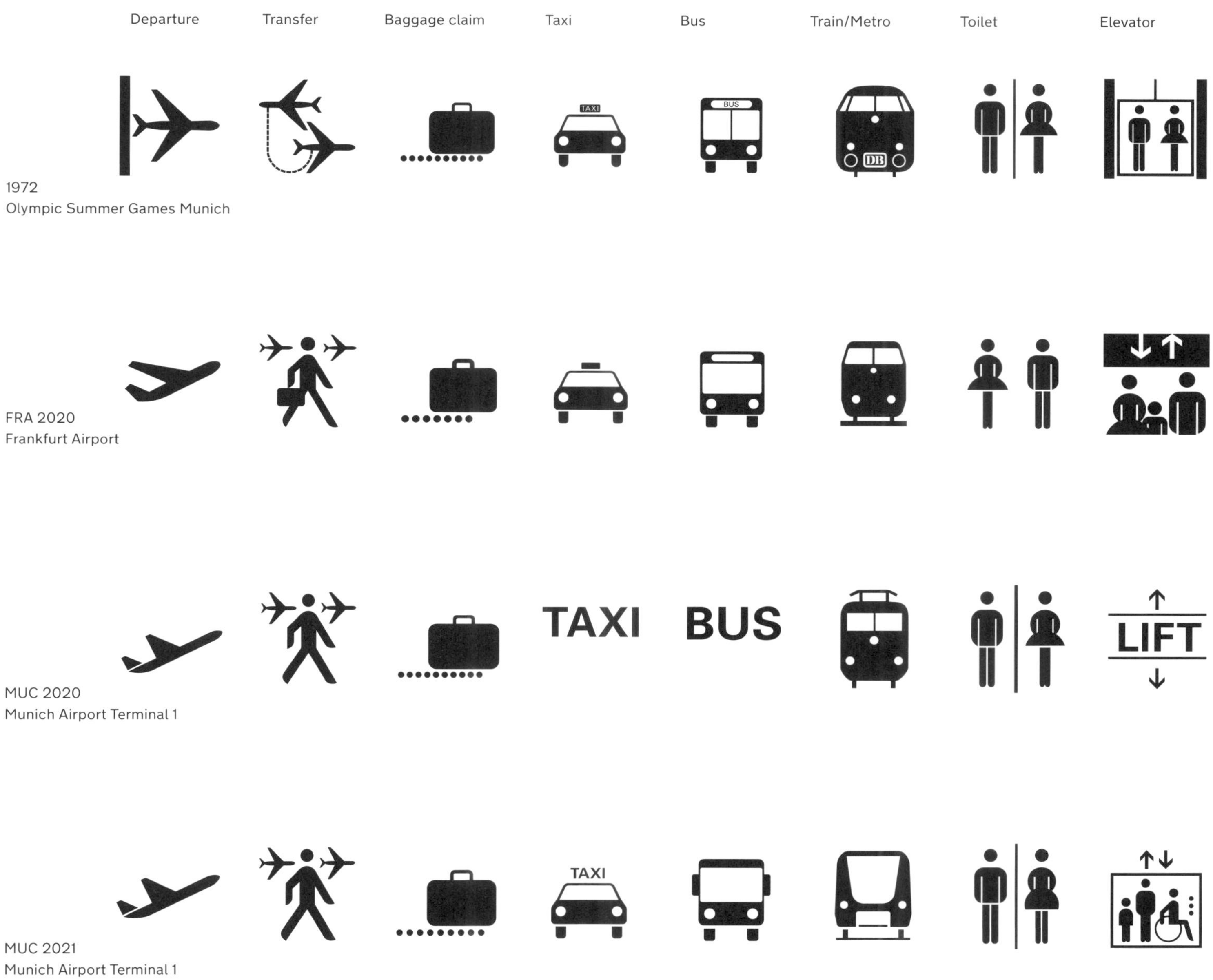

A direct comparison reveals the careful ongoing development of the pictogram set, originally drawn for the Olympic Summer Games Munich 1972. Today it is used for airports in Frankfurt FRA and Munich MUC. For the Munich Airport, the taxi, bus and lift pictograms were replaced by text.

Train

Access to public transport from an airport is important for most travellers. Bus connections are standard at airports around the world, but direct metro service and/or rail connections do not always exist. For major airport hubs, rail-link connections are an essential component of any contemporary, intermodal transport concept. Increasingly, airport and rail operators are working together to create seamless connections between the transport modes as part of an overall strategy to reduce the carbon footprint associated with travel while keeping journey times short. Airports are also launching a number of innovative programmes involving special services, such as Air & Rail check-in counters and combined ticket programmes.

The pictogram representation of the train as a means of transport has developed more conspicuously than that of the bus. With the planning of a station in or next to new large airports, there may be connections to several different types of trains. If this is the case, train pictograms must be differentiated and easily recognisable to distinguish, for example, between a high-speed train and a metro line.

Pictograms are usually shown within a square field or frame that defines the space around the pictogram. Their fields usually contrast in colour so that both stand out against the background, as shown on the next page.

On the following pages, we focus entirely on the symbols. Although we are aware of the significance of the pictogram's field, frame and colour scheme, all pictograms are presented here without a frame and in black-and-white.

Frontal view, perspective or lateral view. Advantages and disadvantages must be weighed up. ISO, for example, recommends the perspective view: by showing the length of the vehicle, the difference to the bus can be better displayed.

Taxi

TXL Berlin Tegel

HND Tokyo

BER Berlin Brandenburg

DOH Doha

LED St Petersburg

VIE Vienna

ORD Chicago

CDG Paris

ZRH Zurich

CGN Cologne Bonn

IKA Tehran

AMS Amsterdam

The taxi pictogram is an excellent example of how a symbol sign can convey the unique identity of a country or airport, as shown here by the example of the Cologne Bonn Airport CGN (on the top right corner). CGN's corporate design and wayfinding system were revamped to create a happy, jovial airport environment that is especially suitable for vacationers.

LHR London

BOM Mumbai

Many travellers are likely to recognise London's Black Cabs immediately. They are an iconic part of the city landscape like Big Ben or the London Eye and generate a positive association for arriving passengers who enjoy watching them pass.

Rickshaws are typical modes of transportation in Asian countries with warm climates. This depiction of the rickshaw from the side with wheels clearly distinguishes it from a taxi.

DEL old
New Delhi

DEL new
New Delhi

Can you guess the meaning of the vehicle on the far left? Most likely only with a bit of prior knowledge and a clue as to where it can be found. There is also one feature one would have to be familiar with in advance: the taximeter installed at the side of the vehicle was a typical feature of Indian taxis from the 1960s to the 1990s. With the disappearance of these types of taxis in the early 2000s, the pictogram also disappeared from the signage at Indira Gandhi International Airport in Delhi DEL. The taximeter was replaced by a driver indicating left-hand road traffic.

Ride sharing

A sign mounted on the roof of the taxi transversely to the direction of travel is the key semantic element that transforms a car into a taxi.

A small tweak can alter the meaning of a sign. With a new trend, such as ride sharing, pictograms are needed that represent different ways of sharing. Both the common use of a vehicle for the transport of persons and the booking of ride sharing over a professional switching agency.

Transfer

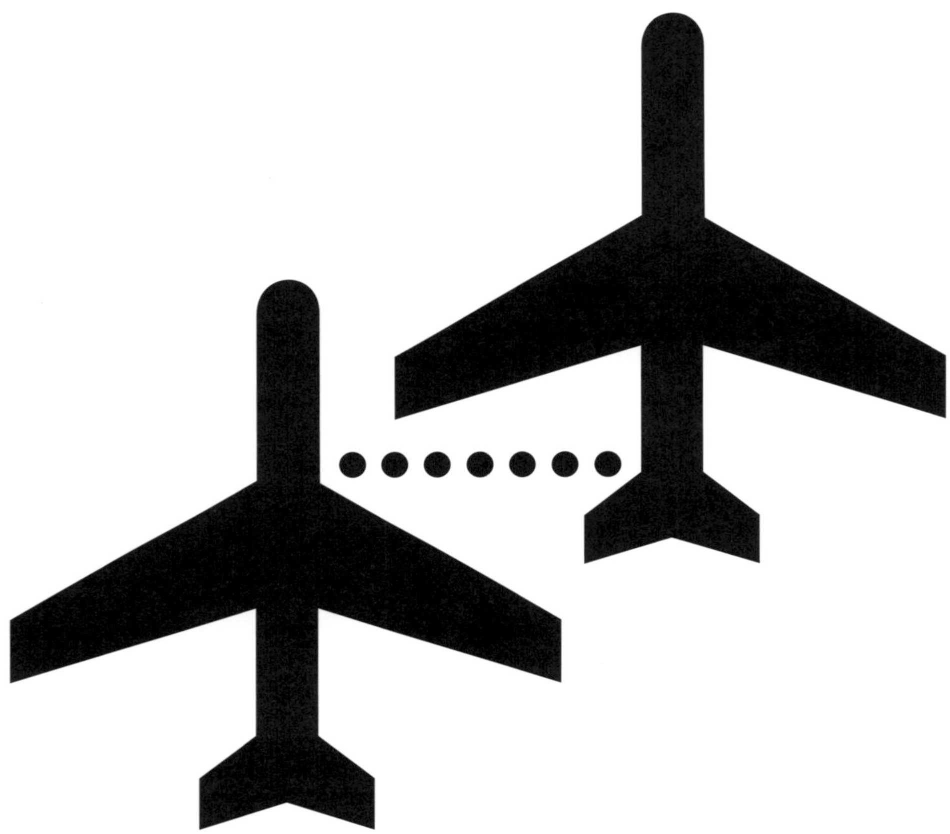

ORD Chicago

When looking at older established pictogram sets, it's easy to see that the "transfer" pictogram was added at a later stage. Transfer or connecting-flight pictograms were not necessary at some airports, because many of them were not connecting hubs. If an airport eventually developed into a hub, the pictogram family expanded to reflect this change.

AMS Amsterdam

HND old Tokyo

LED St Petersburg

CDG Paris

HND new Tokyo

LHR London

MAD Madrid

CGN Cologne Bonn

BER Berlin Brandenburg

Sets

Most of the pictograms on this page correspond to the standards outlined on page 193. In this case O'Hare International Airport in Chicago ORD uses AIGA pictograms, but also features its own unique CTA train pictogram. If a destination is location-specific, or if the standard no longer corresponds to current perception habits, customised pictograms are used. The toilet pictogram at King Khalid International Airport at Riyadh RUH also does not correspond to the AIGA standard.

Designers often have to decide whether to uniformly draw all pictograms of a set from a frontal perspective or not. By not conforming to frontal perspective there is more opportunity for clearly distinguishable individualised pictograms. When pictograms representing busses are depicted from the side, their dissimilarity to the taxi pictogram, which is depicted from the front, is more striking. Each airport needs to answer these questions on an individual basis.

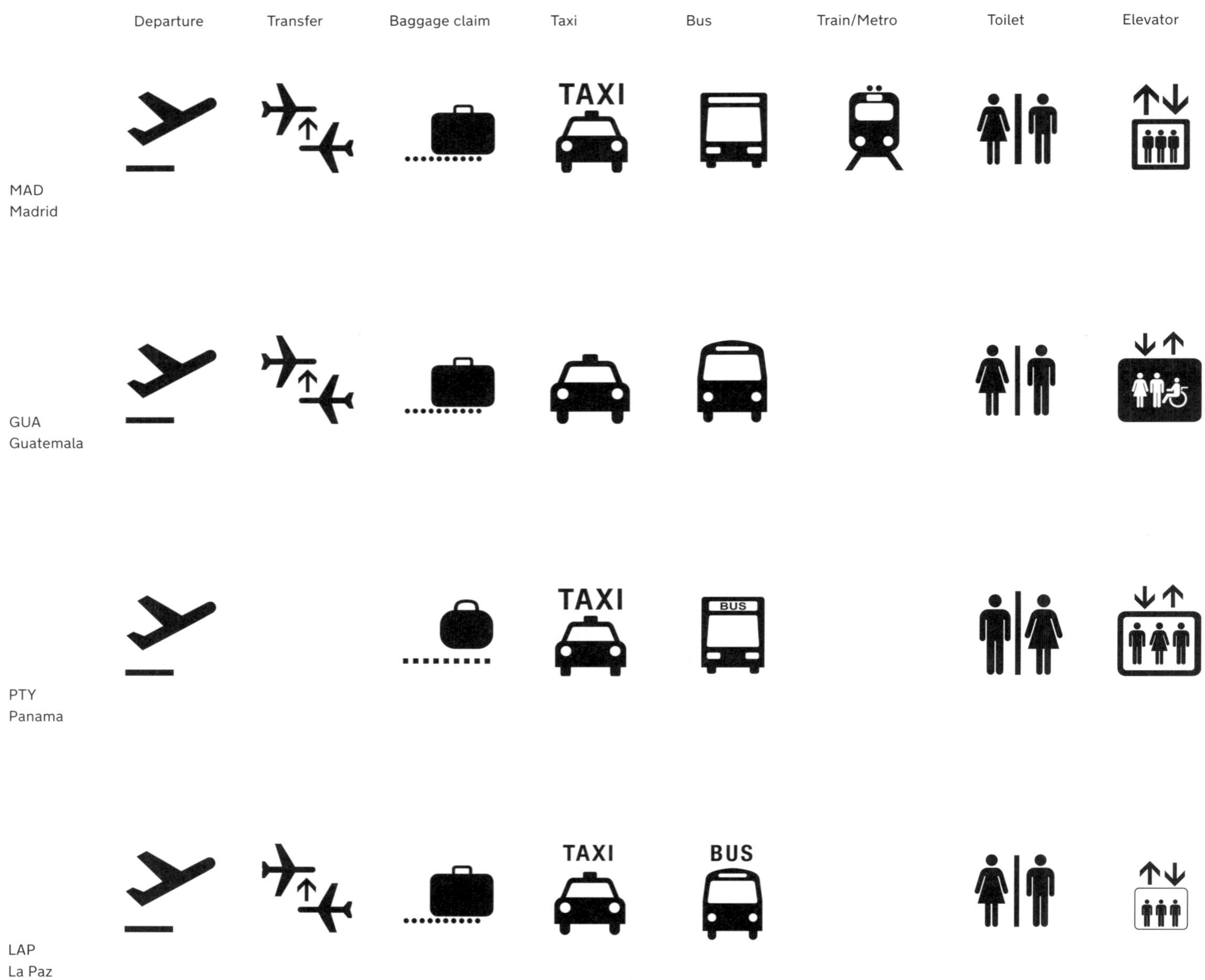

The Spanish airport operator Aena (Aeropuertos Españoles y Navegación Aérea) makes its pictogram set available on its website. These pictograms are used, for example, at Adolfo Suárez Madrid-Barajas Airport MAD, which is operated by Aena. Airports in Latin America, such as La Aurora International Airport in Guatemala City GUA, Tocumen International Airport in Panama PTY and Manuel Márquez de León International Airport in La Paz LAP, use the pictograms created by Aena (or at least very similar versions) in their wayfinding systems.

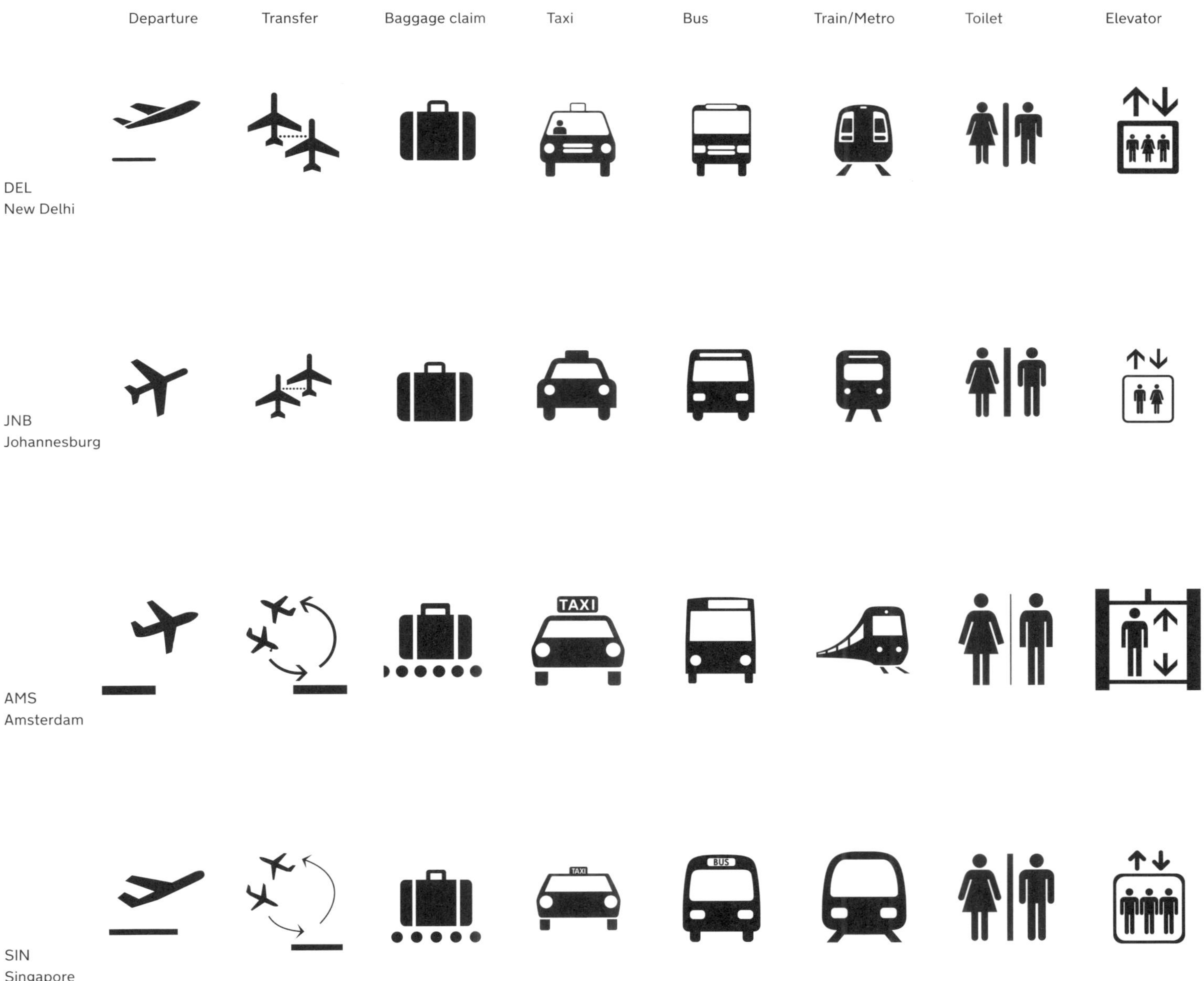

One pictogram that has formally established itself at most airports worldwide is the AIGA toilet depicting a man and woman. The idea of making sure travellers don't confuse the pictogram for toilet with the pictogram for lift corresponds to the notion of a "Design for All". A lift pictogram that features several people of diverse genders and sizes, as well as a wheelchair, would be an effective and inclusive approach.

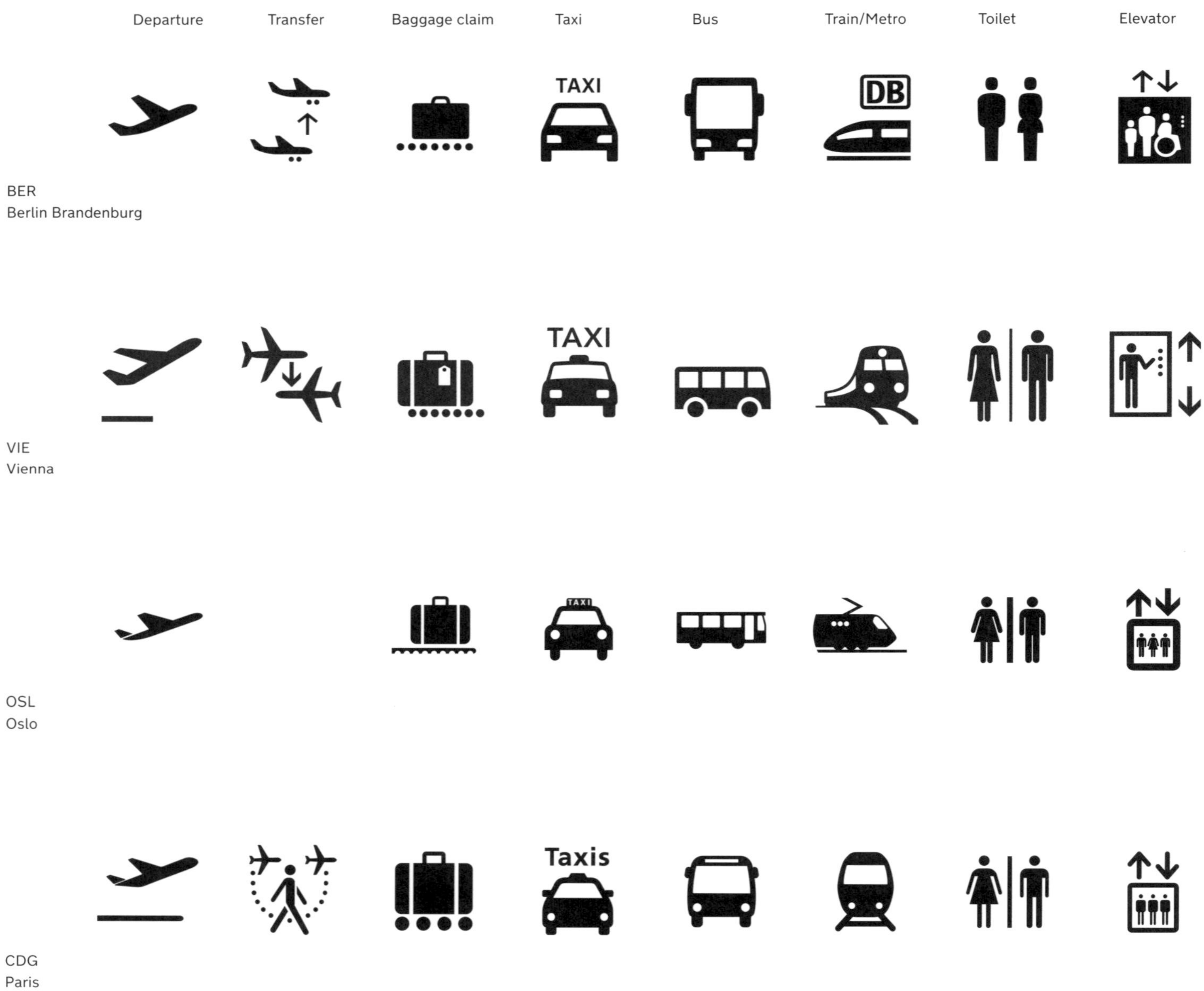

In many sets, stereotypical pictograms such as those for suitcases are in use. Although most travellers today use trolley-type luggage, the meaning of the suitcase image is still well established. But the symbol is currently undergoing an evolution, for example at Pulkovo Airport in St Petersburg LED (see right side).

Pictograms speak a graphic language, whether loud or quiet, subtle or bold, simple or complex. One way to find a formal language for pictograms is to develop them in accordance with the typical characteristics of the font with which they are implemented. This creates a harmonious overall appearance.

Arrows

Left

Arrows show us the way. To the left, to the right, up or down or perhaps around the corner. When an arrow is added to the sign, it becomes a directional sign. Depending on the sign location the straight ahead arrow means up and down as well.

An arrow is drawn as a line (shaft) with a pointed tip (two shanks) at the end of the line. The form can be adjusted to fit the letters and the pictograms. The thickness and length of the line are variable, as is the tip of the arrow. To create an optical balance, the shaft of the vertical arrow pointing upwards and downwards is usually depicted on signs as being somewhat longer than that of the horizontal arrow.

Fig. 1 and fig. 2 are the two arrow types most often used in wayfinding at airports, as they are very easy to read: Fig. 1 is the arrow that has cut the shanks of the arrow tip parallel to the shaft. A straight top and bottom edge between arrow and pictogram thereby emerge on the same line with a text or pictogram. The result is orderly and precise. This type of arrow is recommended by the International Standards Organisation (ISO) 7001. Fig. 2 is the arrow with tip cut off at a right angle. Depending on the size of the arrow, the shanks of the arrow tip protrude either over or under the optical line to the pictogram or text resulting in a more dynamic optic.

Left down

Left straight ahead

fig. 1

fig. 2

Straight ahead

Straight ahead

Right

Left up

Right down

Right up

Straight ahead left

Turn around left

Turn around right

Straight ahead right

214

Visit

Visit—Paul Andreu

During the course of his long career, the French architect Paul Andreu († 2018) designed and planned airports all over the world. His remarkable path began with the legendary Terminal 1 at Charles de Gaulle Airport CDG. This building shaped the very typology of airports. We were very keen to meet with Paul Andreu personally and learn more about his projects and his collaboration with the Swiss typeface designer Adrian Frutiger on the Charles de Gaulle Airport wayfinding system—itself a milestone in graphic design from the early 1970s. Paul Andreu graciously agreed to meet us. With the help of his assistant Madame Carole Rami, we were given an appointment in his studio close to the Place de la Bastille in Paris in October of 2013. The day before our meeting, we ventured to Charles de Gaulle Airport—the second largest in Europe with its Terminals 1, 2 A—F as well as the satellite gates K, L, and M which had just been completed. Andreu developed the master plan for this mega-structure. We descended with one of the many intersecting escalators that traverse this fascinating structure and noted that it has lost none of its futuristic charm. We were struck by the time-less-ness of this iconic structure in the brutalist tradition. It continues to impress despite having undergone many updates over the years. New handling processes, new standards and security regulations had led to a comprehensive renovation, which was now almost complete. On the day of our meeting, we were greeted by Andreu and his colleague Carole Rami. One of the most striking things we learned from Andreu was, how as a very young man, he approached the project at Roissy (as the project was called during the early planning phases). He was courageous, determined to work in interdisciplinary collaboration with a team of experts and he embraced innovation. Also, he was determined to maximise the flexibility that individual motorised travel, by car and bus, could bring to a large infrastructure project.

Andreu and Rami showed us the original Letraset sheets used by Frutiger for Roissy. We were familiar with such transfer sheets from our university days. Frutiger used them to produce his sign mock-ups. He first had to convince Andreu to let him design a new typeface for the airport guidance system. Andreu was keen to use the Peignot font. With use of the mock-ups, Frutiger demonstrated that Univers would be inappropriate for the terminal and that a typeface with improved legibility was the way to go for the new airport. They discussed letterforms, perceptual psychology and such details as the form of the arrows. We learned that these two leading experts in their respective fields shared the conviction that good design can yield good things. Their collaboration on Charles de Gaulle Airport CDG combined function with aesthetics and resulted in the creation of a typeface that has become an international standard at airports all over the world.

1 Charles de Gaulle Airport CDG Terminal 1 represents a completely new concept in many respects in the early seventies, the car park was located on the upper floors of the circular terminal.

2 Paris, October 2013, Heike Nehl, Sibylle Schlaich, with Carole Rami and Paul Andreu

Visit—
Mike Wolff

We visited Mike Wolff in London shortly before the Olympic Games 2012, where the city had prepared well in advance by expanding its infrastructure, renovating public transport and also expanding the London Underground's wayfinding system. London displayed its most wonderful characteristics as host. The public space was inviting and well designed and guests from all over the world were able to orientate and move around the city seamlessly.

The Sign Design Society, of which Wolff was chairman at the time, had organised a conference on orientation, focusing in on the signage system for the Olympic Games, aspects of barrier-free wayfinding but also on the scientific approach to urban connectivity and mobility in the city. The exemplary wayfinding project Legible London was presented at a very inspiring event where all speakers and participants were invited to share their personal passions for the topic of orientation. Wolff had studied geography and, in 1971, his passion for aviation brought him to the then British Airport Authority (BAA) (the operator of three London airports), where, from 1997 to his retirement in 2008, he was Head of Wayfinding and was largely responsible for the development and execution of the signage system at London Heathrow. We took the train to Reading, 40 kilometres west of London to meet him. His open-mindedness, friendliness and curiosity sparked an interesting conversation about the processes involved in planning guidance systems and about strategies and obstacles.

He explained that when constructing new airport terminals, architects and/or operators are inevitably tempted to give the building a unique identity in order to emphasise the achievement and the advancement over the original infrastructure. Whilst he was not opposed to this, Wolff was clear that since Terminal 5, which opened in 2008, was part of an airport complex at Heathrow Airport LHR, and the adopted signing system should coordinate with the four existing terminals. Indeed some 40 per cent of Heathrow's passengers were connecting between flights and often transferring between terminals.

At 81 million passengers per annum (pre-Covid), Heathrow is the largest airport in Europe and expansion had made it a very complex, interconnected structure. Ultimately, for Terminal 5, the signage system was partially redesigned, but the familiar black/yellow base colour combination was retained. After careful scientific testing, a version of Frutiger was chosen to replace the serifed Bembo font first introduced in the 1990s. Wolff explained that this allowed for a cleaner identity for T5 and could be equally functionally effective in the other terminals without requiring immediate replacement of existing signs. The wayfinding guidance system features a very minimal graphic language. It is very clear and precise. The signage is constructed using high-quality materials and the details are extremely well designed. The airport may have cast off a unique element of its brand identity, but in return, it has received an impressively sharpened concept and graphic principles that create an unmistakable image for London Heathrow.

Wolff talked about the special wayfinding requirements for Heathrow as a whole, which he described as the "most complex people moving environment in the world". No other airport operates at such volumes in such a constrained space. Complex processes and procedures are spread across five terminals in three separate geographic areas to handle people from every nation, culture and language group. His prior experience in airport terminal planning, development and operation had convinced him of the importance of a holistic approach to wayfinding and a single team that could act as an interlocutor between airport operation and professional designers. He was an advocate for the notion of the "educated client"—that is, people fully familiar with the airport and its business model, but also able to understand the principles of good design and how best to deploy that for optimal effectiveness. This would contrast with the person "tasked" with signage as part of a much broader portfolio.

His role, created in 1997, was predicated on the importance of wayfinding as a discipline, not just signage. The fundamentals, Wolff said, were that you needed to be mindful of all those influences which assist users' understanding of what they have to do at an airport, where to go and what information they needed en route. Whether it was the shape and position of an entrance, the volume of a space, the position of lighting, escape routes, the logical progression of a journey or the conflict with extraneous influences. The logical, swift and efficient progression through an airport could be influenced as much by, say, the shape and position of an entrance, the volume of a space, the position of lighting, the location of escape routes or the conflict with extraneous and potentially distracting influences, as by the design and placement of signing, flight information, notices and displays or the words staff used to direct people—a big and often underestimated task.

1 Heathrow Airport LHR, Terminal 2A, check-in hall

2 London, April 2012, Sibylle Schlaich, Heike Nehl and Mike Wolff, Head of Wayfinding, Heathrow Airport from 1997 to 2008

Visit—
Jane Davis Doggett

We had been working on wayfinding for many years before we discovered Jane Davis Doggett's work. We stumbled upon an interview with her on the SEGD website. The Society for Experiential Graphic Design (SEGD), is an international non-profit professional association whose members are experienced, interdisciplinary experts that work on spacial design projects around the world. There we learned of Jane Davis Doggett's groundbreaking work on airport wayfinding in the United States since the 1950s. Many basic tenets of her work are still recognisable at major US airports. Her design firm, Architectural Graphics Associates, worked on more than 40 US airport projects. She established basic principles for wayfinding and was hugely innovative in her use of colour and symbol in sign progression. We were deeply impressed by her work and contacted the SEGD to ask if they could help us set up a video call with her. We were delighted when we received a positive response.

Jane Davis Doggett, now 90, lives close to Tampa, Florida. Though she is a designer with a strong sense of aesthetics, she firmly supports the basic Bauhaus tenet that "form follows function" and she believes that design and communication are equal coordinates in cohesively guiding passengers to their destination.

Doggett told us that her time studying architectural and graphics design at Yale graduate school was decisive for her future work. "Architectural Graphics" was a new field that she first became aware of at Yale, It was a mere idea at the time—a theory more verbalised than it was visualised. It was at Yale where she became determined to pursue Architectural Graphics as a design specialisation. One day she would have a firm by that name. Her Yale education gave her a wide base of knowledge to draw from later on. She was at Yale during an incredibly vibrant period and was able to study with some of the most influential names in 20th-century design such as Joseph Albers, Paul Rand, Louis Kahn, Alvin Eisenman and Laszlo and Sibyl Moholy-Nagy. The Yale School was structured in the tradition of the Bauhaus School. Students were encouraged to innovate and adopt a pioneering spirit. It was a Yale connection that led to a design collaboration with Roy Harrover, a Yale-graduated architect, and fellow native of Nashville, Tennessee. Having observed the development of her work at Yale, and her passion for Architectural Graphics, he brought her onto the design team competing for the commission of the new Memphis International Airport MEM. By good fortune, Roy Harrover's firm was selected, and thus began a half-century career for Jane Davis Doggett as a pioneer wayfinding design specialist.

She discovered that, until her firm's founding, graphic design did not exist as a distinctive discipline within the offices of transport planners, architects or engineering firms. Signage was traditionally supplied by tradespeople who were sign-makers or by larger-scale sign manufacturers. These suppliers were specialised in commercial and advertising signs and therefore keen to sell large, illuminated formats because these were the most lucrative. As a result airport signage appeared arbitrary—randomly placed in spaces and lacking in message clarity, information organisation and layout or typography. Lettering was oddly-sized and the illumination very uneven. Airports were in urgent need of Architectural Graphics. The exponential growth in air traffic through the 1950s and 60s led to the expansion of airports and the construction of mega-jetports. Jane Davis Doggett summed up her years of experimentation with airport wayfinding as follows: The more complicated the airport—with many different airlines grouped into separate terminals; various facilities and transit systems; as well as passengers from many different countries—the more efficient the system approach has to be. That is the coding of information and indexing it with simple, basic, large symbols and colours. "When it comes down to overcoming language barriers, the abtract language of mathematics serves us well," says Doggett. "I go back to Galileo who taught us a universal language of mathematics: triangles, circles and other geometrical figures." Her conceptual work went way beyond primary wayfinding. She treated each airport as a gateway with its own thematic identity. As such she gave each its own logo to represent its unique features—geographic, cultural and historic. Typically she would start the roadway signage progression with a main sign to welcome visitors to the airport. This sign was boldly expressed by an airport thematic identity by means of a logo and colours. Often she utilised the airport logo throughout the wayfinding system. Tampa International Airport is the best example where her logo continues to be used in wayfinding for the last 50 years. She repeated the thematic identity of the airport throughout the terminal interior.

We discussed many topics such as pictograms, typeface and colour—all components of wayfinding systems that we deliberate with each project carefully. Though modern airport design has become more complex and international, many of her considerations and concepts have stood the test of time. One of the highlights of our conversation with Jane Davis Doggett was simply enjoying our shared passion for airport wayfinding with her. We showed her our work on the Berlin Brandenburg Airport BER and discovered, that despite the difference in times and the ocean that divides us, that there are many parallels in our approaches.

1

2

1 From 1971—73, Jane Davis Doggett designed the iconic logo as a key visual for the Tampa International Airport wayfinding system. The logo was applied to exterior vehicular airport approach roadways and to terminal interior passenger routings. Her unique system was structured on a two-colour coding of the two sides of the Terminal building. The logo and colour system are still in use at Tampa today, almost half a century later.

2 Florida—Berlin, May 2020, Jane Davis Doggett, Heike Nehl and Sibylle Schlaich meet via video conference.

Visit—
Margaret Calvert

In 2011, we were invited to the Tag der Typografie, an annual symposium in Bern, Switzerland dedicated to typeface design and design with typography. The event is curated by the Zurich Design School and the Union for Media and Communication Workers in Switzerland, syndicon and brings together some of the most interesting typeface designers and design firms from around the world. Our presentation was dedicated to the topic of wayfinding systems. As much as we enjoyed presenting our work, for us the event was a rare opportunity to discuss type and typography with some of the leading experts in the field. The London-based type designer Henrik Kubel held a fascinating presentation on the development of the New Transport font which goes back to a similar font used at Gatwick Airport LGW in the 1960s. Kubel had studied under Margaret Calvert at the Royal College of Art.

In 2008, in collaboration with his colleague Scott Williams, Kubel released New Transport. He recounted the story of the Transport font and explained how Jock Kinneir and Margaret Calvert had developed the first stringent wayfinding system for Gatwick Airport and later for London Heathrow Airport LHR and with what detail they had worked on the typeface and its font sizes, widths and letter spacing for optimal effectiveness in the indoor setting. In this process, Kinneir and Calvert drew their first font which later became Transport. It was adopted for motorways and streets throughout Great Britain. To develop the New Transport, Kubel and Williams worked with Margaret Calvert's original drafts for Transport and carefully reworked them for digital media. We thoroughly enjoyed meeting Henrik Kubel in Bern and stayed in contact.

In 2012, we visited Margaret Calvert in London for a fascinating conversation about her work. She welcomed us to her stylish townhouse in Islington. Commercial graphic artists often work in obscurity, no matter how widespread and ubiquitous their work may be. That had just changed in the case of Margaret Calvert. Her works were featured in an exhibition in the Design Museum London "Margaret Calvert: Woman at Work" and the Victoria & Albert Museum entitled "British Design 1948—2012". This exhibitions are tribute to the immense investment in design training that Britain had undertaken since the Second World War and its recognition of the role of design for innovation and economic development.

Calvert is an enormously important and influential personality in the world of design. We were very grateful for the opportunity to speak with her. She recounted the story of her work as a designer at the outset of the Jet Age and showed us an original BAA Manual. We left this meeting with a strong sense of connection and respect for her as a designer and for her groundbreaking work.

1

2

1 Margaret Calvert best known for the design of the UK's road signing system, together with Jock Kinneir

2 London, April 2012, Heike Nehl, Margaret Calvert and Sibylle Schlaich

222

Digital

3

The social media presence of airports

This map shows the social media activity of the 30 busiest airports in the world (2024). The pie charts indicate how the presence is divided among the platforms, while the size indicates the total number of followers. The map helps to illustrate the value airports attach to social media. It also shows that social media are a popular mode of communicating with passengers.

SOCIAL MEDIA FOLLOWERS 02 Aug 2024	IATA	AIRPORT
5 945 000	SIN	Singapore Changi Airport
1 566 000	LHR	Heathrow Airport
1 291 000	DXB	Dubai International Airport
1 136 000	DEL	Indira Gandhi International Airport
917 000	LAX	Los Angeles International Airport
907 000	ICN	Incheon International Airport
849 000	FRA	Frankfurt Airport
793 000	AMS	Amsterdam Airport Schiphol
646 000	IST	Istanbul Airport
536 000	MCO	Orlando International Airport
467 500	ORD	O'Hare International Airport
463 400	CAN	Guangzhou Baiyun International Airport
450 700	BKK	Suvarnabhumi Airport
431 000	DFW	Dallas Fort Worth International Airport
417 000	PEK	Beijing Capital International Airport
372 000	DEN	Denver International Airport
353 400	BOM	Chhatrapati Shivaji Maharaj International Airport
333 000	CDG	Charles de Gaulle Airport
328 000	ATL	Hartsfield-Jackson Atlanta International Airport
316 000	SFO	San Francisco International Airport
311 000	MIA	Miami International Airport
305 000	HND	Tokyo Haneda International Airport
261 800	SZX	Shenzhen Bao'an International Airport
203 000	LAS	Harry Reid International Airport
189 000	SEA	Seattle-Tacoma International Airport
151 000	PVG	Shanghai Pudong International Airport
121 000	CLT	Charlotte Douglas International Airport
48 000	JFK	John F. Kennedy International Airport
35 000	MAD	Adolfo Suárez Madrid-Barajas Airport
18 800	BCN	Barcelona-El Prat Airport

224

The passenger experience

225

The proliferation of digital technologies in global societies has been as rapid as the expansion of the air travel industry and these technologies have transformed the travel industry overall human mobility. It is impossible to predict how airports will function in the future.

An airport is hard to fathom in its entirety, and some passengers will not be familiar with all processes they encounter, which means they are obliged to place their full trust in the wayfinding and orientation system. Digital orientation tools can be particularly useful because they can be responsive to the individual passenger and the specific situation he or she faces. Is travel to the airport on public transportation delayed due to a disruption in service? Which security check has the shortest line? Is there a change relating to my flight? Does my gate have wheelchair access? As mobility continues to become ever more synchronised, wayfinding will no doubt also have to become more dynamic in the future.

There are several different stations within the airport journey that represent a potential touchpoint in the passenger experience. Each touchpoint can be digitalised and designed to give passengers the most positive experience and safe handling possible. On their airport journey, passengers connect with airlines, airport operators and countless service providers as they navigate through the complex. When these actors all work hand-in-hand, they can create a seamless chain of information flow.

In this chapter, we explore the passenger experience in the three stages of their journey: pre-travel, at the airport and onward travel. In particular, we examine the digital tools currently available at international airports to illustrate how digital applications and signage can merge smoothly with static wayfinding to help improve orientation.

Since digital applications have permeated daily life, the general population has become more digitally adept. Some have reached such a level of competency that they deliberately chose digital options and self-services. The ubiquity of mobile devices and the access to information on demand has been a huge boon to orientation—particularly with regard to the sudden necessity to install new security or health protocols in response to an unfolding health crisis. In the post-Covid-crisis era, digital devices may even become mandatory as a way of guaranteeing safety at airports and making air travel possible at all.

Closer cooperation among airports, airlines, developers and designers is needed in order to foster innovation and the digitalisation of the entire passenger journey. The goal is to think outside the box and bring together different stakeholders and skill sets. Innovation hubs have begun hosting events to bring together creative minds to collectively generate solutions and foster innovation. This form of cooperation will be essential in guaranteeing continued innovation in the aviation industry in the future.

H

Pre-journey

For passengers travelling by air, each trip is a process that begins long before the flight takes off and involves research, planning, preparation and orientation. From the moment passengers book a flight, they are provided with information to help with orientation. No matter the surroundings, people need to understand where they are going, how they should behave and react on their journey and what to expect when they arrive.

1 Airports often keep in touch with passengers via social media, whether it is practical information or just beautiful pictures available through Instagram.

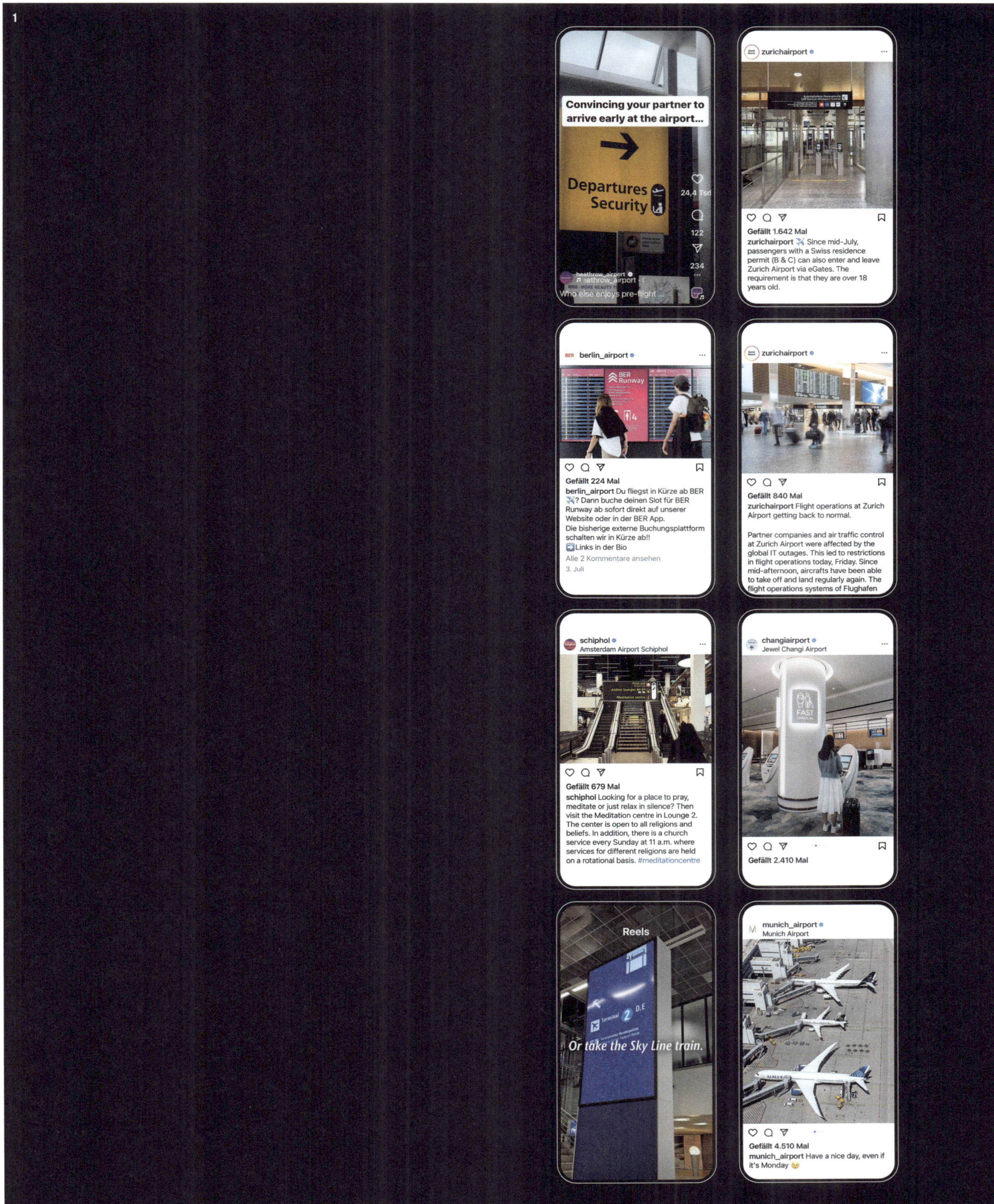
1
Convincing your partner to arrive early at the airport...
Departures
Security
24,4 Tsd
122
234
heathrow_airport
Who else enjoys pre-flight ...
zurichairport
Gefällt 1.642 Mal
zurichairport ✈️ Since mid-July, passengers with a Swiss residence permit (B & C) can also enter and leave Zurich Airport via eGates. The requirement is that they are over 18 years old.
BER berlin_airport
BER Runway
Gefällt 224 Mal
berlin_airport Du fliegst in Kürze ab BER ✈️? Dann buche deinen Slot für BER Runway ab sofort direkt auf unserer Website oder in der BER App.
Die bisherige externe Buchungsplattform schalten wir in Kürze ab!!
➡️Links in der Bio
Alle 2 Kommentare ansehen
3. Juli
zurichairport
Gefällt 840 Mal
zurichairport Flight operations at Zurich Airport getting back to normal.
Partner companies and air traffic control at Zurich Airport were affected by the global IT outages. This led to restrictions in flight operations today, Friday. Since mid-afternoon, aircrafts have been able to take off and land regularly again. The flight operations systems of Flughafen
schiphol
Amsterdam Airport Schiphol
Gefällt 679 Mal
schiphol Looking for a place to pray, meditate or just relax in silence? Then visit the Meditation centre in Lounge 2. The center is open to all religions and beliefs. In addition, there is a church service every Sunday at 11 a.m. where services for different religions are held on a rotational basis. #meditationcentre
changiairport
Jewel Changi Airport
FAST
Gefällt 2.410 Mal
Reels
Terminal 2 D.E
Or take the Sky Line train.
munich_airport
Munich Airport
Gefällt 4.510 Mal
munich_airport Have a nice day, even if it's Monday 😉

Websites

Booking platforms and websites are generally the first touchpoint in the passenger's chain of information. They offer details on services provided by the airline or the airport and where these can be found on-site. The information design—for example, on the various check-in options and self-service baggage kiosks—often differs from the information design travellers encounter during pre-information on websites and what they'll see at the airport. If the differences are minimal, it does not create any problems. Travellers are quite capable of processing different iterations of familiar pictogram motifs. Difficulties only arise when completely new processes or technologies, unfamiliar to passengers, are introduced at airports.

Social media

Airports also use social media to provide passengers with useful information prior to their arrival on-site. For example, they might send out messages about the latest developments at an airport and highlight unique aspects of their brand. These notifications mostly offer information for orientation on-site and are specific to the airport's location and individual identity. They are an excellent opportunity to introduce the passenger to the airport brand and the wayfinding system in the airport complex.

Apps

Today, airlines and airports are developing apps to guide visitors throughout their airport journey. Airlines maintain contact with their passengers from booking until online check-in is completed. Airlines and airport authorities also send out continuous updates on flight information, specific airport conditions, gate changes and public transport delays. These app updates are especially useful to a smaller subset of travellers, such as local residents who frequent the airport on a regular basis and passengers with special information needs.

Some airports coordinate their digital services in order to be able to maximise their usability and efficiency. Alternatively, they might work with third-party service providers who create modules for use at different airports. In this case, the graphic user interface can be adapted to the airport's specific corporate identity and wayfinding system. Airline apps are limited to their own group of users and contain information solely about the destinations to which that airline flies. More general information on airports can be integrated into the wallet function on a smartphone. Even though usage is limited to just a few functions such as check-in or gate position, it provides passengers with useful assistance.

Maps

Today, the use of online maps is ubiquitous thanks to their integration into the operating systems of mobile devices. They are the preferred map for most travellers in public spaces because they do not require any additional installation and most users are familiar with their functionality.

Increasingly, airports are also providing travellers with indoor maps. To enable this service, they cooperate with global mapping service providers to coordinate the destination points in the complex. For effective user orientation, the quality of the site mapping is key. The information on the map must be as close as possible to what passengers actually encounter in the terminal itself and offer high levels of detail. Map services are often biased towards providing information on commercial and retail offerings, whereas in airports the focus is always on flight-related information. In the best case scenarios, coordination between airport operators and map providers can hugely benefit individualised passenger wayfinding and provide different levels of detail. Interactive maps can help navigate passengers to destinations that are more difficult to locate or not included on signage. The static signage can then focus on the most highly frequented targets.

Wayfinding with airport-supplied maps that are both digital and static can be a very reliable source of information provided it uses consistent symbols and illustrations. If it offers visitors a detailed overview of the airport complex, this combination can be particularly helpful in making barrier-free access paths more visible and more effective. Maps can be made available in different formats, such as interactive kiosks, displays and static signs. Due to the continuously changing environment of the airport, it is advisable to install digital maps where appropriate.

1

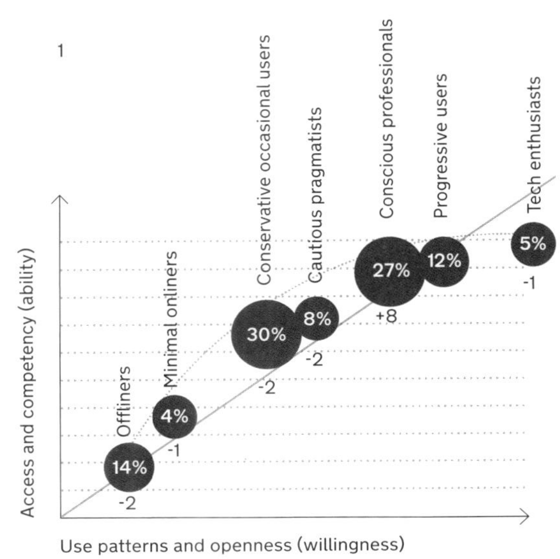

1 Conservative occasional users are still the largest group the largest group in Germany, closely followed by the Conscious professionals—the group with the strongest growth.

At the airport

Departure and arrival

- → Self-service kiosk
- → Flight information displays
- → Adaptive security information
- → Digital displays
- → Data collection
- → Digital wayfinding
- → Real-time customer service
- → Leisure and entertainment

Pre-journey

Research, planning and preparation ... journey to the airport

- → Websites
- → Social media
- → Apps
- → Maps

Onward travel

Journey to the city

- ➔ Follow instructions
- ➔ Parking
- ➔ Setting the framework
- ➔ Additional transportation
- ➔ Digital strategy

1

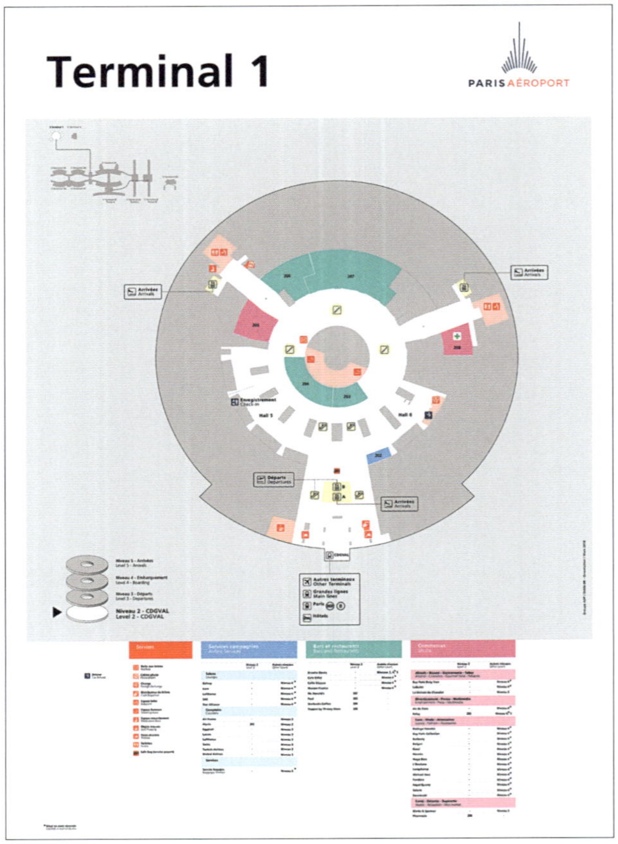

Terminal 1
PARIS AÉROPORT

2

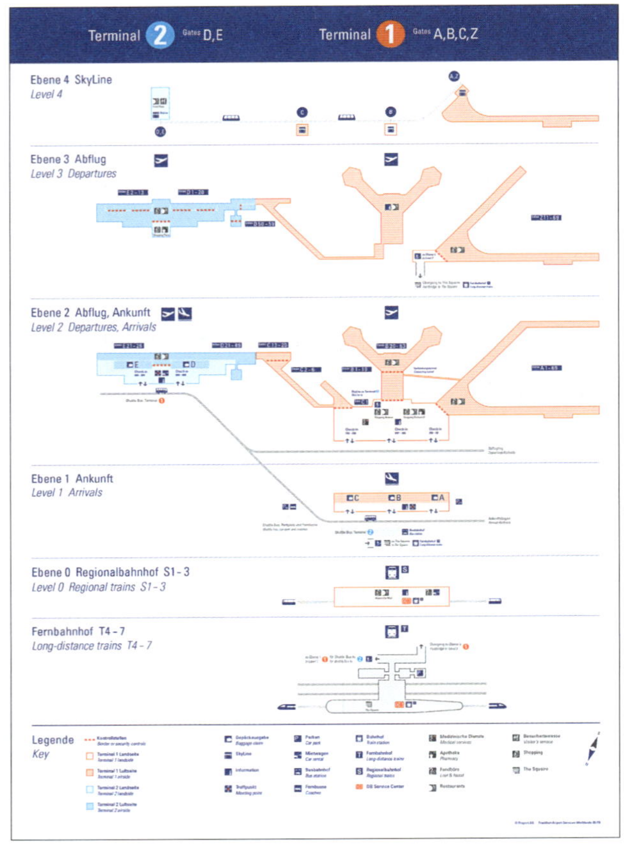

Terminal 2 Gates D,E
Terminal 1 Gates A,B,C,Z
Ebene 4 SkyLine
Level 4
Ebene 3 Abflug
Level 3 Departures
Ebene 2 Abflug, Ankunft
Level 2 Departures, Arrivals
Ebene 1 Ankunft
Level 1 Arrivals
Ebene 0 Regionalbahnhof S1-3
Level 0 Regional trains S1-3
Fernbahnhof T4-7
Long-distance trains T4-7
Legende
Key

3

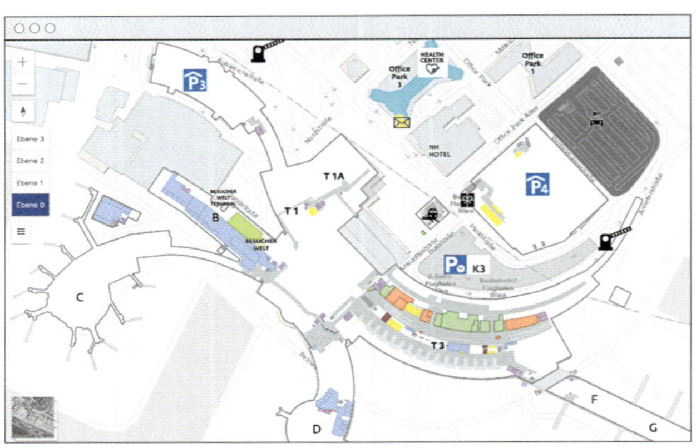

T 1A
T1
T3
C
D
F
G

4

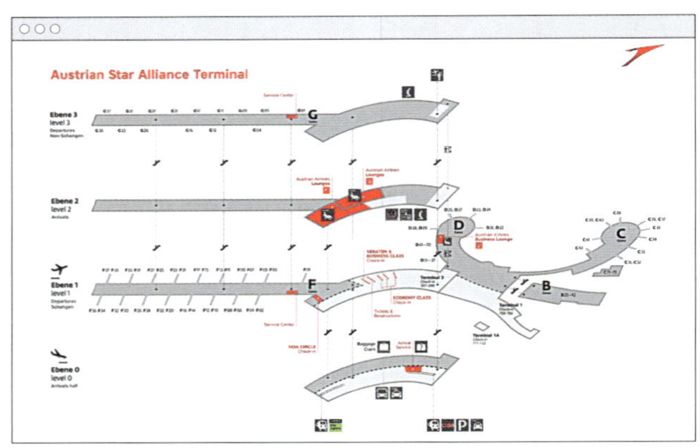

Austrian Star Alliance Terminal

5

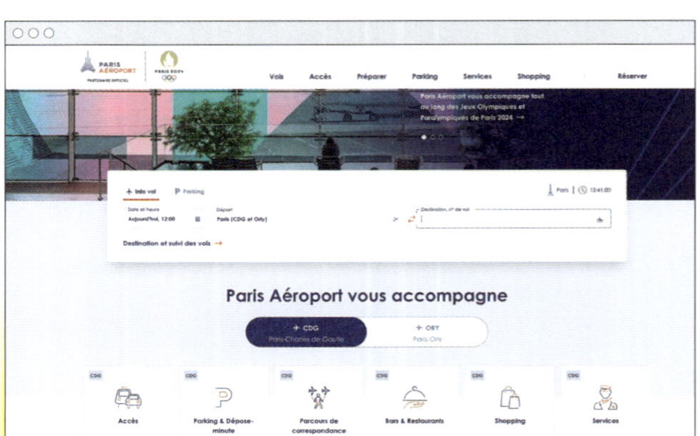

Paris Aéroport vous accompagne

6

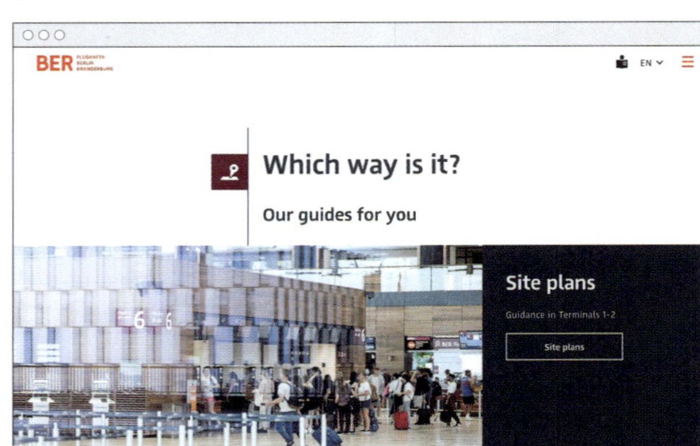

BER
Which way is it?
Our guides for you
Site plans
Site plans

7

8

1 **CDG** Charles de Gaulle Airport map gives travellers valuable information that helps them navigate their way through the terminal.

2 **FRA** The Frankfurt Airport map provides a clear overview of the two terminals.

3/4 **VIE** Vienna International Airport maps show different levels of detail. Each one reveals the bias of the map provider: Vienna International Airport (3), Austrian Airlines (4)

5 **CDG** Charles de Gaulle Airport welcomes visitors to the Olympic Games 2024.

6 **BER** The Berlin Brandenburg Airport website with its consistent use of colour, pictograms and fonts is a rich source of orientation.

7 **ZRH** Zurich was the first airport in the world to be equipped with Google Maps 'Live View' in 2021.

8 **AMS** Amsterdam Airport Schiphol maps are based on OpenStreetMap designed with Mapbox provided on the website.

J

At the airport

Digitalisation makes it possible to handle large numbers of people efficiently at the airport. Digital devices and dynamic wayfinding elements can be extremely helpful tools for moving people effectively and safely to their destinations. Many tasks which previously required the assistance of service staff can now be handled by the passengers themselves. Under enormous time pressure or other forms of stress, people are often faced with the task of using new services and navigating through an environment completely unfamiliar to them. The airport needs to support and guide the passengers as best as possible.

1 **LIS** Air travellers are greeted by kiosks at Lisbon Airport. From check-in to baggage drop-off, passengers can carry out their own check-in procedures completely independently. The infographic explains each individual step, passo 1—passo 2 …

1

passo 2 - entrega de bagagem
A01
A02
check in
passo 1
step 1
check in
passo 1 - quiosque
step 1 - kiosk
check in
step 1 - kiosk

Self-service kiosks

Upon arrival at the airport, passengers are greeted by a row of self-service kiosks. These have been in operation at countless airports for many years now. More and more options are being included. Check-in passengers can now print luggage tags before proceeding to self-service baggage drop-off without interacting with airport or airline personnel. Comprehensive user interfaces and information design is key to fast processing.

Flight information displays

A large-scale flight information display continues to function as landmark in airport buildings. Even though smaller passenger information display systems positioned frequently throughout the entire terminal, the large-scale display remains a central and often imposing element of the departure hall in front of the security at airports to this day. Flights to and from destinations all over the world are displayed here, creating a kind of connectivity dashboard.

Adaptive security information

Today, dynamic signage is the standard at most airports as a means to improve the flow of passengers through security lines and reduce congestion in individual spots. Digital systems anonymously record the number of passengers in the security checkpoint queuing areas and then display information indicating wait times at each checkpoint. Terminal space is limited and passenger numbers are growing. In recent years, a number of airports have changed their airside wayfinding systems to allow all gates to be accessible from each security checkpoint. Security checkpoints are amongst the biggest bottlenecks at airports around the world. It is here that the handling processes of airlines, airports, security authorities and third-party companies converge. All parties in this area have to cooperate and coordinate their processes well in order to facilitate a quick and efficient passenger journey. This requires good interfaces amongst the various parties and a synchronisation of data and processes.

In the future, most of the airport processes will be contactless thanks to digital technologies. Facial recognition software has potential for use in airports as security and passport control and in order to ensure the most efficient flow of travellers. However, this technology is highly controversial, not only due to its racial bias.

Digital displays

Large-scale digital advertising spaces also function as easy-to-remember landmarks for passenger orientation in the terminal. Undeterred by the bustle of the airport, they transport their message to travellers passing by in the form of elaborately produced moving images and photographs, thereby creating an atmosphere reminiscent of a shopping mall. The boundaries bet-ween advertising space and flight-related information are blurry. Erstwhile passenger info systems can be repurposed into advertising spaces, for example, at gates where no aircraft are currently being processed.

Data collection

As airports digitalise, they collect significant amounts of user data. The data shows where travellers are in the terminal, how they move and what their needs are. But who manages this data? And will it always be used to the benefit of passengers? Airports and airlines have a considerable interest in tracking their passengers' every move; it allows them to optimise their operations and also tailor the airport experience to increase potential revenues. Recently, however, growing data privacy concerns have increased pressure to collect data transparently and seek the explicit consent of users as part of an acceptable and successful digital service in the long term.

Digital wayfinding

Traditional wayfinding signage is becoming more dynamic. For example, messages now switch between multiple languages. Signs guide passengers on different paths through airports depending on available capacities and other up-to-the-minute airport conditions. To be effective, their visual appearance should in no way differ from the airport's static signage and integrate seamlessly into its overall appearance. Artificial intelligence and learning programmes can help to forecast passenger flows and manage the frequentation of the terminal. This technology can also display animated graphics which may become a more common requirement in the future.

Leisure and entertainment

When travellers have a connecting flight, their airport stopover can last several hours. Many passengers use the stopover to get a bite to eat, do some shopping or take a break. Airports offer various facilities, such as relaxation areas with massage chairs and rest zones. Showers and fitness rooms can provide a welcome opportunity to rejuvenate before the next flight. Many travellers enjoy leisure options such as films or computer games as a way of passing the time. Many airports also make entertainment and media options available to passengers. Some airports install elaborate installations with some connection to the local culture in order to leave a lasting impression on passengers. For passengers looking for a sense of familiarity and security, airports can create spaces that provide memorable experiences, thereby bringing added value to air travel. The airport complex provides a unique atmosphere, in addition to its function as an transport infrastructure.

1 **SFO** A multiple set of components and a dashboard which includes flight informations and maps is responding to various passenger needs at San Francisco International Airport.

2 **HAJ** The new wayfinding system at Hannover Airport focuses on guiding passengers to individual terminals. The colour-coding remains consistent across all static and dynamic elements from the check-in points all the way to the departure gates.

3 **BER** Berlin Brandenburg Airport—Information graphics such as the passenger information display systems are developed to closely correspond with the wayfinding design concept.

3

Abflug
Departures
14:30
Wartezeit an der Sicherheitskontrolle
Waiting time at the security control
→ 1
→ 2
↑ 4
← 5 Geschlossen
Closed
← Check-in 5–9
511–926
Check-in 0–4 →
011–426

1

Bordkartenkontrolle
Boarding pass control
Gates
G, H, K, L
Voraussichtliche
Wartezeit
Estimated
waiting time
0-3 min
Fluggäste mit
eingeschränkter
Mobilität
Familien mit Kindern
bis 6 Jahre
Bordkartenkontrolle
Boarding pass control
Gates
G, H, K, L
Voraussichtliche
Wartezeit
Estimated
waiting time
6-9 min

2

IN 3 SCHRITTEN ZUR
SCHNELLEREN
SICHERHEITSKONTROLLE:
Book-a-Slot
1. ONLINE SLOT BUCHEN
KOSTENLOS REGISTRIEREN

3

Frankfurt Airport
Im Voraus Entspannung
buchen: mit FRA SmartWay
Sichern Sie sich kostenfrei Ihren Slot für
die Sicherheitskontrolle
Zurück
FRA SmartWay
Exklusiven Zugang zur
Sicherheitskontrolle buchen

Real-time customer service

When passengers scan their boarding passes at kiosk systems or transfer counters, these devices can provide individualised information on connecting flights and routing to the gates. Another way to respond to passenger queries is to communicate via telepresence at info kiosks distributed throughout the airport or mobile devices. Robots can also answer travellers' questions. They are mobile and therefore available everywhere in the airport. Voice interfaces are constantly being improved, so that robots can provide answers to very specific questions. And if the tests and prototypes at international airports are any indication, in the future they will be able to guide passengers safely. At least, robots are also already in use as cleaners in airport buildings.

5

1 **MUC** Dynamic signage for better utilisation of boarding pass control at Munich Airport.

2 **FRA** At an aviation hackathon in Berlin, teams of developers and designers were tasked with inventing new concepts for air travel. Several international airports, airlines and associations made their programming interfaces—so-called APIs—available to aid their prototyping. For example, booking systems for time slots at security check, such as Book-a-slot were developed and tested at Frankfurt Airport.

3 **FRA** With the free service FRA Smart Way you can conveniently book a time slot for the security check from home or while travelling. By booking, you are authorised to use exclusive access to the checkpoints and can avoid long waiting times.

4 **MAD** Facial Recognition Pilot Project at Terminal 4 at Adolfo Suárez Madrid-Barajas Airport with the aim of providing passenger experience at the airport by enabling customers to identify themselves at the boarding gates.

5 **AMS** A so called Passenger Experience Platform serves data to different touch points at Amsterdam Schiphol Airport including personal devices.

5

6

5 **PRG** Digital signage trial, launched for passengers at Vaclav Havel Airport Prague, is available in six language versions. The signage system provides much more information than conventional information boards. It informs departing passengers of their gate and the walk time to reach it. With the help of pictograms, passengers can learn about the services located in the vicinity.

6 **HND** At Tokyo Haneda International Airport, displays switch between Chinese, Korean and Japanese text in addition to English sign messages.

7 **IST** Real-time customer service at self-service kiosks reduces wait times for passengers and costs for Istanbul Airport.

8 **CDG** Wall mounted kiosk displays directories and maps below FIDS at Paris Charles de Gaulles.

9 **SIN** Robots can clean up to 1,600 square metres an hour, spotted here at Singapore Changi Airport. They express their own unique identity.

10 **ZRH** Hard-working floor scrubber robots at Zurich Airport …

11 **MUC** Snack robot is serving drinks.

7

BANA SOR!
ASK ME!
Istanbul Airport

8

Départs - Departures - 出发

9

Flughafen Zürich

11

SERVUS, I'M YOUR
SNACKBOT

K

Onward travel

Spacious information areas provide passengers with an overview of all information in the form of maps, information graphics and public transport schedules for onward travel options. A visual language consistent with the wayfinding creates a seamless chain of information and allows the airport to fulfil its role as a provider and enabler of mobility. Arriving passengers often feel discomfort due to language barriers. Clear and user-friendly graphics are welcoming and enhance the user experience, whether they're travelling via airport express to the city centre or taking an autonomous shuttle to the park decks.

1 **LAX** An Automated People Mover, will connect to six stations: inside the Central Terminal Area, the Economy Parking facility, the Metro Transit Center station and the Rent-A-Car facility at Los Angeles International Airport in 2026.

2 **STR** The new, more representative baggage claim area at Stuttgart Airport: the displays here are integrated into an illuminated belt, offering a pleasing symbiosis of interior and information.

3 **LHR** Clear information design at Heathrow Airport creates a welcoming space for arriving guests and their onward travel.

2

30
STUTTGART AIRPORT
Welcome to Stuttgart
31

3

Information
Information services
Which Terminal?
Information leaflets
Car rental

Follow instructions

When passengers exit the plane, they are often tired and groggy from a long flight. They make their way through the jetbridge that secures their passage from the aircraft to the terminal building and soon have solid ground under their feet. A series of digital services facilitate passengers' official entry and arrival at their destination. Displays located in the baggage claim area, provide passengers with information about baggage status, immigration and customs regulations as well as transport connections to the city. Though passport control is often automated, passengers still have to identify the correct line by using the wayfinding. Here, they follow instructions in the form of a video; and endure the impatience of others standing behind them in the queue. From this point onwards, they are faced with one pressing decision after another: follow connecting flight, exit to the city, railway station, ride sharing ...?

Parking

Passengers with parked cars, those who have rented a car and visitors picking passengers up by car all have to make their way to the parking garage. It is the job of the wayfinding system to guide them there comfortably and clearly. Parking is still a key source of income for airports, and innovations such as car washes and shopping deliveries are bringing parking services to a new level.

Autonomous vehicles facilitate travel between terminals and parking lots. Effective information design is key to explaining this unfamiliar procedure to passengers.

Setting the framework

Many passengers are unfamiliar with their surroundings and how to navigate. The airport wayfinding sets the framework enabling passengers to absorb information in the most comfortable way. By providing Wi-Fi, passengers can use their own devices to navigate their preferred path into the city. Another option is an information kiosk operated by public transport authorities. Each mobility provider has its own visual language which might be confusing to the user. Arriving passengers often feel discomfort due to language barriers and a general fear of making mistakes and therefore often shy away from using self-service machines. Good user interfaces can go a long way towards improving the comfort level, and airports can create the space to minimise stress.

New mobility options

As new modes of transportation and services emerge, they have to be integrated into the airport wayfinding. If a passenger's preference is to use a ride-sharing service, the signage must make it easy for them to find the pick-up point. This is often found in a different location than designated taxi stands and public transport stops.

Digital strategy

To enable a seamless and stress-free passenger journey, an airport's wayfinding system must be closely connected with the airport's digital strategy. In order for passengers and visitors to navigate the airport complex smoothly, the interface points between the digital and the physical navigation tools must work seamlessly. This requires involving all airport sectors in the planning process, including aviation, management, IT, corporate communications, architects and real estate. It also involves keeping independent services in the loop, such as airlines, law enforcement and customs. In this process, the airport's role is that of a provider of infrastructure and a framework for collaboration. Ideally it should act as a moderator, representing the perspective of the passenger in this process.

In the recent past, maximising profitability and expanding capacity were the primary goals of the airport planning process. Today and in the future, with the help of digital tools, planners could fulfil more passenger-centred mobility concepts which prioritise safety, comfort and sustainability.

Digital technology has revolutionised orientation in the entire travel experience. It has made passengers independent through automated processes such as ticket purchases, check-in and baggage tagging. It has enabled individual routing at the airport and allowed airports to adapt quickly to the emergence of new requirements. In short it provides a flexible, unified concept for both content and design across all media in which passengers can place their trust. Instead of objects requiring handling, they are now agents in their own journey and mobility.

248

Beyond

4

249

Relevance of an airport for the city

This map looks at the 30 biggest cities in the world by population (metropolitan area, 2019). The two halves of each circle show the relationship between the number of air travel passengers (white half) and the number of residents (blue half) respectively. The main purpose of this graphic is to demonstrate the importance of an airport to the city it serves and to illustrate how many large cities do not have proportionate airport capacity.

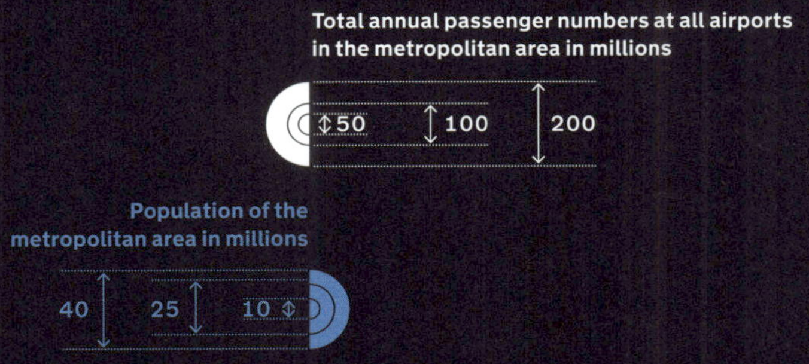

	City	Airports					
1.	Tokyo	HND	NRT				
2.	Delhi	DEL					
3.	Shanghai	PVG	SHA				
4.	São Paulo	GRU	CGH				
5.	Mumbai	BOM					
6.	Mexico City	MEX					
7.	Beijing	PEK					
8.	Osaka	KIX					
9.	Cairo	CAI					
10.	New York	JFK	EWR	LGA			
11.	Dhaka	DAC					
12.	Karachi	KHI					
13.	Buenos Aires	AEP	EZE				
14.	Kolkata	CCU					
15.	Istanbul	IST	SAW				
16.	Chongqing	CKG					
17.	Lagos	LOS					
18.	Manila	MNL					
19.	Rio de Janeiro	GIG	SDU				
20.	Guangzhou	CAN					
21.	Los Angeles	LAX	ONT	SNA	BUR	LGB	
22.	Moscow	SVO	DME	VKO			
23.	Kinshasa	FIH					
24.	Tianjin	TSN					
25.	Paris	CDG	ORY				
26.	Shenzhen	SZX					
27.	Jakarta	CGK	HLP				
28.	London	LHR	LGW	STN	LTN	LCY	SEN
29.	Bangalore	BLR					
30.	Lima	LIM					

250

How airports connect

251

Airports are complex structures that constitute much more than just air traffic. Once outside the terminal, the focus shifts to what happens in the area directly surrounding the terminal and how the airport connects with the city it serves. Here too, orientation is key.

Airports are a crucial part of the mobility infrastructure that connect a city to the world. They make a large contribution to the attractiveness of a city for residents, visitors and investors. Good planning ensures that the airport and the city are successful together and make a positive impact on the regional economy. Good concepts to connect the city centre with the airport—whether it be in close or more remote proximity—can maximise the benefits for both entities. However, airports may well have to redefine themselves as the aviation industry undergoes yet another phase of transformative change. They provide working space to develop and experiment with future innovation.

Airports and the cities they serve are interdependent. As one develops, so does the other sometimes creating unique momentum which, of course, varies from country to country and depends on the local socio-economic situation.

Airports began as strategic locations for military use. Once they started handling freight, they took on economic importance. Today, they are meeting places and attractive shopping and travel destinations. Airports are also drivers of innovation. As the air travel industry strives to become more sustainable and energy efficient, this could very well be a positive evolution.

Airports which have closed and repurposed are chapters in the history of air travel and the aviation industry. How cities have reclaimed the space they occupied is worth examination for those airports set to meet a similar fate in the near future. In this chapter, we also take a closer look at several repurposed airports from around the world and discover how some are still recognisable in their previous form whereas others have dissolved into the city's landscape and how they work with signage in their new form.

L

Airport mobility

Today's wayfinding systems lead far beyond the terminal. An airport site can be as large as an urban district and form its own microcosm. Airports are becoming intermodal transport and mobility hubs. Airport orientation needs to integrate all these aspects and create a continuous information flow.

1 **BER** The Berlin Brandenburg Airport features a comprehensive wayfinding system which includes the terminal and exterior traffic wayfinding system as well as the pedestrian wayfinding systems. Pictograms, typography, colours, and nomenclature are designed consistently.

2 **BKK** Suvarnabhumi International Airport signs are designed to resemble road signage.

3 **ORY** Orly Airport has implemented sculpture-like outdoor signs for terminal orientation after renaming all terminals in 2019.

4 **TPA** Tampa International Airport continues the colour-coding for exterior road signs in the interior.

5 **PKX** The new rapid transit line from Beijing city to Beijing Daxing International Airport starting at Caoqiao station.

6 **OSL** The Flytoget Airport Train connecting Oslo Gardermoen Airport to the city centre has increased the number of passengers arriving by public transport.

1

Terminal 1–2
P1
Airport City
Mietwagen
P2-8

2

3

Orly 2
Orly 2
Orly 3

4

Terminal
CLEARANCE 13'-0"
Terminal
Marriott Airport Hotel
CLEARANCE 13'-0"
SunPass Plus Not Available For Valet

5

6

Oslo Lufthavn

Signage unequivocally indicates the visitors' arrival at the airport site. Destination points such as Car Rental Return, Cargo or General Aviation Terminal (GAT) are clearly visible on the signs next to Departure and Arrival. A large network of one-way streets often runs through the entire complex, with junctions between airport levels or to various multi-storey car parks. The road network also leads to numerous operational services buildings located around the airport. The exterior wayfinding system is often a hybrid version of the terminal guidance system and national traffic signs.

By the early 1960s, individual motorised transport to the airport was becoming the international standard. Huge parking facilities were constructed to accommodate the exponential growth of vehicles at airports such as: Orly Airport, Paris, ORY, George Bush Intercontinental Airport, Houston, IAH, O'Hare International Airport, Chicago, ORD, former airport Berlin Tegel Otto Lilienthal, Berlin, TXL. Parking is still one of the most important revenue streams for airports. Multiple related services have emerged to maximise these revenues such as pre-booking parking spaces, car wash and direct vehicle delivery of purchases. At the same time, car trips are becoming increasingly anachronistic due to their heavy carbon footprint.

Multimodal mobility

Today decarbonising the transport sector is a huge priority. New airports are building high-speed long-distance as well as regional train stations to increase the airport's catchment area and enable short hops to be undertaken by train for connecting to flight. Some airports such as Zurich Airport ZRH already function successfully as mobility hubs. There, passengers can continue journeys seamlessly from aircraft to train and bus for long or shorter distances. Signage can improve intermodal mobility.

The new Beijing Daxing International Airport PKX is connected to the city centre by a high-speed rail line. From the moment one boards the train, the journey resembles a flight. Close coordination between air and rail transport make it possible for passengers to avoid short-haul flights and opt for a train trip to the international airport. Starting in 2020, the Dutch airline KLM has announced that it will offer rail travel from Amsterdam to Brussels to give passengers a lower carbon option. Airlines such as Lufthansa offer a bus shuttle service to the Munich Airport MUC. After having boarded the passengers are already "on board" with the airline and no longer have to worry about getting to the airport on time. The CAT City Airport Train in Vienna is the only airport service in Europe where passengers can check themselves and their baggage in at a central location in the city. Hong Kong has provided this service for many years.

1 **CDG** At the train station Aéroport Charles de Gaulle 2—TGV Paris passengers switch modes from air to rail. The wayfinding system has to guarantee a smooth transition between the two systems.

M

Airport and the city

Airports are built near cities and the areas around them. Today they are becoming cities themselves, often referred to as airport cities. Is this an appropriate description? What distinguishes them from cities that have grown organically? They offer high connectivity and attract companies to locate in their vicinity. They are global meeting places. They foster international exchange.

1 **HEL** Helsinki Airport provides a rich cultural exchange to the city of Vantaa, located north of Helsinki, and acts as a junction where local life meets global exchange. Aviapolis is set to become the gateway from Finland to the world.

2 **DEN** The Denver International Airport Strategic Development Plan creates a roadmap for transforming non-aviation airport land into several development districts for local, national and global commercial and institutional activities.

3 **TXL** The Urban Tech Republic will see the development of a research and industrial park for urban technologies. Berlin reclaimed a part of the city when the airport closed in 2020. A smart residential district comprising more than 5,000 homes will be developed in the immediate vicinity.

4 **THF** In 2008, former Berlin Tempelhof Airport ceased air traffic creating valuable urban space for events and leisure as well as various new tenants.

5 **HKG** 1998, Kai Tak Cruise Terminal with a large rooftop garden, located at the former Kai Tak Airport, now repurposed as a terminal for cruise ships.

1

2

3

4

Flughafen Tempelho
Tempelhof Airport
Vorfeld
Flügel 2
Flügel 1

5

A place for innovation

Lufthansa launched the Lufthansa Innovation Hub to transform its core business into that of a provider of mobility. Airlines are beginning to see themselves as more than just operators of flights, but as service providers along the entire travel value chain. In recent years, numerous mobility startups have emerged and begun to transform the travel industry with the help of digital tools. Airlines have also recognised the necessity to expand their core business by adding new integrated revenue streams. New business models are evolving at the interface between airlines, airports and passengers.

Consequently the airport has become a place where innovative solutions are developed and can be tested immediately. The Zurich Airport has recently set up an Innovation Hub, to transform and improve the passenger experience at the airport. ZRH Innovation Hub offers space for smart solutions and pioneering products across departments and companies. Its mission is to test and develop prototypes based on the latest technologies such as artificial intelligence, big data analytics and predictive maintenance, as well as the internet of things (IoT).

In Munich, the airport operators are building a similar facility. The LabCampus is located in the immediate vicinity of the airport. A workspace of approximately 500,000 square metres will span four quadrants to create a bustling campus on which many different small and medium-sized companies can settle. The developer's intention is to foster productive cross-company collaborations that yield innovative concepts. In order to improve the sustainability and acceptance of the activities at the campus, neighbours, the surrounding municipalities and the wider urban community have open invitations to participate and give their feedback.

Vienna is pursuing a similar concept. The Airport City development project, currently evolving, is focussing specifically on sustainability. The building's energy needs will be met using new sustainable energy technology. The heating system features ground air collectors to preheat ambient air and concrete pillars will conduct geothermic heat throughout the space. A photovoltaic installation on the roof will provide the necessary electricity. The result will be a state-of-the-art work environment.

Hong Kong International Airport HKG is developing SKYCITY, one of the largest commercial real estate projects in the territory. It is set to become an airport city—a destination far beyond the traditional shopping mall. It aims to create a unique experience to attract both tourists and the international business community and establish itself as a dynamic lifestyle and family entertainment hub.

Zurich Airport ZRH has developed a vast commercial complex called The Circle. It features collaborative co-working and meeting spaces, hotels, convention centres and a medical and biotech complex. The retail sector includes brand stores, commercial space for galleries and art markets as well as various food and beverage options. The vision: digital integration throughout the complex will connect various sectors to ensure a smooth customer experience. The developers sought to create a space amidst the bustling activity of the airport, that is both "urban and open-minded" to expand the airport experience for the 150,000 visitors, passengers, commuters and employees that venture to the airport every day.

Airport as a tourist destination

In 2019, a new landside attraction The Jewel opened between the terminals of the Singapore Changi Airport SIN. It is an attractive mixed-use space, encompassing a landscaped park and a variety of leisure and shopping facilities, within a giant greenhouse. With its massive indoor waterfall and terraced green areas, the space is a magnet for visitors, attracting more than 300,000 of them every day. With The Jewel, the airport has created yet another highlight, making the airport a popular tourist destination even for non-flying visitors. The Jewel's motto is "Discover a wondrous world where nature meets retail".

Visitor terraces at airports have traditionally attracted large numbers of guests and are still generously designed to offer an impressive view of the airport airside to visitors who enjoy observing the departing and arriving aircraft. Some airports have added visitor centres that feature interactive exhibits and other attractions. These places are often designed to encourage wanderlust or the desire for international travel to distant countries and exotic destinations. The cosmopolitan flair resonates with every visit and spawns the travel bug. An airport is a built space from which a world of experience beckons.

A second life for airports

A trend which is certain to grow is the transformation of infrastructure towards sustainable transport. Ultimately, this will require certain airport locations to be abandoned and repurposed in order to concentrate national air traffic in such a way that neither the urban nor rural environments are underserved. A concentration of efficient and high-tech airports easily accessible with high-speed rail is one option for the future.

What will become of outdated airports? Particularly those located closer to urban centres are more likely to be phased out to protect residents from noise and air pollutants. These sites are often well connected and attractive for redevelopment.

The municipal government in Berlin is developing an Innovation Campus on sustainable urban technologies on the site of the Tegel Airport TXL. Though this project breathes new life into the old airport, the phasing out of Tegel marks the end of an era. It is part of the city's identity and holds many memories. It was the starting point of numerous journeys, the stage of political events and will now be relegated to the status of a historic monument. The repurposing of the terminal into a technology campus and the transformation of the area into an urban park symbolises a turning point for the German mobility industry.

In Berlin there are no less than three airports which face repurposing. The closure of Tempelhof Airport THF in 2008 was the subject of an emotional, citywide debate. The municipal government wanted to develop the abandoned airfield in the middle of the city to create space for leisure and sports activities in a city park and permit the construction of much-needed residential buildings on the perimeter. The plan was highly controversial. A citizens' petition forced a referendum on the plans with the result that the municipal government was forced to abandon the project and leave the airfield unchanged. Today, it is a popular destination for residents and visitors who enjoy a wide range of outdoor activities in the vast space. Some airport signage was deliberately left on the terminal buildings to comply with the designation of the complex as a historical monument. It is protected and preserved to reflect its colourful history as an airport. The third airport is Schönefeld—the former official airport of East Germany finally closed in 2022 after being part of BER Berlin Brandenburg Airport for a while as Terminal 5.

Former airports of architectural interest will likely be preserved and repurposed. For example, Paris Le Bourget Airport LBG serves as a business airport and a museum of aeronautics and space. It was officially opened in 1919. Charles Lindbergh landed his "Spirit of St. Louis" here in 1927 after his celebrated flight across the Atlantic. Le Bourget has a storied history. In Great Britain, the original terminal building at Gatwick Airport, constructed in 1936, has also been preserved as a historic site. The building referred to as The Beehive due to its circular structure, is an architectural gem in the Art Deco style of the 1930s.

1 New destination at Zurich

180,000 m²

With 180,000 square metres of floor space for retail, hotels, offices, art and culture The Circle at Zurich Airport ZRH, opened in 2020, has become a new attraction for the city.

2 New landmark for Hong Kong

383,000 m²

SKYCITY adjacent to Hong Kong International Airport HKG will be a major development including retail and dining areas, hotels, entertainment facilities and offices. It is poised to become the new landmark of Hong Kong for local and overseas visitors.

3 Unique innovation campus next to Munich Airport

~ 500,000 m²

A total of ~ 500,000 square metres are to be built next to Munich Airport MUC. The LabCampus is designed to bring together international corporations, mid-size companies, and outstanding start-ups for cross-industry innovation.

1

Are airport cities actual cities?

Airport cities offer many of the same functions of a city, such as mobility, shopping, employment, leisure activities and accommodation, but they are not cities. They do not grow organically by and for individuals living in a specific geography over a long period of time. They are built on a drawing board to conform to a global consensus. At the same time, they do capture some aspects of local identity. Airports have no permanent residents and there are few personal or private touches on display. Yet they are intimately connected with urban life. One prerequisite for urbanity is the existence of private and public space. As the need for urban space is expanding, airports and cities are beginning to melt together.

	city	airport
Mobility	public transport railway station ride sharing motorways individual car traffic	public transport railway station ride sharing motorways autonomous vehicles
Education and healthcare system	schools university science, research sports museum	- - innovation labs gym art installation
Supply system Free time	parks cemetery clinic cathedral residential living music events, concerts leisure privacy -	indoor gardens - private clinic chapel, room of silence hotel commercial events leisure - lounges
Economic system	offices shopping pharmacy	offices shopping pharmacy

1 **SIN** Singapore Changi Airport has become a tourist destination. With the opening of The Jewel in 2019, it features a shopping complex within an impressive greenhouse environment.

264

Addendum

265

Page	Image	Credit
17	1	Port Authority of New York and New Jersey
	2	© Landesbildstelle Berlin
	3	Maria Austria Instituut / KLM
	4	Amnat Phuthamrong, Shutterstock
	5	Chicago Department of Aviation & Studio ORD
19	1	Flughafen Stuttgart GmbH
	2	Flughafen Stuttgart GmbH
35	1	Chon Kit Leong, Alamy
40	1	Associated Press
41	2	Information Services Department of the HK Government
	3	Flight Path Museum LAX
44	1	WHA United Archives
	2	Wikipedia in public domain
45	3	Flight Path Museum LAX
48	1	Flughafen Berlin Brandenburg GmbH
49	2	© gmp Archiv
50	1	H. Sander K.G.
	2	Public Records Office, Government Records Service Hong Kong
51	3–5	Department of Airports LAWA
54	1	Flughafen Berlin Brandenburg GmbH
55	2	Alex Mak (photo)
58–59	1–2	Flight Path Museum LAX
63	2	Airport Authority Hong Kong
64	1	Worldwide Cruise Terminals Hong Kong
65	2	Flight Path Museum LAX
69	1	Eugène Hénard
	2	Barrat Homes, William Zeckendorf
	3	Bauhaus Luftfahrt e.V.
	4	© Volocopter
	5	© UNStudio, Plomp, commissioned by: Hardt Hyperloop
82–83	1	Yoshio Futagawa, GA photographers
84	1	Jon Arnold Images Ltd, Alamy
	2	Markus Mainka, Shutterstock
85	3	uskarp, Alamy
	4	Leonardo Finotti
86	1	ansonmiao, gettyimages
	2	Chicago Department of Aviation & Studio ORD
87	3	Leonardo Finotti
	4	i-mad architects
88	1	uskarp, Alamy
89	3	Haptic Architects, MIR
	4	Skidmore, Owings & Merrill (SOM), Robert Polidori (photo), © Mumbai International Airport Pvt. Ltd.
91	4	© LHR Airports Limited
	10	Leonardo Finotti
	11	He Xincheng
	12	Jon Arnold Images Ltd, Alamy
	14	© LHR Airports Limited
93	1	© Kenta Hasegawa
	2	Thomas Koch, Shutterstock
95	1	© Ivan Brodey
	2	GoSleep
	3	Green Furniture Concept
96	4	Chicago Department of Aviation & Studio ORD
	5	Airports Corporation of Vietnam (ACV) and HEERIM ARCHITECTS & PLANNERS
97	6	Benoy
99	1	Royal Schiphol Group
	2	Nutcreatives
	3	Gatwick Airport
103	2	Keiichi Koyama, i Design
	3	Adelaide Airport
	4	© LHR Airports Limited
	5	Royal Schiphol Group
	6	Suradech Singhanat, Shutterstock
	11	Alexander Branczyk
	14	ferna
105	1	Associated Press
	3	United Archives GmbH, Alamy
	4	Yoshio Futagawa, GA photographers
	5	Department of Airports LAWA
	7	LAX, Max Groot Archive
107	2	© LHR Airports Limited
	3	© LHR Airports Limited
	4	Royal Schiphol Group
109	3	Markus Mainka, Alamy
111	2	© LHR Airports Limited
	3	Mariana Reinhardt
	5	Flughafen München GmbH, Peter Engels (photo)
	15	Paul Andreu, Gilles Ehrmann (photo), © VG Bild-Kunst, Bonn 2020
113	2	Katharina Brenner
	4	Lars Harmsen
	12	Jörg Schlaich
115	3	Alexander Branczyk
	6	Andreas Pieper
	9	Alexander Branczyk
	10	Andreas Pieper
	15	Keiichi Koyama, i Design
117	2	Madrid Airport
119	2	Flughafen München GmbH, Bernd Ducke (photo)
121	2	© Stefan Schilling
123	2	ferna
124	1	Public domain
126	2	Majority World CIC, Alamy
127	3	© Kenta Hasegawa
129	10	Terminal Design Inc.
131	1	100km Studio
	2	DLugowski, Alamy Stock Photo
	3	SOPA Images Limited, Alamy Stock Photo
	4	Khun Ta, Alamy Stock Photo
	5	© Kenta Hasegawa
	7	Heorshe, Alamy Stock Photo
	8	ruelleruelle, Alamy Stock Photo
	11	Heorshe, Alamy Stock Photo
	12	Marie Karim Khani
133	1	Gatwick Airport, "Design" Magazine, Design Council
135	1	Gatwick Airport, "Design" Magazine, Design Council
	2–3	Margaret Calvert
137	1	Roger-Viollet
139	1	Matthew Carter
141	1	Matthew Carter
142–143	2	Architectural Press Archive, RIBA Collections, Ian Berry (photo)
145	4	Margaret Calvert
146–147	5	Jock Kinneir Library
149	1	Lehnartz/ullstein bild
150–151	2	Eero Saarinen Collection, Yale University Library
153	1	Yoshio Futagawa, GA photographers
154	1	Walter Rawlings, fotoLibra
	2	Christian Schwartz
155	3	Christian Schwartz
157	1	Collection Het Nieuwe Instituut
158	1	Collection Het Nieuwe Instituut
	2	Amsterdam Schiphol Airport Archive
161	1	Jane Davis Doggett
162–193	1–2	Jane Davis Doggett
165	1	Zurich Airport
167	1	Paul Andreu, Gilles Ehrmann (photo), © VG Bild-Kunst, Bonn 2020
168–169	2	Paul Andreu, Gilles Ehrmann (photo), © VG Bild-Kunst, Bonn 2020
170	1	Paul Andreu, Gilles Ehrmann (photo), © VG Bild-Kunst, Bonn 2020
	2	Zürcher Hochschule der Künste/Museum für Gestaltung Zürich
172–173	1–4	Zürcher Hochschule der Künste / Museum für Gestaltung Zürich
175	1	Jane Davis Doggett
177	2	Hans G. Deumling
179	1	Changi Airport Group
182–183	2	FocusBreatheShoot, Shutterstock
	3	ImagineerInc, Shutterstock
187	7	© LHR Airports Limited
	9	Ely Penner, Shutterstock
	8	© Stratacache
	10	Royal Schiphol Group
	11	Changi Airport Group, Paul Dingman (photo)
197	1	Erco
217	1	© LHR Airports Limited
219	1	Jane Davis Doggett
227		Instagram
232	1, 6	Paris Aéroport
	2	Fraport AG Frankfurt Airport Services Worldwide
	3	Flughafen Wien AG
	4	Austrian Airlines
	5	Flughafen Berlin Brandenburg GmbH
233	7	Zurich Airport, © Google
	8	Amsterdam Schiphol Airport, © Mapbox, © OpenStreetMap
238	1	Jason O'Rear
240	1	Flughafen München GmbH
	2	Moniteurs, Iabsis, Fraport AG
	3	Fraport AG, Clear
	4	Iberia
241	5	Aviation Solutions Schiphol Group
242	5	Prague Airport
	6	Keiichi Koyama, i Design
243	7	TrueConf
	8	Flughafen München GmbH
	9	Changi Airport Group
	10	Zurich Airport
	11	Instagram, Munich Airport
244	1	© Los Angeles World Airports
245	2	Flughafen Stuttgart GmbH, Deniz Calagan (photo)
	3	© LHR Airports Limited
	2	phichak, Shutterstock
	3	Frederic Reglain, Alamy
	5	Shan_shan, Shutterstock
	6	Flytoget
255	1	WorldPix, Alamy
257	1	MASSLAB
	2	Denver International Airport and Sasaki
	3	Tegel Projekt GmbH
	5	Earnest Tse, Shutterstock
261	1	Zurich Airport
	2	Airport Authority Hong Kong
	3	Flughafen München GmbH
262	1	Changi Airport Group

© Moniteurs—
all picture numbers
not counted here

Cover front:
Mike Kelley, Los Angeles International Airport LAX
Cover back:
© LHR Airports Limited
© Hannover Airport (FIDS)

Many thanks to the airports and designers for kindly providing the pictograms shown in this book.

266

Airport index

267

268

Bibliography

The literature and websites selected here have accompanied the creation of this book and also serves for further information.

ACI Airports Council International: **Annual World Airport Traffic Report 2019,** in: https://aci.aero/wp-content/uploads/2019/10/WATR_2019.pdf, access 09.04.2020

Adam-Tkalec, Mariatta: **Schönefeld: Vom Zentralflughafen zum BER,** in: https://www.berliner-zeitung.de/mensch-metropole/schoenefeld-vom-zentralflughafen-zum-ber-li.73929, access 10.11.2020

Aicher, Otl/Krampen, Martin: **Zeichensysteme der visuellen Kommunikation. Handbuch für Designer, Architekten, Planer, Organisatoren,** 1st edition, Stuttgart, Verlagsanstalt Alexander Koch GmbH, 1977

Airport Cooperative Research (ACRP): **Wayfinding and Signing Guidelines for Airport Terminals and Landside,** Volume 52, ACRP report, Transportation Research Board, 2011

Arbeitsgemeinschaft Deutscher Verkehrsflughäfen (ADV): **„Information und Wegweisung": Normen/Standards, Piktogramme zur Orientierung auf Flughäfen/Pictographs for Orientation at Airports,** 3rd edition, Germany, 1974, 1st edition, Germany, 1969

Arthur, Paul/Passini, Romedi: **Wayfinding, People, Signs, and Architecture,** 1st edition, Ontario, Whitby McGraw-Hill, 1992

Association Typographique Internationale (atypi): **Charles Peignot, 1996—1983,** in: https://www.atypi.org/about-us/whos-who/charles-peignot, access 11.04.2020

Atmosfair: **Auswirkungen des Flugverkehrs auf das Klima,** in: https://www.atmosfair.de/de/fliegen_und_klima/, access 03.10.2020

Baines, Phil: **An Interview with Margaret Calvert,** in: Frieze, 10.09.2003, in: https://frieze.com/article/time-signs, access 02.02.2020

Barker, Peter/Fraser, June: **Sign Design Guide. A guide to inclusive signage,** 2nd edition, London, JMU and the Sign Design Society, 2004

Black, Alison/Luna, Paul/Lund, Ole/Walker, Sue: **Information Design. Research and Practice,** 1st edition, Oxon, Routledge, 2017

Blankenship, Edward G.: **The Airport. Architecture. Urban Integration. Ecological Problems,** Stuttgart, Verlag Gerd Hatje, 1974

Bosma, Koos/Berkers, Marieke/Burgers, Iris/Davids, Karel/ El Makhloufi, Abdel/De Mare, Heidi/Nikolaeva, Anna/Willem de Wijn, Jan: **Megastructure Schiphol: Design in Spectacular Simplicity,** Rotterdam, Nai010 publishers, 2013

Bundesministerium für Gesundheit, Referat „Soziale Eingliederung Behinderter Menschen": **Handbuch für Planer und Praktiker,** Bonn, Bad Homburg, Fach-Media-Service-Verl.-Ges. (FMS), 1996

Calvert, Margaret: **Battle of the Serif, Margaret Calvert**, London, 2006, first published in: Bos, Ben/Bos, Elly/AGI: **Graphic Design since 1950**, Thames & Hudson, 2007, in: http://www.newtransport.co.uk/, access 09.04.2020

Cuadra, Manuel/Flagge, Ingeborg: **World Airports,** Hamburg, Junius, 2002

Mijksenaar, Paul: **Wayfinding at Schiphol,** first published 2008, Amsterdam, Mijksenaar, 2012

Der Spiegel: **Airbus plant Wasserstoff-Flugzeug,** Hamburg, 2020, in: https://www.spiegel.de/wissenschaft/technik/airbus-plant-wasserstoff-flugzeug-drei-konzepte-fuer-klimaneutrales-fliegen-vorgestellt-a-95c76ca2-d36d-4cb2-9543-1b63742198b8, access 21.09.2020

Deutsches Luft- und Raumfahrtzentrum: **Der globale Luftverkehr trägt 3,5 Prozent zur Klimaerwärmung bei,** in: https://www.dlr.de/content/de/artikel/news/2020/03/20200903_der-globale-luftverkehr-traegt-3-5-prozent-zur-klimaerwaermung-bei.html, access 10.09.2020

Dümpelmann, Sonja: **Flights of Imagination. Aviation, Landscape, Design,** Charlottesville, University of Virginia Press, 2014

Dümpelmann, Sonja/Waldheim, Charles: **Airport Landscape. Urban Ecologies in the Aerial Age,** in: Harvard Design Studies /Harvard University Cambridge, Harvard University Press, Printing: Die Keure, Belgium, 2016

Edwards, Brian: **The Modern Airport Terminal. New Approaches to Airport Architecture,** 2nd edition, Oxon, Spon Press, 2005

Eero Saarinen, TWA Terminal Building Kennedy Airport, New York. 1956–62 Dulles International Airport (Washington, D.C.), in: GA Global Architecture Magazine No 26, Chantilly, Virginia, 1958–62

Eiselin, Stefan: **Neues Terminal in Schönefeld kommt früher,** 2017, in: http://www.aerotelegraph.com/neues-terminal-in-schoenfeld-kommt-frueher, access 01.10.2020

Eiselin, Stefan/Frommberg, Laura/Gutzmer, Alexander: **Faszination Flughafen. Die schönsten Airports und ihre Geschichten,** Munich, Callwey Verlag, 2015

European Commission: **Transport Modes, Air, What do we want to achieve?,** in: https://ec.europa.eu/transport/modes/air_en, access 11.11.2020

Huygen, Frederike: **The interior of Schiphol: teamwork on a never-ending work in progress,** in: https://www.design-history.nl/2016/the-interior-of-schiphol-teamwork-on-a-never-ending-work-in-progress/, access 02.02.2020

Fuller, Gillian/Harley, Ross: **Aviopolis. A Book about Airports,** London, Black Dog Publishing, 2004

Gibson, David: **The Wayfinding Handbook. Information Design for Public Places,** New York, Princeton Architectural Press, 2009

Gordon, Alastair: **Naked Airport. A Cultural History of the World's Most Revolutionary Structure,** Chicago, University of Chicago Press, 2008

Grundy, Tom: **HISTORY—A Brief Visual History of Hong Kong's Old Airport, Kai Tak**, 2014, in: http://hongwrong.com/kai-tak-airport-photos/, access 10.11.2019

Heinrich-Böll-Stiftung/Airbus Group: **Oben. Ihr Flugbegleiter,** Berlin, 2016

Herdeg, Walter: **Archigraphia. Architectural and Environmental Graphics,** Zurich, The Graphis Press, 1978

Hildebrand Ralph D./Wallbaum, Rainer (eds.): **Der Flughafen München—Ein Jahrhundertwerk,** Munich, Leo-Verlag, 1992

Hong Kong Kai Tak Airport, Public Relations Office, Civil Aviation Department: **Hong Kong (Kai Tak) Air Traffic Statistics (1947–1998),** Hong Kong, 1998

Hora, Mies: **Official Signs & Icons 3,** 1st edition, 1996, 3rd edition, 2017, New York, Utimate Symbol

Jahn, Helmut/Schuler, Matthias/Sobek, Werner: **Suvarnabhumi Airport. Bangkok, Thailand,** Ludwigsburg, Avedition, 2007

Jock Kinneir Library: **Kinneir begins work on signage for Gatwick Airport,** 2017, updated 2019, in: https://jockkinneirlibrary.org/1957-gatwick-airport-signage, access 09.04.2020

Kapitzki, Herbert W.: **Design: Method and Consequence. A Biographical Report,** Stuttgart/London, Edition Axel Menges GmbH, 1997

Kasarda, John D./Lindsay Greg: **Aerotropolis. The Way We'll Live Next,** Farrar, Straus and Giroux, 2012

Küppers, Harald: **Das Grundgesetz der Farbenlehre,** 11th edition, Cologne, DuMont Buchverlag, 2004

LAX Airport: **"#1 World Way"—the Story of Los Angeles International Airport,** in: https://www.youtube.com/watch?v=B4NysCgVQ1Y:, access 11.11.2019

Meuser, Philipp: **Signaletik und Piktogramme. Handbuch und Planungshilfe,** 2nd edition, Berlin, DOM publishers, 2010

Mollerup, Per: **Wayshowing>Wayfinding. Basic & Interactive,** Amsterdam, BisPublishers, 2013

Museum für Gestaltung Zürich: **Adrian Frutiger—Roissy, Frutiger,** in: https://www.eguide.ch/de/ausstellungstexte/adrian-frutiger-roissy-frutiger/, access 04.01.2020

Masters, Nathan: **From Mines Field to LAX. The Early History of L.A. International Airport,** 2012, in: https://www.kcet.org/shows/lost-la/from-mines-field-to-lax-the-early-history-of-la-international-airport, access 01.10.2019

Neurath, Otto/Eve, Matthew (ed.)/ Burke, Christopher (ed.): **From Hieroglyphics to Isotype. A Visual Autobiography,** London, Hyphen Press, 2010

ntv: **Die Geschichte des Flughafens Tempelhof,** 2014, in: http://www.n-tv.de/mediathek/bilderserien/panorama/Die-Geschichte-des-Flughafens-Tempelhof-article12912581.html, access 03.11.2020

Osterer, Heidrun/Stamm, Philipp: **Adrian Frutiger—Schriften. Das Gesamtwerk,** 2nd edition, Basel, Birkhäuser Verlag, 2014

Ringli, Kornel: **Designing TWA. Eero Saarinen's Airport Terminal in New York,** Zurich, Park Books, 2015

Russell, Edward: **How form and function helped make BWI the D.C. area's busiest airport,** in: https://dc.curbed.com/2018/10/17/17989092/, access 12.04.2020

Schlaich, Sibylle/Meier-Walter, Anita: **The evolution if the elevator pictogram,** in: idJ Special Issue: Information Visualization, Volume 25, No 1, Information Design Journal, Amsterdam, Netherlands, John Benjamins Publishing Company, 2019

Schönberger, Angela: **Airports. IDZ-Hochschulprojekt, Entwürfe für einen Flughafen Berlin Brandenburg International,** Berlin, Ernst & Sohn, 1997

Shaw, Paul: **Helvetica and the New York City Subway System,** revised edition, Cambridge, MIT Press, 2011

Siebert, Jürgen: **Die 100 besten Schriften,** Berlin, FontShop, 2007

Skytrax: **The World's Best Airports of 2023,** in: https://www.worldairportawards.com/worlds-top-100-airports-2024/, access 03.08.2024

Smart Cities World: **Collaboration aims to create an urban air infrastructure,** in: https://www.smartcitiesworld.net/news/collaboration-aims-to-create-an-urban-air-infrastructure--5544 w.smartcitiesworld.net, access 15.08.2020

Society for Experiential Graphic Design (SEGD): **2018 SEGD Conference Experience Minneapolis—Fellow Award —Jane Davis Doggett,** in: https://vimeo.com/275899191, access 11.04.2020

Statista: **Number of scheduled passengers boarded by the global airline industry from 2004 to 2021,** in: https://www.statista.com/statistics/564717/airline-industry-passenger-traffic-globally/, access 03.04.2020

Stay Grounded: **Report Degrowth of aviation,** Stay Grounded/Kollektiv Periskop, Vienna, 2019

Stiehl, Reinhard/Over, Daniel/Gehrmann, Kai: **otl aicher piktogramme und die Olympischen Spiele 1972,** in: https://www.piktogramm.de/de/#c53/, access 12.04.2020

The Elliott Museum lecture series "To Open The Eyes", Albers & Heirs: **Josef Albers, Neil Welliver, Jane Davis Doggett,** in: https://www.youtube.com/watch?v=M-HQl1XoEKjA, access 11.04.2020

The History of London's Heathrow Airport, in: https://www.bbc.com/news/av/uk-england-london-37753262/the-history-of-london-s-heathrow-airport, access 02.01.2020

Turner, Tracy: **Environmental Graphics Pioneer,** in: eg magazine No 07, 2013, in: https://segd.org/jane-davis-doggett-environmental-graphics-pioneer, access 11.04.2020

van Uffelen, Chris: **Airport Architecture,** 1st edition, Salenstein, Braun Publishing, 2012

Umweltbundesamt (ed.): **Schwerpunkt Fliegen,** Dessau-Roßlau, Das Magazin des Umweltbundesamtes 2/2019, 2019

Umweltbundesamt (ed.): **Wohin geht die Reise?** Dessau-Roßlau, UBA Forum 2019, Luftverkehr der Zunkunft, 2019

US population 2019: **Population of Los Angeles 2019,** in: https://uspopulation2019.com/population-of-los-angeles-2019.html, access 22.05.2020

von Vegesack, Alexander (ed.)/ Eisenbrand, Jochen (ed.): **Airworld. Design and Architecture for Air Travel,** Weil am Rhein, Vitra Design Museum, 2004

Waller, Robert: **Comparing Typefaces for Airport Signs,** in: Information Design Journal No 15, Amsterdam, Netherlands, John Benjamins Publishing Company, 2007, in: https://www.academia.edu/39798325/Comparing_typefaces_for_airport_signs, access 09.02.2020

Walters, John L.: **Britain's signature,** in: eye magazine No 71, Vol 18, 2009, in: http://www.eyemagazine.com/feature/article/britains-signature, access 01.05.2020

Warnholtz, Anna: **Wir werden ein Weltklasse-Airport,** Welt, 03.02.2012, in: https://www.welt.de/reise/article13847183/Wir-werden-ein-Weltklasse-Airport.html, access 01.06.2020

Wasmuth, Georg: **Der Flughafen Tempelhof als Kandidat für die European Tentative List,** Berlin, ICOMOS-WORKSHOP, kunsttexte.de, No 1, 2010, in: https://edoc.hu-berlin.de/bitstream/handle/18452/7796/wasmuth.pdf?sequence=1&isAllowed=y, access 01.06.2020

Wikipedia: **List of busiest airports by passenger traffic,** 2023 statistics, in: https://en.wikipedia.org/wiki/List_of_busiest_airports_by_passenger_traffic#2023_statistics, access 16.08.2024

Wikipedia: **Berlin Brandenburg Airport,** https://en.wikipedia.org/wiki/Berlin_Brandenburg_Airport, access 16.8.2024

Williams, Pat (producer)/ Wehlage, Ben (ed.)/ Jones, Jeff (director): **Jane Davis Doggett: Wayfinder in the Jet Age,** Oolite Arts, 2019, in: https://www.youtube.com/watch?v=VTkuU39js7E, access 11.04.2020

Winchcombe, Simon/Sillery, Clare/Hornsby, Gaby: **The Secret Life of an Airport,** BBC Four, London, 2009

World Biogas Association: **Global Potential of Biogas,** 2019, in: https://www.worldbiogasassociation.org/wp-content/uploads/2019/09/WBA-execsummary-4ppa4_digital-Sept-2019.pdf, access 14.10.2020

Die Zeit: **Klinikatmosphäre am Flughafen,** Hamburg, 25.04.2020, https://www.zeit.de/wirtschaft/2020-04/flugreisen-coronavirus-aenderungen-massnahmen/komplettansicht, access 25.04.2020

worldometers: **Countries in the world by population (2020),** in: https://www.worldometers.info/world-population/population-by-country/, access 22.05.2020

Wuppertal Institut: **Wie Deutschland bis 2035 CO2-neutral werden kann,** in: https://wupperinst.org/a/wi/a/s/ad/5169/, access 13.10.2020

Information graphics:
1 Evolving
The Guardian: **In flight: see the planes in the sky right now,** in: https://www.theguardian.com/world/ng-interactive/2014/aviation-100-years, 2014, access 29.05.2020

https://www.statista.com/statistics/564717/airline-industry-passenger-traffic-globally/, access 09.08.2024

https://www.statista.com/statistics/564769/airline-industry-number-of-flights/, access 09.08.2024

2 Identity
https://en.wikipedia.org/wiki/List_of_busiest_airports_by_passenger_traffic (2023) and the opening paragraphs of the English Wikipedia page of the airports

3 Digital
https://en.wikipedia.org/wiki/List_of_busiest_airports_by_passenger_traffic, access 29.05.2020

www.instagram.com, access 03.8.2024
www.weibo.com, access 03.8.2024
www.tiktok.com, access 03.8.2024
www.facebook.com, access 03.8.2024
www.douyin.com, access 03.8.2024

4 Beyond
https://www.worldatlas.com/citypops.htm, access 29.05.2020

Maps on pages 13, 75, 77, 223, 249: AuthaGraph map
AuthaGraph is an equal-area type map projection, meaning it tries to show the world with as little area distortion as possible. The map keeps sizes of all oceans and continents, to give the user a better picture of the earth. This projection also opens up the possibility of centering the map on any part of the globe.

It was invented by the Japanese architect Hajime Narukawa in 1999: http://narukawa-lab.jp/archives/authagraph-map/, access 07.04.2020

The sources and authors are named to the best of our knowledge and belief. Illustrations and information material not listed in the picture credits are from Moniteurs and from collections of the text authors or are in the public domain.

270

Acknowledgements

So many friends and colleagues contributed to making this book happen. They discussed themes and concepts with us, brought in ideas, criticised and motivated us, and we thank you all very much! First and foremost, of course, our thanks go to Alexander Branczyk and Andreas Pieper for challenging and cheering us on.

Thanks also to Marla Luther and Julie Hagedorn for transferring our text from German to English and for keeping an eye on all the important details. To Annette Wüsthoff and Anna Gaissmaier for helping to shape the design of the book. To Lars Harmsen for his interjections from the edge of the pitch. To Jürgen Siebert for his experienced review of the typography chapter, and to Anita Meier-Walter for the pictogram flight control. To Jane Davis Doggett, Margaret Calvert, Henrik Kubel, Mike Wolff, Carole Rami and Paul Andreu, who passed away in 2018, for opening their doors to us and providing us with deep insights into their work. To Ethel Pattison, the heart of LAX. To Keiichi Koyama for the steadfast link to Japan. To Keith Perry, Sharon Dowson and Michael Furze from Heathrow Airport for their generosity and for sharing their wonderfully diverse library with us. To Anfas Suhail, Marwin Nehl and Yat Kiu Joshua Lo for their information design and research. To Feia Nehl and Elena Wünschmann for juggling one million contemporary and historical photos. To Sannia Ho Mei Ling for her invaluable tenacity in HKG. To Hubert Nienhoff and Hajo Paap for bringing us to the runway in 2005. We would also like to thank our talented and wonderful Moniteurs team, whose great support makes our projects possible in the first place.

Most patient of all were our families, not only over the course of all those years spent at countless airports, wait time again and again, until we had carefully inspected and photographed all the signs we could. They also stood patiently by until this book was finally finished! Many thanks to Feia, Lele, Marwin, Jule and Luise.

271

The authors

Heike Nehl studied Visual Communication at the FH Bielefeld University of Applied Sciences, completing a thesis on contemporary British graphic design. In 1990, she began working at MetaDesign in Berlin, which was followed in 1993 by a period in the USA at MetaWest in San Francisco. At MetaDesign she met Sibylle Schlaich and worked with her on the wayfinding for the Berlin Public Transport Operator. After founding Moniteurs communication design with Sibylle Schlaich and another partner in 1994, they focused their work on information design and wayfinding after a few years.

The experience gained from working on numerous wayfinding projects—a selection: Berlin Brandenburg Airport, Hannover Airport, Zurich Airport, Kulturpalast Dresden, BMW FIZ Future, Merck group—and dealing with mobility projects has made her an expert in the field of information design.

Heike Nehl has taught at different design universities, Typography and Information Design at the Bauhaus University in Weimar and Interaction Design at the FH Bielefeld University of Applied Sciences. In 2013 she taught as guest professor at the Chinese German Academy of the Arts in Hangzhou, China. In 2024 she was appointed honorary professor at the Hochschule der Bildenden Künste Saar (HBKsaar). She has given talks at conferences such as Creative Mornings, Typographic Design Munich, Day of Typography Bern, Dimensions of Mobility/Dessau, or at the Smart Airport conference in Singapore.

She is the co-author of the books "emotional digital—A Sourcebook of Contemporary Typographics", "Look Book Informationsdesign" and "1:1 Orientation, Signage, Identity".

Sibylle Schlaich studied Visual Communication at the HfG University of Design Schwäbisch Gmünd and at the Berlin University of the Arts, the diploma was the thesis on the use of renewable energies, visualised with data and information graphics. She worked for MetaDesign in Berlin, where she met Heike Nehl and worked with her on the wayfinding for the Berlin Public Transport Operator. After founding Moniteurs communication design with Heike Nehl and another partner in 1994, they focused their work on information design and wayfinding after a few years.

The experience gained from working on numerous wayfinding projects—a selection: Berlin Brandenburg Airport, Munich Airport, Stuttgart Airport, Kunsthalle Mannheim, BMW plant Leipzig, Continental company—and dealing with mobility projects has made her an expert in the field of information design.

Since 2000, Sibylle Schlaich has taught in the fields of Information Design and Typography, among others at the Leibniz University in Hanover at Faculty of Architecture, at the Bauhaus University in Weimar and she has been a guest professor at the CDK, the Chinese German Academy of the Arts in Hangzhou. In 2024 she was appointed honorary professor at the Hochschule der Bildenden Künste Saar (HBKsaar). She has given numerous talks, such as at the international design conference TYPO Berlin, at the Smart Airport Conference in Vienna or at the Nirma University in Ahmedabad, India. She has also been a jury member of various selection panels.

She is the co-author of the books "1:1 Orientation, Signage, Identity", "Look Book Informationsdesign", "emotional digital—A Sourcebook of Contemporary Typographics" and "Erneuerbare Energien nutzen".

Imprint

The Deutsche Nationalbibliothek lists this publication in the Deutsche Nationalbibliografie; detailed bibliographic data are available on the Internet at http://dnb.dnb.de

ISBN 978-3-7212-1014-9

www.niggli.ch

2nd edition 2024

Authors and editors: Heike Nehl, Sibylle Schlaich
Concept and design: Heike Nehl, Sibylle Schlaich
Layout and setting: Annette Wüsthoff, Anna Gaissmaier
Translation and proofreading: Marla Luther, Julie Hagedorn
Reproduction: Bild1Druck GmbH, Berlin
Font: New Transport

Cover front

LAX 2017—Los Angeles International Airport,
Tom Bradley International Terminal from a bird's-eye view.

Cover back

Left:
LHR 2013—Heathrow Airport, London.

Right above:
BER DOH SIN CGN—Departure pictograms clockwise from top left.

Right below:
HAJ 2021—Hannover Airport, flight information display system (FIDS).